A Watchman's Warning to Israel in Dispersion

Volume V

By Pastor Dan Gayman

A Watchman's Warning to Israel in Dispersion, Volume V

1

AMERICA: A NATION UNDER COVENANT SANCTIONS

Winter 2007

The plain fact is that we are now under the sanctions imposed by the covenant Law of our God. The curses are starting to fall in unmeasured sorrow upon this land. One merely need to turn to Deuteronomy 28 or Leviticus 26, two important portions of the covenant Law under which our nation was settled, to determine where we stand.

America is a nation established by the authority of our covenant God and is under the terms of His covenantal Law. Every home, every church, every sphere of civil government in this land of 300 million people has a compelling need to know that America was established as a covenantal nation and is bound by the Law of God as found in His Word. No power can transcend, abrogate, or annul this contract with Jehovah. This covenant is based on Bible Law and is ratified by the very blood of Jesus Christ, the

Son of God! The clergy and civil leaders now at the helm have a compelling need to know the covenant nexus America has with God.

The first settlers to arrive upon this soil from the European fatherland were the Pilgrims, followed by the Puritans and successive waves of European Christians who survived and thrived here. In spite of different languages and variant labels of Christianity, all shared one ethnic, cultural world vision! Europeans colonized America under the terms of God's covenant Law. They developed this country according to God's ways as best as they knew how. They cleared the land of briars, nettles, and trees and tilled the soil to produce food to sustain them. They build houses and established cottage industries. Small villages grew out of a primeval wilderness, church steeples adorned the land, and everyone honored the Sabbath of rest and worship.

The spirit and soul of America were anchored in the covenant Law of God. Statutory law reflected biblical principles and was enacted throughout the early colonial settlements. Whatever God's Word declared to be the standard became the template for the home, church, community, and state. Under covenantal contract with God and moving in terms of His Law, America quickly rose to prominence. In less than two centuries, America was able to defend herself in a protracted war against the might of the British Empire, among the strongest nations on earth. America was a biblical theocracy because God and the rule of His Law held supremacy.

From the first settlement in Jamestown, Virginia in 1607 to the end of World War II 1945, some 338 years, America rose to become the strongest military, economic, and political power on earth. In 1945, American military and economic might dwarfed the rest of the nations on earth. However, in 2006, some sixty years later, America is fighting for her very survival. In less than one century, America has mounted the largest national debt among the nations of the world. In less than half a century, our mighty military has been stretched thin over vast regions of the earth, reaching into Afghanistan, Iraq, Bosnia, Kuwait, South Korea, and elsewhere. In less than fifty years, the powerful and mighty American nation has gone from its highest peak of power to being buffeted and bullied by rogue nations like North Korea, Iran, Venezuela, and Cuba.

Fifty years ago, almost every household item in the home and industry was made in the U.S.A. In 2006, America is a nation awash in goods made by the slave labor of China. In less than half a century, America has lost its place as the leading manufacturing nation on earth. Our industry is all but shut down as the nation fills itself with foreign goods made in China, Japan, Korea, and the Far East. Our standard of living, once the highest among all the nations of the earth, is now plunging. The great American middle class, once the envy of the world, is being reduced to a pittance of what it once was.

Since 1945—in less than half a century—America has been transformed from being nearly all Caucasian to a nation constituted of a multitude of races. Since 1965, the racial face of America has gone from snow white to dark brown. No nation in the history of the world has witnessed such a tidal wave of unrestricted immigration into its borders in such a short period as fifty years. A majority of these newly arrived immigrants came from different cultures, heritages, religions, and moral backgrounds than the former generations from Europe who populated America. People who grew up before World War II days can no longer identify with the America that the 21st Century witnesses.

The strong moral values and biblical principles that once glued the American people into one homogeneous nation sharing one cultural worldview and religious faith are no more. Our moral standards have become like those of a common alley cat. Heinous crimes like abortion, sodomy, miscegenation, adultery, fornication, and bestiality have trumped the former biblical standards by which America lived. Divorce, once a rare occurrence, is now the common lifestyle for more than half of Americans. Our homes have become mostly dysfunctional, while one third of all children born are illegitimate and being raised by a single parent. In the midst of a multi-racial, multi-cultural, anti-biblical moral climate, America is coming apart at the seams.

In the face of this national crisis and impending judgment from a sovereign God, it is past time for the fathers, ministers, and civil leaders in this land to pause and reflect upon the fact that America is a covenant land, established under the terms of a Covenant God. Nothing is going to change this fact. Because America was colonized and developed under terms of a covenant contract with Jehovah God, where we promised to be His people and obey His laws, we will either live in obedience to His covenant Law and reap unending blessings, or we will suffer covenantal sanctions and reap unending curses. Visit if you will the words found in Deuteronomy 28:15-68. Engage yourselves in a fact-finding inventory of the present state of our Union and determine what sanctions and curses are visiting this covenant land. Our rejection of God and disobedience to His covenant Law are bringing horrific sanctions upon our land. In fact, the following survey barely touches the developing events in our American fatherland.

Cities Will Be Cursed!

"Cursed shalt thou be in the city, and cursed shalt thou be in the field" (Deuteronomy 28:16).

American cities are under a curse. Most of them are in financial crisis, burgeoning with debt, squalor, ghettoes, and slums where only the bravest dare go. The mafia controls New York City. The Sodomites control San Francisco. Gambling lords run Las Vegas. Gang lords rule the streets of Los Angeles. Drive through the inner districts of Chicago, Detroit, Miami, Atlanta, St. Louis, Kansas City, Seattle, or Denver and witness the blights of poverty, squalor, violence, drugs, and soaring crime that now plague America's cities.

Our cities have become concrete jungles where booze, drug lords, street gangs, government-subsidized housing slums, and squalor abound. White flight out of the inner cities to the suburbs has been followed by inner city slum dwellers to these same suburbs, forcing yet another wave of white flight into the rural areas surrounding every city in the United States. Security guards and armed policemen must now stand guard in many urban schools to prevent violence, rape, and murder.

Sickness and Disease

"The LORD will smite thee with the both of Egypt, and with emerods, and with the scab, and with the itch, whereof thou canst not be healed . . . Also every sickness, and every plague, which is not written in the book of this law, them will the LORD bring upon thee, until thou be destroyed" (Deuteronomy 28:27,60).

On October 3, 1965, while standing at the foot beneath the Statue of Liberty, Lyndon Johnson signed the Immigration Act of 1965. This opened the floodgates to the third world to come into America. With them came all of the diseases and plagues common to them. *"'The U. S. Centers for Disease Control and Prevention,' writes author-columnist Phyllis Schlafly, 'reported 38,291 California cases of tuberculosis that included Multiple Drug Resistant Tuberculosis, which is 60 percent fatal and for which treatment costs $200,000 to $1,200.00 per patient. Illegal aliens are also bringing in syphilis and gonorrhea. Bedbugs have invaded the United States for the first time in 50 years, with 28 states reporting recent infestations'"* (State of Emergency, The Third World Invasion and Conquest of America, Patrick Buchanan, 2006, p. 29). *"In May the 2006, the New York Times reported that one in every seven East Asian immigrants in the city, as many as 100,000 people, is a carrier of hepatitis B—an infection rate thirty-five times that of the general population. Almost all the new measles cases in America are brought in from abroad."*

Many Americans do not realize that the tidal wave of aliens, most of them illegal, pouring into this county from Mexico and throughout the world is bringing infectious and deadly diseases with them. This includes Hepatitis A, B, & C, tuberculosis, leprosy, and Chagas Disease (a serious parasitic bug indigenous throughout Latin America of which 18 million people are infected and 50,000 die annually). One can only wonder how quickly these infectious diseases will spread through our population by means of the public schools, restaurants, movie theatres, and shopping malls.

Consider the skyrocketing rise in degenerative diseases that now afflict millions of Americans: heart disease, cancer, diabetes, crippling arthritis, AIDS, etc., are filling the hospitals of this land. Health care has become the largest industry, totaling billions in America. We cannot build hospitals fast enough. The cost of health insurance is soaring beyond the reach of millions of Americans.

Serious Drought Upon the Land

"And thy heaven that is over thy head shall be brass, and the earth that is under thee shall be iron. The LORD shall make the rain of thy land powder and dust: from heaven shall it come down upon thee, until thou be destroyed" (Deuteronomy 28:23-24).

Weather patterns over the United States have undergone tremendous changes in recent years. Searing, hot temperatures roasted much of the Midwest in the summer of 2006. Pasture lands from Texas north into Missouri and Nebraska have been baked by lack of rain. We now have prolonged drought in the American breadbasket, while other parts of the country are flooded with unprecedented rainfall. Fires in the Western States, many of them out of control, have consumed millions of acres in recent years. The Southeastern coast from Louisiana to Florida has been hit by a succession of violent hurricanes in recent years.

Almighty God has imposed sanctions upon the weather over North America. This nation has forgotten God, so He is withdrawing His covenantal blessings from this land. Fruitful rains and abundant harvests are directly related to the morality of the covenant people. The spiritual famine in America is gradually going to bring about a land of powder and dust and a corresponding famine for bread and good drinking water.

Authorities who chart weather patterns in the United States have recorded an increase in the number and intensity of killer tornadoes. Hurricanes have been extremely destructive on the Southeastern coasts of America, from Louisiana all the way to Florida and north into the Carolinas. Floods, fires, and severe weather patterns have ravaged much of the United States. Most Americans have forgotten that a covenant keeping God *" . . . hath his way in the whirlwind and in the storm . . ." (Nahum 1:3). "Then the earth shook and trembled; the foundations also of the hills moved and were shaken, because he was wroth" (Psa. 18:7).*

Loss of Military Victory

"The LORD shall cause thee to be smitten before thine enemies: thou shalt go out one way against them, and flee seven ways before them: and shalt be removed into all the kingdoms of the earth" (Deuteronomy 28:25).

Breaking covenant with Jehovah God has brought sanctions upon military victories on the field of battle. America began its course of serious covenant breaking after the end of World War II (1945). Since that time, American armies have retreated without victory from the battlefields of Korea (1950-1953) and from Vietnam (1963-1973). United Nations rules of engagement, entangling alliances, riches sought by international bankers from the House of Esau-Edom, biased news media, and incompetent politicians have contributed to our military defeats around the world. In truth, God has withdrawn His grace from the wars that America now wages in the name of democracy.

More than 100,000 Americans died in these no-win wars. American armies have remained in Korea since 1953, with some 37,000 soldiers stationed there to this day and no victory in sight. American armies have been stationed in Germany since 1945; they remain there this day. America has armies in Bosnia and Kuwait, and we are bogged down in Afghanistan (since 2002) and Iraq (since March, 2003), with no victory in sight. American casualties in Iraq total 2900 killed in action, with another 50,000 sustaining wounds, and thousands of them losing limbs from various types of explosives.

Foreign Invasion in Our Land

"The LORD shall bring a nation against thee from far, from the end of the earth, as swift as the eagle flieth; a nation whose tongue thou shalt not understand; a nation of fierce countenance, which shall not regard the person of the old, nor shew favour to the young" (Deuteronomy 28:49-50).

The present Mexican invasion of the United States is one of the most blatant foreign invasions upon any people since the Germanic tribes over-ran the Roman Empire in the years before its fall in AD 476. Some forty million illegal Mexicans have crossed the Rio Grande into America since the last amnesty was granted under President Regan in 1986. These Latinos are not and never will be assimilated into the American culture. They come here demanding that America adopt their language, their culture, their morals, and their sub-culture life style. Unlike the successive waves of Europeans who poured into the American landscape between 1607-1945, the Latinos are a different race with a decidedly different language, culture, morals, and worldview.

American prisons house almost 100,00 illegal aliens. Soaring crime rates have followed the arrival of forty million Latinos since

1973. Our schools, hospitals, and other infrastructure are going bust with the burdens imposed by this foreign invasion. Thousands of these illegals operate as street gangs and drug cartels in the cities across America. Low wages and a plunging standard of living are all covenant sanctions coming upon America because of our breaking covenant with Jehovah God. The racial face of America is undergoing profound change, so that by 2020, the old, indigenous Caucasian population will be a minority amid a sea of non-white, third-world aliens packed into slums and living in squalor throughout the urban areas of the United States.

Strangers Will Become the Head

"The stranger that is within thee shall get up above thee very high; and thou shalt come down very low. He shall lend to thee, and thou shalt not lend to him: he shall be the head, and thou shalt be the tail." (Deuteronomy 28:43-44).

Between the settlement at Jamestown 1607 and the year 1890, the American banking system remained in American hands. Because America was connected to God and His covenant Law, this nation prospered and was the economic showcase of the earth. After 1890, however, millions of Ashkenaz Khazarian Jews arrived into the U.S. from Eastern Europe. They quickly gained control of the financial and banking institutions and by 1913 had successfully orchestrated passage of the Federal Reserve Act. Through contracting, expanding, deflating, and inflating the currency, the international bankers control the financial markets of the world. This was a private banking corporation that took over the exclusive control and management of America's money.

In 1935, strangers from the House of Esau-Edom managed to work behind the scenes until gold backing was removed from American currency (1935) and silver backing was withdrawn in 1965. The interest on America's nine trillion-dollar debt is now so enormous that paying the principal is almost impossible.

These strangers very quickly assumed increasingly greater control of the economic and monetary interests of America. In the 21st Century, these strangers have become the head, leaving the native-born Caucasian Americans to become the tail. We now borrow from the privately-owned Federal Reserve Banks, while the strangers become enormously wealthy at the expense of the U. S. Government and its taxpayers. Our nine trillion-dollar public debt is the highest in the world.

Declining Population

"And ye shall be left few in number, whereas ye were as the stars of heaven for multitude; because thou wouldest not obey the voice of the LORD thy God" (Deuteronomy 28:62).

Throughout the early history of America and continuing to about midway through the 20th Century, America favored and loved children, so large families were common. However, our disconnection from God and the family has brought an alarming drop in the birth rate. Caucasian women average just barely more than one child per capita among the general population, causing the Caucasian population of America to shrink rapidly. The older population is dying out, and the declining birth rate is reaching zero population growth.

Plunging birth rates in Europe, the British Isles, Scandinavia, Canada, the United States, Australia, and elsewhere among the indigenous Anglo-Saxon peoples is alarming. Germany now offers a government subsidy to couples who will have children. White children have become an endangered species in Anglo-Saxon lands. The great nations of the Christian West are being depopulated of their Caucasian stock and repopulated by non-white, third world people who swarm into these Israelite nations and bring with them poverty, disease, large numbers of children, and an alien language, culture, and moral code.

Ethnically pure Caucasian children are becoming an endangered species; if the trend toward **childlessness** continues, the non-whites will forever change the racial face of America. The high birth rate and unrestricted immigration of non-whites into America signal the end of Caucasian America. The transformation of America from a white Christian nation to a non-white secular state will insure the demise of this nation.

What Must We Do?

As Jehovah God imposes divine sanctions upon America in response to our persistent breaking of His covenant, what must the God-fearing, blood-washed, Bible-believing, Spirit-filled Christians do? Living among a nation that has chosen to love, worship, and serve other gods and live in continual violation of the covenant Law of the Living God, what must we do?

First: All husbands/fathers must examine their own lives and those of their family members and come to full repentance by faith in the Lord Jesus Christ. This repentance should be confirmed by our turning from all forms of wickedness and our fervent desire to live in obedience to the Commandments of God, with full allegiance to the testimony of Jesus Christ, the Son of God.

Second: There should be a complete separation from the immoral, anti-biblical standards of abortion, birth control, sodomy, miscegenation, adultery, fornication, pornography, gambling, drunkenness, drugs, and other types of immorality. God is looking for a holy and sanctified people who will live in obedience to His covenant Law.

Third: The spiritual strength and physical increase of the family should be the highest priority for every husband and wife. The multiplication of children should be the first goal of every marriage. Let God determine **when** and **how many** children He wants in your family. Home school your children or place them in a proven Christian school. Do not place your children in a government school. Curb the insatiable American appetite for bigger and better homes, cars, and recreational toys, and invest in children instead.

Fourth: Seek the cover of a Christ-centered, Bible-based local church that stands strong against abortion, birth control, sodomy, and race mixing. If you cannot find a local church with biblical standards, open a home church under the cover of an organized church that does conform to the standards of God and Scripture.

Fifth: Flee the concrete, urban jungles and look for a place in rural America where you can worship and associate with others who share a common ethnic heritage, faith, and worldview.

Sixth: Set your financial house in order. Limit debt to the purchase of land, a home, or business. If you cannot manage credit cards and avoid high interest charges, burn these plastic slave cards. Think outside of the box and find a skill or business that cannot be outsourced to India, off-shored to China, or eliminated by the changing times. Work out a biblical partnership with God, develop a consistently good work ethic, pay God's tithe faithfully, help the poor, and be blessed above all you can imagine.

Seventh: Make evangelism a high priority in your life. **Protest the evil of this generation!** Bear your testimony to the truth of Jesus Christ and the Gospel of the Kingdom! Share a tape, a book, a tract, or a testimony with every potential person the Holy Spirit inspires you to evangelize. Support those who stand on the frontline firing bullets of truth into the enemy armies that now seek the brainwashing and demise of the Anglo-Saxon population of this country.

A Final Word: Time and history are moving us irrevocably toward the day when ***"The Kingdoms of this world are become the kingdoms of our Lord, and of His Christ; and he shall reign for ever and ever"*** (Rev. 11:15). ***" . . . For the elect's sake those days shall be shortened"*** (Matt. 24:22). ***"And when these things begin to come to pass, then look up, and lift up your heads; for your redemption draweth nigh"*** (Luke 21:28).

Make every day, a gift from God, count! Be all that you can be! Take time every day to consult with God! Read His Word! Husbands, be the spiritual leader of your wife and children! Worship and rest on the biblical Sabbath and work hard the other six days of the week. Be a good foot soldier of Jesus Christ and face Satan, the world, and your own sin nature with courage, resolve, and conviction. Run the race to win (I Cor. 9:24)!

2

THE ONLY ANSWER FOR AMERICA: RETURN TO A BIBLICAL THEOCRACY

Spring 2007

The America we love and pray for daily is in a free fall from glory, and we have yet to reach the bottom! The political process in America is locked in total paralysis, with the largest debt in history mounting during the last five years. We have saddled our children with trillions in debt, plus compound interest, that will burden them for untold generations. Our armies are bogged down in imperialistic wars waged by politically correct rules under UN oversight, with no victory in sight. America is awash in immorality that has fostered the heinous crimes of abortion, lethal birth control, sodomy, miscegenation, fornication, adultery, pornography, drunkenness, gambling, and drug culture mania.

In the midst of our love of racial diversity and multiculturalism, we worship the heathen gods that former generations of Americans disdained. We have rejected the one true God and His revealed Word. Mainstream pulpits and the U. S. Supreme Court have denounced the statutory laws that once reflected God and Scripture. Secular Humanism has become the official religion in America, with Federal and State approval. Our public schools, state-supported colleges and universities, media outlets, and mainstream pulpits parrot the tenets of humanism. America is drowning in a sea of racial diversity, over-run by an invasion of millions of third world people from Mexico and throughout the world. Most God-fearing Americans are overwhelmed, feeling hopeless. What can we do? There is one answer. Are you ready to take the plunge?

America must return to its former status as a biblical theocracy. Yes, a biblical theocracy is the only solution for this country! Anything less than this insures America's continued slide into the dust bin of history, where the former empires of the world met their demise. America is not a democracy, and our founding fathers never intended it to be. This country was formed into a republic, with elected representatives of the people, bound to and governed by the rule of law. Progressive secularists can scream democracy forever, but it will only push America into the abyss of political, economic, social, moral, and spiritual suicide.

A theocracy is submission to the rule of our sovereign God over every man, woman, and child. A theocracy demands that the people, convicted in the heart, follow God and His Word, willingly submitting themselves to God's Law, as is reflected in the elected representatives of the people. A theocracy demands that God's Law, not man's, be the rule by which every man, every home, every church, community, state, and nation lives. All elected representatives must mirror this law in the legislative process that governs the affairs of each community, state, and nation at large. In a theocracy, God—not the state—is the lord and ruler of men. A biblical theocracy where God and the rule of His law prevail is not new to this country.

When God and the Bible Ruled!

Consider this: the founding fathers of this country framed a republic in which the sovereign power was lodged in representatives elected by the people. Most of the framers of the U. S. Constitution and the various state Constitutions were Christian. The people and their elected representatives chose to make God and His Law the rule by which this nation would be governed. As officials enacted the various state and federal statutes, they clearly reflected the Bible, God's rulebook for men and nations. The framers of the U. S. Constitution designed this instrument for a Christian people. As America ceases to be a Christian nation, the constitution will work increasingly less efficiently.

From Jamestown in 1607 to the middle of the 20th Century, our statutory laws reflected God and His rule of Law as contained in the Bible. A cursory examination of our nation's history should convince the most stubborn humanist that the template that governed America for most of its history was that which is found in the Bible. In this sense, America was and continued to be a biblical theocracy until midway through the 20th Century. A return to this form of government is the only solution that will rescue America in its present freefall.

That biblical Christianity was the foundation upon which America was established is confirmed in the Supreme Court case Holy Trinity Church v. The United States, 143 U.S. 457 (1892). The High Court argued among other things that *" . . . From the discovery of this continent to the present hour, there is a single voice making this affirmation . . . There is a universal language pervading them all, having one meaning. They affirm and reaffirm that this is a religious nation. These are not individual sayings, declarations of private persons. They are organic utterances. They speak the voice of the entire people . . . These and many other matters which might be noticed, add a volume of unofficial declarations to the mass of organic utterances that this is a Christian nation"* (Emphasis ours).

That America was a nation under God's Law is clearly punctuated in a number of U.S. Supreme Court cases that overturned historic legislation that reflected God's rulebook. Examine carefully a few salient examples of how America has progressively disconnected from God and His Law, thus rejecting a biblical theocracy. As you reflect upon America's disconnect from a biblical theocracy, recall that an elitist band of American clergy in mainstream America had been the cheerleaders pushing for the overturn of God's law in this nation. The High Court merely followed the lead of liberal, humanist clergy.

Compelling evidence shows that the spiritual climate among rank and file clergy in mainstream Christianity was moving toward radical changes in the historic view of Christianity in this country. This new modernism was reflected early in Europe and birthed the **World Council of Churches** organized in 1948. Liberation theology was seeking to make radical changes in the social and moral structure of America. This is clearly evident in the work of the **National Council of the Churches of Christ in the United States of America**, an organization established in 1950 by the merger of the **Federal Council of Churches of Christ** and some seven other religious agencies. Among other goals was the dumping of the **Authorized King James Bible**, which was accomplished in 1952 with the publication of the **Revised Standard Version.**

The growing rationalism, fueled by evolutionary humanism and the liberalization of Christianity, created a climate in the 1950s for the overthrow of the long-established biblical theocracy in America. Inspired by a generation of humanist clergy and a surging movement to overthrow the foundations of historic Christianity, the climate had ripened for the assault upon our theocracy. A spate of decisions soon came from the U. S. Supreme Court that was packed with liberal justices clamoring for social changes in the structure of American life. The moral standards of the Bible needed, in their minds, to be replaced by the tenets of a new religion, **Secular Humanism.** These changes were not long in coming as the following High Court decisions show.

The End of Racial Segregation

The U. S. Supreme Court ended all segregation in American public schools in **Brown v. Board of Education of Topeka**, 347 U.S. 483 (1954). This was the beginning of the complete overthrow of a major biblical statute that forbade the amalgamation and fusion of the distinct and separate races which God had created. From Jamestown in 1607 to 1954—some 337 years—American public schools had practiced racial segregation. The biblical doctrine of Separatism, already being threatened by many leading clergy, now became the new policy of the American government. This new radical humanism did not come without cost. Tens of thousands of federal troops were mobilized and sent throughout the South to enforce the integration of U.S. public schools and silence all opposition.

The end of segregation in the public schools had been preceded by the integration of the American Armed Forces under President Harry S. Truman in 1946. Liberal clergy were demanding the integration of American churches. Billy Graham, a well-known evangelist, pushed for full integration of his crusades in the 1950s. The integration of American public schools and churches was the first step toward ending the established separation of the races and endorsing interracial marriage in America.

1954 marked the beginning of the end for racial segregation in America. The covenant people who colonized, settled, and developed America had long endeavored to practice the doctrine of separatism. As American settlers pushed the savage, uncultured Indians from their unsettled hunting grounds, they were doing precisely what Jehovah commanded in His covenant law: *"Ye shall inherit their land, and I will give it unto you to possess it, a land that floweth with milk and honey: I am the LORD your God, which have separated you from other people . . . And ye shall be holy unto me: for I the LORD am holy, and have severed you from other people, that ye should be mine" (Lev. 20:24, 26).*

In 1491 BC, Jehovah endorsed racial segregation in these words from Moses regarding the people of Israel: *"For wherein shall it be known here that I and thy people have found grace in thy sight? Is it not in that thou goest with us? So shall we be separated, I and thy people, from all the people that are upon the face of the earth" (Exodus 33:16).* Solomon validated this segregation of Israel from other people some five hundred later, as is confirmed in I Kings 8:53: *"For thou didst separate them from among all the people of the earth, to be thine inheritance, as thou spakest by the hand of Moses thy servant . . ."* Yet another five hundred later, about 445 BC, the Israelites continued to practice racial segregation: *"Now it came to pass, when they had heard the law, that they separated from Israel all the mixed multitude" (Neh. 13:3).*

Belief in God Is not a Requirement for Public Office

That Jehovah was the one true God, the supreme Creator and Ruler of the universe, was a common belief in early America. This was reflected in the various Colonial and later State Constitutions. This belief in God was a requirement for public office holders, but was terminated when the U.S. Supreme Court in **Torcaso v Watkins,** 367 U.S. 488 (1961) overthrew a Maryland statute that required this conviction. Thus, another cornerstone was removed from our biblical theocracy. The removal of God from the public life of America was a major assault upon the idea of a nation being governed by God and His Law. If there is no God, there can be no rule of law that trumps the edicts of man.

The Overthrow of Prayer

Prayer is a fundamental right for a Christian. When it was a theocracy, America was a nation that prayed. The first English settlers who disembarked at Jamestown in 1607 and at Plymouth Colony in 1620 prayed as soon as they set foot on American soil and continued thereafter throughout our nation's history. However, in the infamous U. S. Supreme Court decision in 1962 in the case of **Engel v Vitale,** 370 U.S. 421, the High Court struck down the following prayer that the Board of Regents for the State of New York had endorsed: **"Almighty God, we acknowledge our dependence upon Thee, and beg Thy blessings upon us, our teachers, and our country."**

This anti-prayer decision in 1962 had a chilling affect upon the spiritual status of all public schools in America. Moreover, there were ripple effects felt in all public educational forums across the nation, and beyond that into public buildings, gymnasiums, football stadiums, etc. In 1961, America rejected belief in God as a test for holding public office. In 1962, America quit praying in public schools. The long-established biblical theocracy in America was unraveling.

The Removal of the Bible

In 1961, a belief in God was no longer a requirement for those holding public office in America. In 1962, American school children were denied the long-established practice of prayer in public schools as the unraveling of a biblical theocracy continued. In 1963, the U.S. Supreme Court struck down as unconstitutional the reading of the Bible in public schools in **Abington School District v. Schempp,** 374 U.S. 203, 83 S. Ct. 1560 (1963). In Pennsylvania, students attending public schools had been required to read at least ten verses from the Bible and recite the Lord's Prayer. However, the High Court ruled that these religious exercises violated the religious freedom of students under the First and Fourteenth Amendments.

Humanists first removed God, then prayer, and finally the Bible from the public life of America. Systematically, secular humanists began removing the very foundations that supported a biblical theocracy. The removal of the Bible from the public life of America was further enforced in 1964 when the U. S. Supreme Court in **Chamberlin v. Dade County [FL] Board of Public Instruction,** 377 U.S. 402 (1964) decided that devotional Bible reading and prayers, previously required by statute, were unconstitutional in Florida public schools.

Statutes Against Interracial Marriage Rescinded

The first flagrant cases of interracial dating and marriage began occurring in liberal churches. The forced integration of American public schools and the rolling back of centuries of separatism opened the door to interracial marriage. By 1967, the integrated Churches and public schools were beginning to accept interracial marriage. The issue came to full boil in 1967 when the U.S. Supreme Court in **Loving v. Virginia**, 1967, struck down a Virginia statute against interracial marriage. The High Court declared the Virginia ban against the marriage of two people of a different race to be unconstitutional.

What had been a biblical ban against interracial marriage for some 360 years was all at once determined wrong. What God and Scripture declared to be unlawful, the U.S. Supreme Court and many leading clergy found to be right. Is this not reminiscent of Isaiah 5:20, which reads: *"Woe unto them that call evil good, and good evil: that put darkness for light, and light for darkness . . ."?*

For centuries, America had followed Jehovah and His covenant Law, which ruled that each kind or species must reproduce after its own kind (Genesis chapter 1). However, the preachers and judges suddenly forgotten that God is not color blind and that the Creator placed His mark of ownership on the original design of each separate and distinct race and called all of His creation good (Genesis 1:31). In the principle of original design, the Creator ordained that every race must have its own physical build, cranial structure, brain convolutions and weight, skin color, skeleton design, blood composition, and endless other qualities that distinguish it from the others.

Throughout Scripture, Jehovah God is careful to limit marriage to one man and one woman of the same flesh or race. Eve was formed from the rib of Adam. When the living creatures passed before Adam, including all the other races (certainly the animals were not candidates for marriage), the Bible says, *" . . . but for Adam there was not found an help meet for him (Genesis. 2:20).* But, upon viewing the newly formed woman, Adam declared, *"This is now bone of my bones, and flesh of my flesh: . . . Therefore shall a man leave his father and his mother, and shall cleave unto his wife: and they shall be one* (or the same) *flesh" (Genesis 2:23-24).*

As Israel prepared to conquer Canaan, God specifically told them to make no covenant with the heathen Canaanites, a mongrelized race of people already dwelling in the land. The covenant contract with Jehovah forbade the interracial mixing of God's people with these heathen mongrels then indigenous to Canaan. *"Neither shalt thou make marriages with them; thy daughter thou shalt not give unto his son, nor his daughter shalt thou take unto thy son" (Deut. 7:3).* When some Israelites ignored this covenant command, Jehovah became angry with His people, saying, *"And they took their daughters to be their wives, and gave their daughters to their sons, and served their gods . . . Therefore the anger of the LORD was hot against Israel, and he sold them into the hand of Chushan-rishathaim king of Mesopotamia: and the children of Israel served Chushan-rishathaim eight years" (Judges 3:6, 8).*

Both Ezra (chapters 9 & 10) and Nehemiah (chapters 9 & 10) vigorously contend with those who violated the covenant injunction against interracial mixing: *"And I contended with them, and cursed them, and smote certain of them, and plucked off their hair, and made them swear by God, saying,*

Ye shall not give your daughters unto their sons, nor take their daughters unto your sons, or for yourselves" (Nehemiah 13:25). Nehemiah's ire rose because of the covenant oath made earlier with the Israelites when they declared *". . . that we would not give our daughters unto the people of the land, nor take their daughters for our sons"* (Nehemiah 10:30).

Bibical Bans Against Abortion Overturned

Throughout the history of the United States, the unborn child in the womb of a mother has been protected as a life under covenant law (Exodus 21:22-25). Biblical law forbids abortion! For some 366, years children in the womb were protected against murder. To the disgrace of this country, however, the activist U. S. Supreme Court, following the lead of liberal clergy among the high and mighty in America, handed down a stunning decision in **Roe v. Wade** 410 U.S. 113 (1973). The High Court struck down the Texas ban against abortion, giving a woman complete autonomy over the child during the first trimester, and defined different levels of state interest for the second and third trimesters. In the aftermath of this decision, forty-six states gave the nod for the mother to commit unborn children to the death chambers.

Since the biblical ban against abortion was overturned in **Roe v. Wade** (1973), some forty million innocent and helpless children have been put to death in the abortion murder mills of this country. The abortion killing fields in America now allow for the murder of full-term babies; some 2700 of these little ones are murdered annually. In making the unlawful act of abortion legal under color of law, America has joined the barbaric nations of history who in the final stages of their moral freefall sacrificed their own children in barbaric and savage rituals. Of interest to note is that since 1973, about the same number of illegal Latinos have invaded the United States as children committed to death in abortion clinics. Perhaps no single issue punctuates the dissolution of the biblical theocracy in America more than does the sadistic murder of unborn children.

Biblical Views on Birth Control Ignored

Throughout most of the history of America, our people have highly valued and fully endorsed the multiplicity of children. Only in recent decades, especially since the end of World War II in 1945, has the trend toward fewer children become popular. In the 21st Century, America is moving toward a "childless" mentality among the educated classes of the Caucasian population. The Caucasian birth rate in America is in steady decline, with just a little more than one child per capita for Caucasian women of childbearing age. The more highly educated couples within the rank and file of the Caucasian population are choosing to remain childless or else adopt.

Until about 1930, Protestant, Roman Catholic, and Evangelical churches taught against birth control. Pre-marriage counseling encouraged newlyweds to become parents. The multiplication of children, not the addition of children, is what God commanded in Genesis 1:28 in the command to *"be fruitful, multiply, and replenish"* God's earth. The multiplication of godly children is imperative to the successful perpetuation of a biblical theocracy.

Historically, the Caucasian people who colonized, settled, and developed America favored large families. **When** and **how many** children should be born were up to God. America's plunge into immorality in the past fifty years has witnessed wholesale endorsement of birth control. A free love society demands the pleasure of conjugal relations without the burden of children.

The arrival of the 21st Century clearly indicates that birth control, a basic tenet of the religion of Secular Humanism, is now deeply rooted among a vast majority of the Caucasian population, both in and out of the Church. Churches now endorse birth control, and pastors freely advise young couples in pre-marital counseling to make decisions on the type of birth control they plan to use. A decided majority of Caucasian married couples believe that when and how many children to have are no longer left to God's sovereignty. Indeed, millions of couples practice lethal forms of birth control that kill the child not long after conception. Statistically, couples abort <u>ten times</u> the number of children via lethal forms of birth control as are put to death in abortion clinics. Shameful!

Aborting enormous numbers of children via birth control has become sandard practice among the Caucasian population of America. The Church is largely silent on this issue, and even among Roman Catholics, the trend is toward birth control. Friend, it is my duty to inform you of the fact that birth control is in direct violation of God's Word and undermines the authority of a biblical theocracy as much as anything that has occurred in American society in the last one hundred years. The Church and the Government have both endorsed and promoted birth control, while the FDA consistently approves of more lethal forms of birth control to insure the death of the conceived children in this country.

Ten Commandments
Removed from Public Schools

The posting of the Ten Commandments in public places has been a longstanding custom throughout the nation from its earliest beginnings. The **Ten Commandments** represent the summary of the most fundamentals laws that enable a biblical theocracy. The very fabric of American society has been reflected historically in these ten laws that derive their existence from the Bible and were first revealed from Heaven and then posted in 1491 BC among the Hebrew people. These ten laws were carved into the stone walls of the judicial headquarters for the U.S. Supreme Court. They are posted, carved, or inscribed in public buildings throughout the nation and are as American as apple pie.

The assault upon the Ten Commandments began in earnest when parents in Kentucky sued to have them removed from the school classrooms, as Kentucky law had previously required. In **Stone v. Graham,** 449 U.S. 39 (1980), the U. S. Supreme Court held the Kentucky law to be unconstitutional, so the posting of the Ten Commandments in public classrooms ended. This was the first of many assaults upon the Ten Commandments. For the past twenty-five years, this assault has continued, and the Ten Commandments have essentially been removed from all public buildings in this country. Ironically, they do remain carved in stone in the judicial building where the U. S. Supreme Court decreed them to be unconstitutional.

The assault upon the Ten Commandments confirms the long-standing biblical theocracy that was foundational to our nation. The war against the Ten Commandments was central to the dissolution of the biblical foundation of law that has long characterized American society. The Ten Commandments were the foundation for hundreds of statutory laws enacted by the state legislatures and other governing bodies within the borders of the United States throughout our nation's history. The goal of Secular Humanism is to remove every vestige of a biblical theocracy from the minds and hearts of the people and from public view throughout the land.

Biblical Separatism
Punished by Federal Government

Racial separatism is another long-established moral and social practice of many within America. Many colleges and universities were established for a particular race. Bob Jones University and Goldsboro Christian Schools are among two of many schools that practiced separatism. Bob Jones University believed that the Bible prohibited interracial dating and marriage. Hence, this behavior was not permitted on their campus. Goldsboro Christian Schools maintained a racially discriminatory admissions policy which they believed was supported by the Bible and therefore accepted only Caucasian students.

In a yet again historic decision, the U. S. Supreme Court in **Bob Jones v. United States,** 461 U.S. 574 (1983) denied tax exemption status to both Bob Jones University and Goldsboro Christian Schools. The Court declared that racial discrimination in education violated a "fundamental national public policy." This High Court decree essentially ended the biblical practice of separatism in both schools and established a precedent that allowed and encouraged interracial dating and marriages in tax-exempt schools throughout the United States. With this move, the High Court imposed a great hardship on any school or college in America that insisted on practicing the biblical principle of **separatism.** In order to qualify for tax-exempt status, schools and colleges must allow interracial dating and marriage. What had been a biblically correct practice for more than 350 years in America suddenly became wrong. And, the assault on the biblical theocracy in America continued, knowing no limits.

Teaching Creation Science
Banned in Public Schools

The belief that God created heaven and earth and all things therein is a basic tenet of the American worldview and is deeply rooted in the spiritual and moral fabric of our society. The creation demands belief in a Creator. The grand design of the universe means there must have been a designer. Holding to this major tenet of a biblical theocracy, the state of Louisiana passed a law entitled the "Balanced Treatment for Creation-Science and Evolution-Science in Public School Instruction Act" prohibiting the teaching of the theory of evolution in the public schools unless that instruction was accompanied by the teaching of creation science, a biblical belief that advanced the idea that forms of life appeared abruptly on Earth. Louisiana schools were not forced to teach creation science. However, if either topic were to be addressed, teachers were obligated to discuss the other, as well. When this case went before the Supreme Court it was held to be unconstitutional. The High Court in **Edwards v. Aguillard,** 482 U.S. 578 (1987) struck down the Louisiana statute that mandated the teaching of supernatural creation when evolution was going to be taught in the classroom.

Among other points emphasized by Justice Brennan was that the primary effect of the law was to advance the viewpoint that a *"supernatural being created humankind . . ."* This decision marked a major victory for the religion of Secular Humanism. At the same time, it assaulted a basic tenet of biblical theocracy, namely that Almighty God created, sustains, governs, and will one day judge the world.

This important court decision marked a significant point along the road to dissolving the biblical theocracy in America. As it now stands, Creationism is considered a theory advanced by Christianity and cannot be taught as science because it is a tenet of a particular religion. At the same time, evolution, a tenet of the religion of Secular Humanism, can be taught because it is science and is not considered part of religion. All of this is in spite of the fact that the U. S. Supreme Court in **Torcaso v. Watkins,** 367 US 488 (1961) ruled that Secular Humanism is a religion. The Court ruled that the First Amendment grants the same protection and imposes the same limitations on the *"religion of Secular Humanism"* as are applicable to other religions.

In the new America, biblical Creationism, a basic tenet of biblical theocracy, cannot be taught because it is central to belief in Christ. At the same time, evolution can and must be taught as science, and yet it remains a basic tenet of the religion of Secular Humanism. In truth, evolution is the religion of Secular Humanism in the very same way that Creationism is the belief in Christianity. Neither qualifies as science because the scientific process cannot be repeated by either. Christians believe that there is a God Who created all things, and the Bible is the record of that creation. Evolutionists have no record, no witnesses, and no proof of the continuous process of evolution and are incapable of proving anything!

Biblical Ban on Sodomy Overturned

Statutory law in the United States had prohibited the heinous crime of sodomy and related acts of perversion, including bestiality.

As late as 1960, all fifty states had laws on their books restricting the sin of sodomy. The Bible case against sodomy was deeply engrained in our moral code. From the earliest beginnings of our nation's history, laws against sodomy were common. This hallmark moral code of a biblical theocracy came under assault by the U. S. Supreme Court in **Lawrence and Garner v. Texas,** 539 U.S. 558 (2003). In this landmark case, six judges held the majority opinion that Justice Anthony M. Kennedy delivered: the Court held that the Texas statute making it a crime for two persons of the same sex to engage in certain intimate sexual conduct violates the Due Process Clause.

This High Court decision to provide government protection to the crime of sodomy came on the heels of growing acceptance of homosexuals in most of the mainstream Churches. Several of the older and most well-established Protestant churches began to ordain homosexuals, allowing them into the ministry, and the pews became home to growing numbers of sodomites. The Supreme Court simply followed the American clergy in giving a hearty welcome to the sodomites. With encouragement from both the church and the State, the sodomite agenda in this country picked up speed and went on the offensive. They now represent one of the most radical and outspoken lobby groups in America. Those who revel in this sin of perversion now share a place of honor in every facet of American society, both in and out of the Church.

The removal of the statutory ban against the crime of sodomy in America proves several things. First, it demonstrates that the Court had to strike down this phase of a centuries-old biblical theocracy in order to remove the statutory prohibitions against sodomy. Secondly, it serves as a barometer to demonstrate the moral freefall that America now suffers. Thirdly, it has and will continue to lead to the toleration of a growing number of perversions that God condemns. Finally, it serves notice on how close America is to a Sodom and Gomorrah society.

Summary

America is in a moral freefall, and God alone knows when we will hit bottom. There are no moral absolutes left in modern America. There is no right or wrong unless you choose to believe in God and the Bible. All moral restraints have been lifted, leaving us in an amoral universe where moral values have been annulled. Evolution has left Americans believing that only the strong survive, and the weak must be exterminated. Hence, we murder our children while they are still in the womb. Human life is cheap. Acts of violence are random and without motive. People kill for the sake and thrill of the kill. Our public schools have been turned into bloody scenes of terror, and the bloodletting knows no limits. The moral vacuum created in the absence of God and His moral absolutes has turned our nation into a jungle. Young people have no consciousness of God and His moral absolutes and of a coming day of judgment. Life is only for the moment. If it feels good, do it. There is no God, no heaven, no hell, and no day of accounting for one's deeds. Progressive Secular Humanists are turning America into a jungle of immorality, murder, and violence, and any Christian who protests this evil is vilified, maligned, and ostracized.

Nothing less than a biblical theocracy can save America. We must bite the bullet and take the cure, or America will join the Roman Empire and all other nations that have rejected God in the scrapheap of history. True Christians stand as embattled soldiers of Jesus Christ fighting for the crown rights of our King.

This nation must roll back sixty years of U. S. Supreme Court decisions and reinstate biblical statutes that for hundreds of years prohibited racial integration, interracial marriage, abortion, sodomy, bestiality, and other acts of perversion. We must rescind every Court decree that ruled against the public and time-honored practices of prayer, Bible reading, teaching of Creationism, and posting symbols of the Ten Commandments and other historic symbols in public buildings, parks, and other public areas in America.

Failure to return to a biblical theocracy will turn American into a living hell and place the nation on death row. We must not only stand our ground, but also wage an offensive war for our King! With the Bible in our hands and His Word in our hearts, let us take His truth into the camp of the enemy and in the name and power of Jesus Christ let His truth sift the wheat from the chaff, the sheep from the goats, and true believers from the serpents, scorpions, and devils of darkness. Let us not live to be a martyr, but live to make martyrs.

3

THE CAUCASIAN
DEMOGRAPHIC CRISIS

Summer 2007

My hope is that every God-fearing, Bible-believing, Caucasian Christian in this land would heed this warning! A crisis is looming in America that trumps all other considerations. Yes, the war in Iraq, the thousands of Mexicans crossing the border into our country every day, record trade deficits that threaten the future of the American economy, public and private debt soaring beyond human calculation, drugs, alcoholism, and a flood tide of immorality that would make the inhabitants of ancient Sodom and Gomorrah blush do not even come close to being as serious as the fact that Caucasians have all but quit having children.

The population of any country grows by natural increase of its own people and through immigration. The racial face of America is undergoing profound change because of non-white immigration from Mexico, Latin America, Africa, India, and Asia. At the same time, the birth rate among the native Caucasian population in America, like Europe and most all of the Anglo-Saxon nations, is dropping below replacement levels. A fertility rate of 2.1 children per capita is necessary to maintain a stable population. The population growth of Caucasians in America has dropped to 1.6, the same as France, while the Hispanic birth rate is soaring.

Demographics is the science of vital and social statistics, including stats on birth, deaths, diseases, marriages, and the measurement of a population of a country. The one common problem shared by every European and Scandinavian country is that they are running out of babies. Caucasian people have elected to live childless. Greece currently has a fertility rate hovering just below 1.3 births per couple, the point of "lowest-low" and from which no nation has ever recovered, according to demographic experts. But wait! It gets even worse! Italy has a fertility rate of 1.2 and Spain 1.1. More Caucasians are dying in Europe than are being born. By 2020, less than fifteen years, Caucasian Europe will cease to exist.

The Caucasian population of America, Canada, Britain, Scandinavia, and all of Europe is aging rapidly. Combine that with the sharp decline in fertility rates, and there simply is an insufficient number of children being born to sustain our civilization as we know it. Money has become one of the most effective birth control programs in history. Millions of married women are now in the work place, no longer stay-at-home moms having babies.

Fertility rates soared in the United States following the Second World War, and these children have sustained the great wave of entitlements including Social Security and other government programs. This great wave of baby boomers born between 1946 and 1964 is aging, dropping out of the system. The problem arises when they are not being replaced in sufficient numbers to sustain the government entitlement and welfare programs. The same holds true for all of Europe. Large European entitlements, six-week vacations, lucrative pensions, and a high tax base require a surging population base. Caucasians in Europe are not having babies, and what is the result? They have relied on a tidal wave of Muslim immigration into Europe, which now dwarfs the Caucasian population. The most popular name in Amsterdam, Brussels, Berlin, Munich, Paris, Copenhagen, and elsewhere in Europe is Muhammad. Why? Because the Arab descendants of Ishmael are having all the babies, while the descendants of Isaac are on birth control pills.

The birth rate in Russia is dropping so sharply that they are simply running out of people. By 2050, the population of Russia will be smaller than the surging Arab population in tiny Yemen. With one-sixth of the earth's land surface, Russia is running out of people. You have only one guess to imagine who will fill the landscape in Russia by the middle of the 21st Century. Every day more Caucasian people are dying in Russia than are being born, so you guessed it: Russia will fill up with Chinese by the middle of the 21st Century.

The most accurate way to determine who will hold political, economic, and military control of a country, a continent, and even the world is to explore the science of demographics. The population growth of a given people will insure them a place on this earth. They will gain territory either by waging war or by the sheer force of colonization. Witness the current colonization of America by forty million Mexicans and more arriving every day. In 1900, one of the highest fertility rates on the planet was among Caucasians throughout the Anglo-Saxon world. This high fertility rate insured their political, economic, and military control of the world.

The 9/11 event on America soil suddenly brought to light a demographic reality that most had not realized. For the past several decades, the Arab population has been 'exploding, with one of the highest fertility rates on the planet. This surging Arab fertility rate makes Muslims the center of population gravity throughout Central Asia, and they are rapidly seizing control of Europe.

Almost every hot spot on earth now involves Arabs, as Mark Steyn explains in his book *America Alone, The End of the World As We Know It,* Regnery Publishing, Inc. 2006. It is Muslims vs. Jews in Palestine, Muslims vs. Hindus in Kashmir, Muslims vs. Christians vs. everyone else in Africa, Muslims vs. Christians in Bosnia, Muslims vs. Buddhists in Thailand, Muslims vs. Russians in the Caucasus, Muslims vs. Danish cartoonists in Scandinavia, Muslims vs. British in the subway bombings in London, Muslims vs. Spain in the Madrid train bombings, and on and on it goes. Arab women are at home having babies while Caucasian women in America and throughout the Anglo-Saxon world are pursuing careers and engaged in everything but having babies.

Europe has become Eurabia, with a surging Muslim population that within a few years will transform Europe into an Islamic stronghold. The tidal wave of Arab immigration necessary to fill the void left by childless Europeans now moves toward political and economic control of the entire European Fatherland. Turks in Germany are surging in numbers and influence. In France, the Muslim population threatens to obscure the old Caucasian France of history. In Britain, Spain, and throughout Scandinavia, the Arab population is surging while the Caucasian fertility rate drops into the cellar!

In the face of the greatest challenge ever to befall the Celtic, Anglo-Saxon, Germanic peoples of history, the pulpits, news media, and even remnant Christians are deathly silent. No one wants to talk about the single greatest problem facing our people. We have quit having babies, but no one seems to care! Sadly, the young Caucasian couples who hold the very key to their own future by having offspring really do not want to be bothered with children. So, the Arabs, Mexicans, Hindus, and Asians declare they will have the babies, and lots of them!

Yes, it is one thing for the Caucasian liberals, Democrats, Communists, Socialists, Fascists, Feminists, Lesbians, Sodomites, Planned Parenthood, Tree Huggers, and abortionists to push for minus zero population growth. Amen! Thank God that all of the named enemies of God do not want or cannot have offspring. Praise God that the Sodomites and Lesbians do not procreate. Thank God the liberals have very few children. Praise the Lord God Almighty that the Communists, Socialists, Democrats, Feminists, and assorted people do not want children! However, it is altogether another thing for honest, God-fearing Christian couples to practice birth control while living in denial of the most basic command God gives to His children in all of Scripture: *"Be Fruitful, and multiply, and replenish the earth, and subdue it: and have dominion over . . . every living thing that moveth upon the earth"* *(Genesis 1:28).* The most flagrant sin among the children of God in modern America is the willful exclusion of children by means of birth control and planned parenthood among the Caucasian Christian (if you can call them that) population of this country. Shame on this childless generation!

There is an urgent and compelling need for our covenant people to revisit the truth of God's Word regarding children and God's call for high fertility rates among His people. Dominion of the earth occurs only when babies are born as God requires in His Word. Forfeiture of a family name, a town, county, and country occurs when people deny the births of children.

The **sin** of childlessness has enabled the invasion of this country by Mexican nationals. The Caucasian population of this country is aging, dying off, and not being replaced by new births. A non-white racial mix is filling the landscape of America, and as it does, the entire spiritual, moral, economic, and social structure of this nation will plummet into a third world condition of poverty, crime, immorality, disease, squalor, and unemployment.

The clock is ticking, and most Americans, sadly even those who call themselves Christian, are too busy to add another child to their Caucasian quiver and secure their own future with their offspring. The spirit of the age is posited against children. Is it not strange that we reject the very ones who can insure our future as a race?

Consider this: One man, Jacob, moved his family of seventy souls into Egypt about 1706 BC (Genesis 46). Some two hundred and fifteen years later, by 1491 BC, this one family of seventy souls, through the simple practice of **multiplying children,** grew to a nation of just under three million people. A high fertility rate among the Israelites very quickly (Exodus 1:7-10) overwhelmed the Egyptian government. Planned parenthood with a government edict to kill all male children quickly stepped in. The Israelites continued to multiply children, even under extremely harsh conditions, and within one more generation, they were sufficiently strong with the power of Jehovah to make an exodus from Egypt.

It is too late for the Caucasian population in America to recover from the sin of birth control. The invasion of our country by non-whites is already too advanced to change the course of our history. However, it is not too late for remnant Christians to repent, return to the fundamental foundations of our faith, and have children. I ask every Caucasian family who can bear children to consider how quickly one family, consistently multiplying children to the fourth and fifth generation, can take dominion of a given geographical area.

If you are a single young man or woman, move forward in marriage and multiply children. If you are a young couple or still youthful enough to become parents, go for it. If you already have a family and are still able to bear offspring, have some more children. Humble yourselves, swallow your pride, and with contrition of heart open your Bible, which reads: ***"The LORD God of your fathers make you a thousand times so many more as ye are, and bless you, as he hath promised you" (Deut. 1:11). "Hear therefore, O Israel, and observe to do*** *it; that it may be well with thee, and that ye may increase mightily, as the LORD God of thy fathers hath promised thee . . . And he will love thee, and bless thee, and multiply thee: he will also bless the fruit of thy womb, and the fruit of thy land . . . Thou shalt be blessed above all people: there shall not be male or female barren among you, or among your cattle"* (Deut. 6:3, 7:13-14).

Bibliography

Bawer, Bruce, *While Europe Slept,* Doubleday Publishers, 2006.

Berlinski, Claire, *Menace in Europe and Why the Continent's Crisis is America's Too,* Crown Publishers, 2006.

Buchanan, Patrick J., *Death of the West,* Thomas Dunne Books, 2002.

——————, *State of Emergency,* Thomas Dunne Books, 2006.

Malkin, Michelle, *Invasion,* Regnery Publishing, Inc., 2002.

McDaniel, George, Taylor, Jared, *A Race Against Time, Racial Heresies for the 21st Century,* New Century Books, 2003.

Pendell, Elmer, PH.D., *Sex Versus Civilization,* The Noontide Press, 1967.

Raspail, Jean, *The Camp of the Saints,* The Social Contract Press, 1973.

Steyn, Mark, *America Alone, The End of the World As We Know It,* Regnery Pulishing, Inc., 2006.

4

THE FEAST DAYS OF JEHOVAH

Fall 2007

The holy days of Jehovah occupy a significant place in Scripture and the practical lives of the covenant people. What role do the festivals play in your life? Have you nailed the biblical holy days to the cross as so many millions of other Christian have? Do you observe the biblical holy days? Do the festivals of both Old and New Testaments have any relevance for Christians today? And what about you? Do you really believe the Bible is a book of faith and practice? Are you content to pick and choose or ignore the biblical holy days? What about the preacher whom you support? Does he teach and observe these holy days? If your children follow your example, will they be festival keepers or covenant breakers?

The weekly Sabbath and annual festivals of Jehovah are central to the faith imparted to ancient Israel. The weekly Sabbath of the seventh day and the annual festivals of the first, third, and seventh month of the biblical year is inseparable from Israel the people of the book. Belief in the preservation of physical Israel is inseparable from the weekly Sabbath and annual festivals of the Bible. Biblical Israelites are inseparably and irrevocably linked to the Sabbath and holy days of Scripture. You really cannot have one without the other.

If Israel can be found on the earth today, we ought to be able to find a people who observe the biblical Sabbath and incorporate the festivals of Jehovah. The people of Esau-Edom, correctly identified as the modern Khazarian/Ashkenaz/Mongol Jews, have validated their *stolen identity* of being biblical Israel by adopting both the Sabbath and the biblical holy days. Two millennia of deception do **not** validate Esau-Edom as the racial descendants of Jacob-Israel. This case of stolen identity would be much easier exposed if genuine Israelites would remain in their covenant with Jehovah and observe the Sabbath and festivals that rightly belong to them, **not** Esau-Edom.

Genuine Israelites who observe Sunday as their weekly Sabbath and replace the biblical festivals with Easter, Christmas, and other religious holidays greatly assist the imposters of history who for almost twenty centuries have masqueraded around the world as the covenant seed of Abraham. The children of Esau-Edom launched their program of *stolen Identity* about 126 BC, when through military force John Hyrcanus, a Maccabean Judean, overran the Edomites (descendants of Esau) together with various Canaanite cities and allowed them to avoid death by embracing the religious customs of ancient Israel, including circumcision, the Sabbath, annual festivals, dietary laws, and other aspects of the covenant embraced by ancient Israel. The Esau/Edom/Canaanite peoples quickly submitted to these requirements and in return gained full status in the covenantal and religious life of the indigenous Israelite population of Judea.

The snake children of Esau/Edom, together with their Canaanite kinsmen, swiftly and deceitfully intermingled among the indigenous Israelite stock of Judea. Not many years passed before they began to gain significant influence and power among the Pharisees and Sadducees, the two most powerful religious parties in the land. The growing influence of the Idumean (Edomite) imposters may be clearly shown by the fact that Herod the Great, appointed by the Imperial Roman government, ruled in Palestine from 37 to about 4 BC. This Edomite dynasty held a firm grip upon the political reins of Palestine until AD 100.

The animosity and enmity of this Idumean family for the indigenous Israelite population can be attested to by the attempt of Herod the Great to massacre all of the young male children, two years and younger, who lived in the land of Judea (Matthew 2:16). Herod Antipas, a son of Herod the Great, was the sly, crafty fox who called for the beheading of John the Baptist (Matthew 14:1-10); he also was the outspoken enemy of Jesus Christ. Herod Agrippa I, a grandson of Herod the Great, ultimately governed all of Palestine. By his order, the Apostle James was murdered and Peter was imprisoned (Acts 12:1-3).

Herod Agrippa II, the son of Herod Agrippa I, had been appointed king of Chalcis, an area in the hill country of Lebanon, by the Roman government. He was invited during a visit to Festus, the Roman governor of Judea, to hear St. Paul's defense and appeal to the emperor (Acts 25:13-26:1-32). Herod Agrippa II joined the Romans in the plunder and destruction of the Kingdom of Judea in AD 70 under the armies of Titus. All the ruling Herods, together with the Herodian religious party (Matther 22:16, Mark 3:6, Mark 12:13), were hostile to the Israelites, particularly to the spiritual leaders of early Christianity, such as John the Baptist, James, and Jesus Christ.

By the early years of the first Century of the Christian era, the Esau-Edom-Canaanite crowd had infiltrated the full social, religious, and political life of the Kingdom of Judea then under the rule of Imperial Rome, masquerading as the stock of Abraham, Isaac, and Jacob. One need not read very long or deep into the New Testament to sense the growing presence of this wicked seed. During the ministry of our Lord Jesus Christ, the *stolen identity* of biblical Israel had been fully implemented by the snake people of Esau/Edom. The Gospel of John chapter 8 is a glaring example of how this wicked Idumean seed had advanced itself as being true Israel. In this instance, the Lord Jesus Christ was involved in a dialogue with members of the Pharisees, consisting of genuine Israelites and the imposters who now claimed full *identification* with biblical Israel. As Jesus engaged the Pharisees, they answered Him, saying, *"We be Abraham's seed, and were never in bondage to any man . . ." (John 8:33).* Recall that biblical Israelites had been slaves in Egypt for well over two centuries (1706 BC to the time of the Exodus, 1491 BC). The Edomites could well say they had not been in bondage. Jesus responded and said among other things the following: *"I know that ye are Abraham's seed; but ye seek to kill me, because my word hath no place in you. I speak that which I have seen with my Father: and ye do that which ye have seen with your father" (John 8:37).*

Jesus acknowledged that the Edomites were Abraham's seed by virtue of their being born through the line of Esau. This did not mean, however, that they were *covenant seed* descended from Jacob. Moreover, Jesus indicated two different fathers, clearly showing that these imposters were not legitimate descendents of the covenant seed of Abraham, Isaac, and Jacob-Israel. Jesus went on to declare, *"If ye were Abraham's children, ye would do the works of Abraham. But now ye seek to kill me, a man that hath told you the truth, which I have heard of God: this did not Abraham" (John 8:39-40).*

As this narrative continues, Jesus Christ makes it clear that the snake people, seeking to steal the identity of biblical Israel, did not fool the Son of God. *"If God were your Father, ye would love me: for I proceeded forth and came from God . . . Why do ye not understand my speech? Even because ye cannot hear my word. Ye are of your father the devil, and the lusts of your father ye will do. He was a murderer from the beginning, and abode not in the truth, because there is no truth in him. When he speaketh a lie, he speaketh of his own: for he is a liar, and the father of it" (John 8:42-44).*

Jesus Christ clearly exposed and linked this spurious and wicked seed to Satan himself (Genesis 3:15). Moreover, Jesus Christ further let it be known that these people who claimed to be Judeans (real Jews) were indeed not descended from the tribe of Judah, nor from any of the other sons/tribes from Jacob-Israel, but were in truth the very synagogue of Satan. *" . . . I know the blasphemy of them which say they are Jews, and are not, but are the synagogue of Satan . . . Behold, I will make them of the synagogue of Satan, which say they are Jews, and are not, but do lie; behold, I will make them to come and worship before thy feet . . ." (Rev. 2:9; 3:9).*

The Esau/Edom/Canaanite faction that began to call themselves Jews more than one hundred years before the birth of Jesus Christ were advocates of the Talmud, not the Old Testament. They were much more addicted to the oral laws and traditions of the Elders than they ever were with the Law, Prophets, Psalms, or History of the genuine Old Testament. The Talmud, Midrashim, Hagada, and the Kabbala were the favorite teachings of those who had assumed the identity of true biblical Israel. With the destruction of Jerusalem and most of the infrastructure of the Kingdom of Judah in AD 70 by the armies of Imperial Rome, hundreds of thousands of genuine Israelites from the tribes of Judah, Benjamin, and Levi were murdered.

As previously mentioned, the Herodians and other factions of the Idumean/Canaanite people living in Palestine joined with the Romans in the destruction of Jerusalem and in the death and expulsion of the Israelites (real Jews) from Palestine. Most of the Idumeans themselves abandoned the land and were dispersed in areas outside of Palestine. At least some of the Edomite/Canaanite population that fled Palestine became a rather prominent player in the history of another nation called the Khazars.

The Khazars flourished from the seventh to the eleventh century in an area extending from the Black Sea to the Caspian, and from the Caucasus to the Volga River in Russia. The powerful Khazars had repelled the Muslim advances against Byzantium in the east at the same time the sword of Islam was sweeping across northern Africa and into Spain. The Khazars had rejected both Christianity in the West and Islam from the East, but that did not prevent them from falling prey to another religion. With the arrival of the Edomite/Canaanites who fled Palestine on the heels of the Roman plunder and military ruin of Palestine in AD 70, the Khazars welcomed and then embraced Pharisaism, the religion of the Edomites. The Khazars quickly adopted the religious beliefs and rituals of Pharisaism (more commonly known as Judaism in contemporary times). For the first time in history, a powerful nation had embraced the religion of the Edomites/Canaanites.

The conversion of the Khazars to Judaism (more correctly Pharisaism) occurred around the year AD 740. Within a short span of time, the Khazarian Empire was devoted to the religion of Pharisaism and endorsing the Talmud and other oral traditions of the elders. Arthur Koestler states on page 19 of his book *The Thirteenth Tribe* (Random House, New York, 1976) this comment about the Khazars: "Until the ninth century, the Khazars had no rivals to their supremacy in the regions north of the Black Sea and the adjoining steppe and forest regions of the Dnieper. The Khazars were the supreme masters of the southern half of Eastern Europe for a century and a half, and presented a mighty bulwark, blocking the Ural-Caspian gateway from Asia into Europe."

The dissolution of the Khazarian Empire in the eleventh century witnessed the migration of large numbers of Khazarian/Ashkenaz

Jews into Eastern Europe. The whole of Eastern Europe became the new seedbed out of which the vast majority of modern Jews originated. Contemporary Jews do not derive their origin from Abraham, Isaac, and Jacob-Israel, but are descended from the Turkish/Mongol/Edomite/Canaanite peoples from ancient Khazaria. Koestler, a well known Jewish writer speaking of modern Jews, comments that they *"came not from the Jordan but from the Volga, not from Canaan but from the Caucasus, once believed to be the cradle of the Aryan race; and that genetically they are more closely related to the Hun, Uigur and Magyar tribes than to the seed of Abraham, Isaac and Jacob"* (Koestler, *The Thirteen Tribe*, p. 17).

By the late 1800s, the Khazarian/Jewish population of Southern and Eastern Europe, embracing the religion of Judaism (Pharisaism), was beginning to migrate in masse into the major cities of the Anglo-Saxon world including New York, Los Angeles, Chicago, London, Paris, and others. We read: *"During the late 1800's and early 1900's, European immigration continued at a high rate. More than 7 of every 10 immigrants came from southern and eastern Europe. In 1907, the United States admitted a record number of 1,285,349 immigrants"* (*World Book Encyclopedia,* Field Enterprises Educational Corporation, 1960, p. 72).

These Khazarian/Ashkenaz Jews with genetics reaching back to Esau-Edom and Canaanite ancestry poured into the United States and quickly integrated into the university and college campuses as professors of almost every discipline. They rapidly entered the arts, entertainment, and all forms of media including radio, newspapers, and later television and the cinema industry. They soon were prolific in banking, on Wall Street, and in every type of financial institution. Esau-Edom soon became advisors to Presidents and formed a powerful lobby in the U. S. Congress. Having stolen the identity of Jacob-Israel, these contemporary Jews from Southern and Eastern Europe soon prevailed in convincing the American public, particularly evangelical Christians, that they were Hebrews, descended from Abraham, and were Israelites, inheritors of all the promises made to Abraham, including the land of Canaan.

Modern Jews have carefully clothed themselves in enough Old Testament laws, including circumcision, weekly Sabbath keeping, annual holy day celebrations, dietary laws, etc. to legitimize themselves be fully endorsed as God's chosen people, with all the rights and privileges of the ancient Israelites—including the land of Palestine. Millions of Christians and their clergy have been duped into accepting Esau-Edom as the rightful descendants of Jacob and the twelve tribes of Israel. The most brazen case of identity theft in history is a success indeed. The strength of this identity theft is measured by the fact that anyone who dares question the racial origin of most Jews and exposes their Khazarian Empire origin will be labeled a bigoted anti-Semite.

Mainstream Christianity has given a tremendous amount of aid and comfort to these imposters. In fact, most Christians believe something not defensible in the Bible. While they reject the weekly Sabbath of the seventh day in preference for Sunday and completely disregard Jehovah's holy days (Passover & Unleavened Bread, Pentecost, and Trumpets, Atonement, and Tabernacles) they embrace man's holidays: Easter, Christmas, Valentine's Day, Halloween, and assorted other pagan celebrations. Contemporary Christians have discarded almost all of the laws of the Old Testament (the tithe law excepted) and instead crafted a religion divorced from the Bible.

Those who wish to claim the faith of Jesus Christ need to carefully retrace their steps and practice the truths of Scripture. Christianity can be validated only when we follow the steps of Jesus Christ and embrace biblical laws and customs. This means that we will circumcise our male children on the eighth day of life to mark them as the seed of Abraham (Genesis 17:13). The biblical Sabbath of the seventh day of the week should be honored in place of the Roman Catholic Sunday worship established outside biblical authority. Christmas, Easter, Valentine's Day, Halloween, and other Babylonian holidays should be rejected in preference for Passover, Pentecost, Trumpets, Atonement, and Tabernacles. Instead of rejecting God's Law Christians need to legitimize their faith by embracing a lifestyle that reflects biblical Christianity.

As long as Christians continue to embrace the Sunday Sabbath, Babylonian holidays, and essentially reject God's Law, they are guilty of sanctioning the stolen identity that Esau-Edom has carefully crafted and implanted so firmly in the minds of this generation. Until or unless we Christians lay claim to the biblical requirements that Jesus Christ embraced, we are blowing religious smoke in the face of Easu-Edom and his Canaanite worldview.

What legacy, then, will you give your children? When you depart this earth, will you leave them with a faith that embraces biblical Christianity or the counterfeit religion that receives a pass from most Christians? Will you leave them with Sunday worship or the biblical Sabbath? Will your sons and daughters embrace Passover or Easter? Will they practice Tabernacles or Christmas? Will they circumcise their male children on the eighth day or allow them to grow up as unmarked seed of Abraham? At what point will the true heirs of Abraham, Isaac, and Jacob get real with God? Must we wait until our economic and political chains are unbearable and we have no recourse but to seek the face of our God?

At least for the present, the snake people of Esau-Edom can rest content in maintaining their stolen identity. They need not fear exposure of their carefully guarded myth because most Christians give credence to the biggest case of *stolen identity* in the history of the world by their simple refusal to practice the religion of Jesus Christ, the Apostles, and the Old Testament Prophets. Those who break this chain of bondage and assume full responsibility for being a Christian Israelite will most assuredly expose the forgery now practiced by modern Jewry.

Remnant Christians, let us work for the full reformation of Christianity. Our Christian Reformation Fathers—including Martin Luther, John Calvin, Huldrich Zwingli, John Knox, and others—took us a long way back to the foundations of Bible truth. Unfortunately, they left much work to do for us. Sadly, the generations who followed did little beyond fossilizing the work of the Reformation Fathers. God's holy Law has been left in spiritual limbo and the work of the Reformation Fathers unfinished. This void has been filled by an artificial, counterfeit version of Christianity that has produced a lifeless people and shrinking numbers in the mainline Protestant churches growing out of the great Reformation Fathers. This hemorrhage cannot be halted without shedding the counterfeit Christianity and returning to the pathway marked in Scripture.

This pastor is determined to work tirelessly for the full work of reformation in the church of Jesus Christ, which includes our return to full biblical Christianity and nothing less. The birthright belongs to Jacob-Israel, but having defaulted on our obedience to Jehovah God, we have forfeited the birthright, albeit temporarily, to Esau-Edom. A counterfeit people now pass themselves off as heirs of Abraham, Isaac, and Jacob, while the whole religious world bows down to these snake people and calls them the chosen of God. How shameful! The *stolen identity* of Esau-Edom can never be exposed and defeated until the rightful heirs of Abraham, Isaac, and Jacob stand up, believe, and practice the faith once delivered to the saints! Will true biblical Israel please stand up and be counted?

5

DOMINION STRATEGY FOR THE COVENANT PEOPLE

Winter 2008

Will your children keep the faith, preserve their ethnic heritage and biblical morality, and exercise dominion in a secular, non-white America? Hear, O House of Jacob! Greetings to the redeemed children of the twelve tribes of Israel living in exile throughout the nations of the Anglo-Saxon world. Grace be to you, and peace, from God our Father, and from the Lord Jesus Christ. Consider this a mayday call to the Christian remnant living in the hinterlands of America and throughout nations where biblical Israel resides. The 21st Century has ushered in the greatest spiritual, moral, racial, and economic challenge to face our covenant people for the past several centuries.

Every city and village in America has been affected by the invasion and colonization from forty million Mexicans now on the ground, with more pouring in every day across our porous borders. Mexicans have colonized California, Arizona, New Mexico, Colorado, and Texas and are now infesting almost every community across the land. One hundred million people of color inhabit America. The Caucasian population in our land is recording the lowest birth rate (1.6 children per family) ever. The high fertility of the non-white population of America, combined with the tidal wave of non-white immigration, poses an imminent danger to every Caucasian family.

This is a call for every God-fearing, Bible-believing Caucasian father to a plan of action. For the glory of your God, the future of your children, and the collective good of your racial heritage, you must become involved in a strategy for dominion in the face of the greatest spiritual, moral, and racial crisis to face our covenant people in the United States of America. Please heed this mayday for spiritual revival and renewal among the Christian remnant, which has an urgent need for spiritual renewal. A spiritual and moral famine grips the American population. The pulpits have abandoned God's Law and are dispensing cheap salvation grace without sacrifice, commitment, duty, or responsibility. There is a terrible falling away in the rank and file of mainstream Christianity; remnant Christians are in danger of losing their spiritual fire and first love of the Gospel. Theological aberrations and heresies abound among remnant Christians. We are left with an urgent need to restore the apostolic and Christian foundations of our covenantal faith in Jesus Christ, the invincibility of God's transcendent Word, and the power of the Holy Spirit.

We need a moral resurgence among all Christians. We must hold the line on the unchanging moral absolutes of God's Law. Remnant clergy must give no ground, no compromise, no quarter whatsoever to abortion, miscegenation, sodomy, pedophilia, fornication, adultery, gambling, alcohol, drugs, or any habit, compulsion, or addiction that threatens the spiritual, mental, and physical energy and finance of Christians. The transcendent moral standard revealed from Jehovah to His covenant people must forever be the rule by which remnant Christians live.

The ethnic heritage of the covenant people must not be compromised at the altar of tolerance and pity. There is no place in the time-honored standard of Jesus Christ and Scripture for the amalgamation of people of different races. Christians have written this law of kind after its kind off and completely ignored the entire first chapter of Genesis. The wholesale sin of miscegenation occurring in America is a stench that reaches to the highest heaven. Racial separatism in our marriages, families, private schools, churches, and communities is an absolute imperative for preserving the ethnic integrity and heritage of Caucasians.

Relative to the economy, this is the time for every family in the Christian remnant to exercise prudence and dominion. America is fully merged in a global economy. The outsourcing of jobs to cheap foreign labor and the off shoring of American companies to foreign lands have all but ended our manufacturing jobs. Free trade policies engineered by American politicians have destroyed the economy of the United States and are in the process of eliminating the Middle Class. Catastrophic trade deficits are turning America into a debtor nation, with the U.S. dollar plunging in purchasing value at the expense of our economy.

The US is becoming a land of urban slums, welfare recipients, and land serfs, with more and more of the nation's wealth concentrated in the hands of the super rich. Remnant Christians must be innovative as they seek to build an economic future outside the confines of corporate Babylon. The goal is to build a future that cannot be outsourced, off shored, or torpedoed by the emerging economic union of the U.S., Canada, and Mexico.

Remnant Christians must understand the reality of where the American political system has landed us in the 21st Century. Caucasian, native-born Americans have become disenfranchised from government at the national level. Both major parties are owned and controlled by special interest groups, multinational corporations, and the Esau-Edom money and media sharks. Both parties and their candidates are moving the country toward full-blown socialism, a massive welfare state, soaring taxes, and government policies that insure the ascendancy of a non-white majority and the end of White Christian Protestant America. Remnant Christians need to be savvy, smart, and energized to take charge of grass roots politics in the local governments where they live. God-fearing Christians should stand up, speak up, and seize every opportunity to run for office at the local level.

Strategy for Dominion

This is no time for remnant Christians to run or seek refuge in the hills. This is the day for remnant Christians to do what Christ told His people to do: "Occupy till I come" (Luke 19:13). This is a time for those who know the truth to speak the truth, stand strong, and in the fear of God and energized by the Holy Spirit know that one with God is a majority. The challenge before remnant Christians is to do what our covenant God told us in His Word. We do not need a new strategy, a new paradigm to deliver us from the quagmire in which we find ourselves. We simply need to be humble and obedient and focus all our energy, time, and wealth on executing the plan which the King gave the covenant people in His divinely inspired and preserved Word of truth. What, then, are the steps that redeemed Israel must take?

First: Set You Spiritual House in Order

1)   Know that your daily discipline of prayer, Bible study, and connection to an organized, Christ-centered church on point with the Bible is urgent. If you do not have a local church, you need to identify with and be under the spiritual cover of a church that is compatible with your view of God and Scripture.

2)   We need to evangelize every member of our family. Every son and daughter, all the grandchildren, and all members of the extended family need to be evangelized. We need to place their

salvation and spiritual state as the highest priority of life. Evangelism begins with the children in your home. If your children are grown, continue to engage them and their children in spiritual and biblical matters. Do not be discouraged if they resist your spiritual meddling into their lives. God will bless you, and one day they may reverse their hostilities and render their eternal gratitude.

3)   You desperately need a biblical worldview that embraces the Gospel of the Kingdom, complete with trust in Jesus Christ, the covenants, the Kingdom, and the knowledge of Israel's identity.

Second: Choose God's Moral Standard and No Other

1)   The transcendent, inspired, and divinely preserved Word of God for   English-speaking people is the Authorized King James Bible of record.

2)   Purpose that you, your family, and collective body (the church) will live by this inspired standard of God's moral absolutes alone.

3)   Make no compromise with the sins of abortion, miscegenation,   sodomy, pedophilia, adultery, fornication, alcoholism, or drugs.

Third: Preserve Your Ethnic Heritage

1)   Teach your children, grandchildren, and extended family members the importance of racial purity (Gen. 6:9).

2)   Teach your sons and daughters early in life the racial truth of Separatism. Keep your offspring out of the public "fool" system and do not allow them to fraternize with friends outside their race.

3)   Preserve by whatever sacrifice necessary the racial purity of the family, the church, and social gatherings.   Become Separatists in the home, the church, and in recreation!

Fourth: Set Your Financial House in Order

1)   Be prudent and frugal in managing the financial resources entrusted into your care by the Living God.

2)   Avoid every form of debt that you can. Do not accrue debt that does not involve the purchase of a home, business, land, or tools for use on the job. Avoid credit card debt with a passion.

3)   Silver (at $15.00 an ounce) and gold (at $820.00) an ounce (as of 11/10/07) continue to hold strong against a declining dollar which may ultimately be replaced by the Amero (God forbid).

4)   Remember it is God Who gives the wisdom and power to get wealth (Deut. 8:18); you owe Him the tenth of all the increase (Lev. 27:30; Mal. 3:10, II Cor. 9:6-7).

5)   Seek a job, establish a business, and provide a product or a service that cannot be outsourced, sent off shore, or terminated as in corporate Babylon. Find a profession, a trade, a business, and an area of expertise that is always in demand.

Fifth: Stand Strong for
Western Christian Culture Standards

1)   Be proud to be a Caucasian American with Western, European Christian roots and heritage. Learn the history of our people and proudly defend it.

2)   Encourage at every point the use of English as the first and only language for America. Aquaint yourself with the great works of English literature.

3)   Encourage the wholesome music of our race, with the great masters of music including Bach, Beethoven, Mozart, Handel, Schubert, Wagner, Strauss, et al, plus Christian hymns, spiritual songs, some Southern Gospel, folk, and bluegrass music. Stand against every form of rock, "Christian" (?) rock, soft rock, rap, country bar-room/cheating music, and music of the jungle.

Sixth: Select Your Geographical Area Carefully

1)   Select semi-rural or rural areas of the country that are populated with indigenous Caucasians who retain a flavor of pro-American, conservative values. Find an area as far removed from a major urban or industrial area, high military target, or nuclear facility as possible.

2)   Work hard to cluster and covenant in a Christian community where you already live, or find one that you can fit into regarding faith, racial heritage, and biblical moral standards.

3)   You need to work to become as self-sufficient as you can without compromising your valuable time, energy, and money. I am not suggesting you live like Old Order Amish (a group presently surging in many areas of the country).

Seventh: Stand in the Gap and Build the Hedge

1)   Every Christian father/husband should be a watchman standing guard over the heritage of God. We need to be a Paul Revere, sound the alarm, and hold fast to the Christian and Patriotic principles upon which our country was built.

2)   We need to make intercessory prayer for our people and our country and pray for repentance and a complete turning from the wickedness that proliferates throughout our country. Prayer is an essential tool!

3)   We need to encourage men to run for office in the local government, write letters to the editor, pass out literature when we can, and live an exemplary life by keeping the biblical Sabbath day holy unto God.

The challenge is now before us. What will we do? Will our sons and daughters stand in the gap and build the hedge when it comes their turn to defend God, faith, race, and country? I pray that we will give heart and soul, mind and strength to serving the King of all kings. Only one life to live— only one King to serve! Let this life be for the cause of Jesus

Christ and His Kingdom! This little theme song fits well with standing in the gap and building the hedge.

> *Have your eyes caught the vision?*
> *Has your heart felt the thrill?*
> *To the call of the Master*
> *Do you answer, "I will"?*
> *For the conflict of the ages*
> *Taught by prophets and by sages*
> *Is upon us, is upon us today!*

6

ISRAEL AND THE KINGDOM: LOST IN MODERN CHRISTIANITY

Spring 2008

The one great theme of the Bible, Genesis 1:1 to the maps, is Israel and her restoration from sin to the earthly Kingdom and Jesus Christ's mission to restore to Israel what she lost because of sin and rebellion. The origin of the people called Israel begins with the call of Abraham from Ur of the Chaldees and the unconditional covenant of promise established in Genesis 12:1 and succeeding revelations from Jehovah recorded in Genesis chapters 13, 15, 17, 18, and 22. The primary thrust of the Law, History, Psalms, and Prophets of the Old Testament is Israel and the marvelous means by which Jehovah ultimately would redeem and reconcile her unto Himself—by the very blood and righteousness of Jesus Christ the Son of God. The ultimate destiny for Israel is the restored, theocratic Kingdom over which Jesus Christ will be King.

This beautiful theme of Israel and the Kingdom is not lost in the New Testament. Rather, the Gospels, Epistles, and the Revelation Letter maintain the clear concept of the redeemed of Israel and the restoration of the Kingdom to Israel as the ultimate end of salvation history. The single person responsible for bringing all of these threads of salvation together is Jesus Christ, the eternal Son of God! To this end, every author whom the Holy Spirit used to write the Bible was an Israelite. Beginning with Moses and ending with John, all were Israelites! There are no exceptions. Moreover, all these writers profile Israel as the redeemed people of God and the heirs of the Kingdom of God on earth.

When Israel and the Kingdom are eliminated from Scripture, all that remains is a blighted and distorted role of Jesus Christ as the Messiah of the Law, the Psalms, and the Prophets. Moreover, the purpose for God's Law is lost, as is the promise and hope for Israel. The entire course of salvation history is distorted and convoluted when biblical Israel is removed from Scripture. Disconnected from Israel and the hope of the Kingdom, the believer is estranged from the mainland of Bible truth and left standing isolated and aloof on the tiny island of John 3:16.

Catholics and Protestants

Tragically, both Roman Catholic and Protestant theologians have left a legacy of replacement theology. For them, the *Gentile, multiracial church* is the new Israel, and the Old Testament forecast of the Kingdom has been fulfilled in this Gentile church. Both Israel and the Kingdom have been absolutely lost from the spiritual menu served from the pulpits of Protestant and Roman Catholic churches to the spiritually anemic sheep in the pews. For these millions of Christians and clergy, God has replaced Israel of the Old Testament with a *new* Israel whom they identify as the *Gentile bride*, or the church redeemed from every race under heaven. Simultaneously, they teach that the Kingdom promised in the Old Testament finds its completion in the church itself. Physical Israel has been spiritualized into a *spiritual Israel,* composed of all races on the planet. The literal Kingdom has been reshaped to fit the mold of the church. The physical throne of David, of which the Bible has much to say, is now synonymous with *"My Father's throne" (Rev. 3:21).* And, instead of Jesus Christ coming to rule upon the *"throne of his father David" (Luke 1:32)* and reigning *"over the house of Jacob for ever" (Luke 1:33),* He now rules in the heart of the believer. The literal throne of David has been placed in spiritual mothballs. The Kingdom over which Christ rules and for which *"there shall be no end" (Luke 1:33)* has been morphed into the church. Thus, biblical Christianity has been lost and is left just a spiritual wasteland of empty promises, broken covenants, and shattered hopes.

Roman Catholics and their Protestant offspring have lost any hope of living in a literal Kingdom on earth, with Jesus Christ ruling upon the throne of David. The goal of Protestants and Catholics is simply to die and go to heaven, spending all eternity in some ethereal existence about which the Bible is silent. The literal reality of the people called Israel, the Kingdom, the throne of David, and a future reign of Jesus Christ upon this earth— these all are lost to modern Christianity. The sum and substance of Scripture has been lost in the replacement theology crafted by clergy who have traded literal Israel for a *spiritual Israel* called the Gentile church. At the same time, the literal, physical Kingdom promised to Israel (Acts 1:6-7) is fulfilled in the church. The Gentile church, both a people (spiritual Israel) and an institution, has replaced any promise of the literal, earthly Kingdom of God.

Moreover, the throne of David of which the Bible speaks so much about does not admit anywhere in Scripture to being a spiritual or imaginary throne in the heart. The throne of David is just as real and literal as any throne in any kingdom on this earth. Moreover, Jesus Christ is King of the Kingdom of God, but He is not King of the church. Christ is Head of the church and King of His Kingdom.

The substance of the Old and New Testaments has been stripped of its spiritual vitality, leaving the covenants, charters, and pledges of a sovereign God to His people shredded, forgotten, and trashed. The heart and soul of Scripture have been ripped out of the Bible, and a cotton candy theology of marsh mellow fluff has been crafted to occupy the minds of those being baptized into the multiracial, multicultural churches bearing Protestant and Roman Catholic labels. The fruit of this theology is coming to full harvest, with a hemorrhage of people leaving the mainline Protestant churches, which have to close their doors for want of parishioners. And, Roman Catholics are forced to fill their pews with third world immigrants flocking to the United States.

Young men preparing for ministry in the Roman Catholic priesthood or any one of the mainline Protestant churches are schooled in the theology of Supercessionism. This doctrine simply means that all that God and Scripture promises to physical Israel in the Old Testament has been transferred to a multiracial, Gentile church. Furthermore, all that the Bible teaches about the Kingdom has been fulfilled in the Church. To achieve this rock-hard doctrine, entire segments of the Old Testament have been spiritualized. Moreover, the New Testament Scripture has been crafted to fit this new paradigm of theology so that the substance of the whole Word of God has been emptied of its covenantal foundations to Israel and the promise of the Kingdom of God. The end result is that the biblical foundations for genuine Christianity have been traded for a light, ambiguous Gospel.

Evangelical Christians

The evangelical world, including most flavors of Baptists, has evolved a completely different theology. But like Protestants and Roman Catholics, evangelicals have crafted a multiracial, Gentile church to account for their inability to know what happened to the lost ten tribes of Israel. Assuming that the Gentiles, Heathen, Scythians, and Barbarians of the New Testament are a composite of all races, they have simply labeled them as *spiritual Israel—*

all collected in the Gentile, New Testament church. Simultaneously they have made a certain place for the *modern Jews*, particularly those gathered into Palestine, regarding them as the surviving Israelite stock of ancient Israel. To these Jews they accord all the covenants, charters, and promises of the Old Testament given to the collective twelve tribes of Israel.

Like railroad tracks running in tandem, they have one track for the multiracial, Gentile church and another place for the Jews, whom they assume to be all that survives of ancient Israel. Some evangelicals revere the Jews to the point that they are willing to allow them another pathway to salvation apart from the Lord Jesus Christ. However, those numbered in the Gentile church are required to confess Jesus Christ and be baptized in His name before they can qualify for eternal life. The Jews are special: they have access to eternal life because of who they are, while members of the Gentile church must qualify through Jesus Christ. The Jews are so special that they are granted immunity from repentance, confession of sin, profession of Jesus Christ, and baptism. They are bound to Jehovah God by virtue of the unconditional covenant of promise given to Abraham.

As you can see, Evangelical Christians have accorded a very special place for the Jews, to whom they interchangeably refer as Israel. Evangelicals believe that the Jews represent collectively all twelve tribes of Israel. They make absolutely no pretense of trying to identify the vast numbers of Israelites from all the other tribes taken into captivity by the Assyrians and later the Babylonians centuries before the birth of Jesus Christ. The refusal of the vast majority of Jews to accept Jesus Christ and name Him as their Redeemer does not dent at all the minds of Evangelicals. They have created a *spiritual asylum* for the Jews so that they are immune from the normal requirements for being a Christian. They have eternal life by virtue of covenant—apart from the Person of Jesus Christ.

This favored people treatment has fostered the idea that the Jewish Israeli State is hallowed ground that marks the spot for the return of biblical Israel to the land of their fathers, with the ultimate goal of restoring a literal, earthly Kingdom over which Jesus Christ will rule when He returns. Millions of evangelicals have been schooled by their clergy that America must defend the Jewish Israelis State at all costs and that our foreign policy should be crafted so that what is good for the Jews is good for America. Even before 1948, evangelical Christians lobbied for the support of the Jewish State in Palestine. The theology of evangelical Christians in respect to the Jews has helped shape American foreign policy for more than sixty years.

The spiritual falling away from mainstream Christianity is quite the large event, whether one look at the situation in America, Britain, Scandinavia, Europe, Australia, New Zealand, or anywhere else in the Anglo-Saxon world. However, what is flourishing is the explosion of small Bible study groups seeking a biblically based Christianity. Mega churches are an indication of the malnutrition prevalent in 21st Century America. These churches teach little but the "tell me how good I am," "increase my self esteem" prosperity Gospel. Otherwise known as the "name it and claim it, blab it and grab it" theology, this brand of Christianity has no problem gathering great crowds. The word *sin* is verboten in modern preaching. God's Law is certainly not taught, for it would surely cause the wicked to feel bad or guilty. In the absence of God's Law, the guilt of sin remains unknown, and the blood of Jesus Christ has no meaning.

If you are looking for a biblically based Christianity, Israel and the Kingdom provide your answer. If your personal faith walk is not biblically based, you are living in deception, and this fraudulent faith will be exposed at the judgment of God (John 12:48). Those who build faith apart from the truth of God's Word (John 1:1) will surely come up short when they stand before the Judge on Judgment Day. Consider carefully the indispensable truth of Israel and the Kingdom when choosing a church and appropriating your hard-earned tithe.

Indisputable Points on Israel and the Kingdom

1)   Our sovereign God is the author of His Word; He alone determines the truths contained therein. *"Every word of God is pure: he is a shield unto them that put their trust in him.   Add thou not unto his words, lest he reprove thee, and thou be found a liar"* *(Proverbs 30:5-6; also Psa. 12:6-7, 119:160; Deut. 4:2, 29:29).*

2)   God the Father chose Israel in election before the foundation of the world (Isa. 41:8, 44:1, 45:4; I Pet. 1:2; Eph. 1:4-5; II Tim: 1:9; Rom.8:28-30). He promised this election with His sworn oath to Abraham (Deut. 7:8; Luke 1:73; Heb. 6:17) and ratified it by terms of the New (Messianic) Covenant of Grace (Jer. 31:31-34; Heb. 8:7-13, 10:14-17), secured by the very blood of Jesus Christ (Isa. 43:1; Matt. 26:28; Luke 1:68-77; I Pet. 1:18-19; Rom. 3:24-25, 5:9-11; Col. 1:13-14; Rev. 1:5).

3)   Israel, chosen in election, redeemed by the blood of Jesus Christ, and sanctified by the Holy Spirit, cannot be lost to the divine favor of God (John 10:26-20; Matt. 19:28; Mark 13:27; Luke 22:29-30; Isa. 41:8-9, 44:21-22, 46:3-4, 49:15-16, 54:17, 59:21, II Sam. 7:24; I Chr. 17:21-22; Isa. 66:22; Jer. 31:35-37; Rev. 7:1-8; 21:9-12).

4)   Jehovah is bound to Israel by unconditional covenants that cannot be broken (Genesis 12, 17, 18, 22, Jer. 31:31-34, 32:37-44; Ezek. 37:26).

5)   The Kingdom of God is the ultimate end of salvation history and is a major theme throughout the Bible (EX. 19:5-6; ISA. 2:1-5, 11:6-16, 65:17-25, Ezek. 37:21-28, Dan. 2:44-45, 7:18, 27; Joel 3:16-21; Amos 9:11-15; Obadiah 18-21; Micah 4:1-5; Zech. 2:12-13, 14:8-21; Matt. 19:28; 21:42-44; 25:31-34; Luke 1:31-33, 13:28-30, 22:28-30; 23:42-43; John 18:36, Acts 1:3, 6, 8:12, 14:22, 19:8, 20:25, 28:23, 31; I Cor. 15:24, 50, Heb. 12:27, 28; Rev. 11:15, 21, 22).

6)   The land of promise given in perpetuity to Abraham, Isaac, and Jacob-Israel will be the headquarters for the theocratic Kingdom of Jesus Christ (Genesis 12:1, 7, 13:14-17, 15:18, 17:6-8, 26:3, 28:4, 35:12; Exod. 6:4, 8; Deut. 30:1-5; II Sam. 7:10; Psa. 105:6-11; Acts 7:5; Heb. 11:8, 9; Zech. 2:12, 14:8, 16-21; Jer. 3:17, 18, 16:15; Ezek. 37:25; Joel 3:17; Amos 9:14, 15).

7)   The throne of David is secured by an unconditional and perpetual covenant made with David and is destined to be the throne upon which Jesus Christ will rule in His Kingdom (II Sam. 7:13-16; Psa. 89:1-4, 28-37, 132:11; Isa. 9:6, 7; Jer. 23:5,6, 33:14-26; Ezek. 34:23, 24, 37:22-24; Zech. 14:9; Matt. 19:28, 25:31; Luke 1:31-33; Acts 2:29-31).

8)   Entrance into this Kingdom can be attained only with a spiritual rebirth by faith in the Lord Jesus Christ and the effectual working of the Holy Spirit as He makes effectual what God the Father purposed and Jesus Christ made possible by His sacrificial Crucifixion and Resurrection from the dead (John 3:1-8; John 3:36, 5:24; 14:6; 17:3; 20:31; Acts 4:12; 16:30,31; Romans 6:3-6; 10:9,10; I John 5: 1,11,12, 20).

All Bible-believing, blood-washed, Spirit-filled Christians will hold tenaciously to a belief in the permanent existence of all twelve tribes of Israel and the promise of the restoration of the Kingdom of God in this earth at the Second Coming of Jesus Christ. Citizenship in the Kingdom of God should be the highest priority of anyone (Matt. 6:33). A devoted, committed disciple of Jesus Christ is what the King of this coming Kingdom requires of every Christian.

Anyone who examines the landscape of modern Christianity must confess that something profoundly wrong has taken over. The Christian faith in America no longer molds the culture. Rather, the pagan secular humanist culture is remolding Christianity in its image. It is not the church in the world, but the world in the

Church. The loss of life and spirit in Christianity is clearly demonstrated in the murder of the unborn. The national endorsement of abortion since *Roe v Wade 1973* has witnessed the murder of nearly fifty million unborn children!

And, homosexuality, once condemned and declared intolerable and an abomination by the church, is now condoned. Likewise, miscegenation was once considered shameful, but is now accepted inside the sanctuary and at large throughout society. What the church used to label as sin and absolutely unacceptable has now found a place of honor. Abortion, sodomy, miscegenation, fornication, adultery, gambling, and other heinous crimes against God are rampant in American society. More tragically, some of these sins have found a place of comfort in many churches.

For these and other reasons, devout Bible students are seeking alternative routes to worshiping God and making a place for the faith of Jesus Christ in their lives. Mega churches that draw tens of thousands of people appear on the surface to serve God. However, upon closer examination, these congregations are fully multiracial. They do not proclaim God's Law, but in fact minimize it at every hand so sinners have no guilt for their sin. Thus, the value of the cross has been almost extinguished.

In the face of this spiritual falling away, remnant Christians must square their shoulders and be resolved to live fully committed lives to the glory of Jesus Christ. Full attention must be given to children and youth, encouraging them to be a generation that will carry the faith forward through the 21st Century. Last but certainly not least is the compelling need to keep the identity of Israel and the knowledge of God's Kingdom as cornerstones in the theological belief system of these children and youth. Let us all be encouraged to keep the faith once delivered to the saints!

7

ON THE PRECIPICE
OF CATASTROPHE

Summer 2008

*B*low ye the trumpet in Zion, and sound an alarm
in my holy mountain: let all the inhabitants of the
land tremble: for the day of the LORD cometh for
it is nigh at hand" *(Joel 2:1)*. To whom it may concern among
the twelve tribes in dispersion among the Celtic, Anglo, Saxon,
Germanic, Scandinavian and kindred peoples of the United States
of America and abroad throughout the British Isles, Europe,
Scandinavia, Australia, New Zealand, South Africa, Rhodesia,
Canada, greetings! Consider this newsletter a mayday call to the
covenant people of Jehovah. I feel compelled to send this
newsletter to those I love in Jesus Christ whose hearts have been
inspired by the **Gospel of the Kingdom** and know who they
are and have found security in the covenants of God. Looking
at the world through my window in Western Missouri, particularly

with such troublesome current events, I sense urgency beyond anything I have known in all my years of ministry for Jesus Christ and His Kingdom. I humbly submit that we are on the precipice of a catastrophic series of events. Yes, I personally feel spiritually secure in Jesus Christ, trusting Him for salvation and knowing that He is sovereign and has the whole world and every one of His sheep in His spiritual arms. No weapon formed can destroy the covenant people of Jehovah (Isaiah 54:17). As long as the sun, moon, stars, heaven, and earth endure, God has promised that Israel, His people, would never cease from being a people on this earth (Jeremiah 31:35-27). God will forever take care of His own sheep.

I go to bed in peace and sleep securely at night because I know that He Who watches over the sparrows (Matthew 10:29-31) has even more concern for His very own children. Worry is interest paid on trouble that generally never happens. The God Whom we love and serve is working out all things according to the council of His own will (Eph. 1:11) and will let us know when He needs our assistance. Every sword wielded on this planet is under His control; all the princes, judges, kings, presidents, and potentates of this earth rule by His sovereign decree.

As a minister charged with being a watchman for Israel, I would be remiss if I did not remind you that we live in a world coming under the judgment and wrath of the Living God. All of our lives will be impacted by the events presently underway. Troublesome times will certainly escalate as the days unfold. Consequently, we need to be in right spiritual and moral relationship with God, living with a penitent and humble attitude and standing strong and tall in the battle for the King and His Kingdom!

God's Hand in Nature

The world cannot process one catastrophic event before another is underway. While relief workers were trying to assess the death toll and destruction of one of the largest cyclones recorded in Burma, a major earthquake, the largest and most destructive in seventy-five years, rocked China, burying tens of thousands in the rubble. Meanwhile, tornadoes rip across the Middle and Southeastern United States, leaving a path of destruction and death.

Fires, floods, hurricanes, tornadoes, droughts, and even earthquakes have repeatedly threatened America. An earthquake shook portions of Illinois, Kentucky, and Missouri along the New Madrid fault line without more than a ripple of notice from the average American. In the face of unprecedented natural disasters in America, there is no sign of national repentance.

Blame for these planetary disasters is laid at the step of global warming, Soviet weather experimentation, and a variety of other exaggerations. Few are willing to admit that the sovereign hand of God might indeed be in charge of the world He created.

Economic Woes Abound

America's disconnect from God, the principles of His Word, and the long-standing values that once guided Her has brought us to the brink of financial disaster. Monetary policies of the privately owned Federal Reserve Bank that governs the economic affairs of America, a nine trillion dollar national debt, unprecedented trade deficits, soaring personal debt, off-shoring of manufacturing, outsourcing of jobs, government red tape and bureaucracy, and multiple free trade agreements that favor other nations over America are rapidly reducing this country to third world status.

Skyrocketing Gasoline Prices

The price of crude oil, now topping $139.00 a barrel and with predictions of $200.00 a barrel and gasoline soaring to unbelievable new levels of five and six dollars a gallon (even $9.00 in foreign countries!) is sending shock waves throughout the

American economy. We are not prepared for what soaring gasoline and diesel fuel prices might mean for us. Absolutely every segment of society will be impacted by the soaring costs of energy. Our entire economy will be jeopardized, and social upheaval will commence, with riots in major cities. If massive food shortages develop and transportation slows or shuts down, rioting could set major American cities on fire, with martial law imposed and gasoline and food rationing ordered by the Federal Government.

Projected Food Shortages

The confluence of several factors is creating worldwide food shortages. First is adverse weather conditions in America and elsewhere in the current growing season; grain and other food surpluses could be in short supply. Second is the proliferation of ethanol fuel production, which is accelerating demand for corn. Third, grain surpluses in the U.S. have consistently been short for several years running. Any major disruption of the trucking industry, and all major food supermarkets might have to close their doors within hours.

The Mexican Invasion of America

The tidal wave of Mexicans pouring into the U. S. since the late 1970s means that between forty and fifty million Mexicans have colonized and seized control of most of the Southwestern United States. The Federal Government has no intention of stopping the flow of illegals entering the U.S. across our Southern and Northern borders. The North American Union linking the U.S. with Mexico and Canada is now well underway. No President, no Congress, nor anyone is going to seal our borders. Open borders and a tidal wave of illegal immigrants is the official policy of most elected officials regardless of Party affiliation.

The entire racial face of America is turning brown. Moreover, terrorists from the Middle East and elsewhere have slipped through these porous borders and have formed deadly cells of potential terrorism within the border of this country. Factions of radical

Islam are recruiting and training would-be terrorists inside the U.S.A. America is rapidly becoming a nation of non- assimilated races, religions, languages, and cultures.

The American-Israeli Love Affair

America was officially wed to the Jewish State of Israel on May 14, 1948, when U.S. President Harry Truman welcomed the new Jewish State and promised aid of every kind. Since that date, every American President and Congress elected to office has courted, loved, and financially pampered this Jewish country. America's love affair with the Israelis has been the deciding factor in shaping our foreign policy for the past sixty years. The fruits of this love affair have been devastating for the U.S. Our nation has been alienated against the Arab Middle East. Curses, not blessings, have come to America since Israeli came into existence in 1948.

America has not won a decisive military victory in any country since we married the Israelis in 1948. Our current Middle East Wars are in large part the result of the love affair the U.S. has with the Jews in Palestine. A major reason for the soaring price of gasoline stems from Islam's bitterness of America's long standing support of the Israelis Jews. American generosity for the Israelis Jews has yielded curses, not blessings, for the last sixty years. The Israelis are one of the most well armed nuclear powers in the world, thanks to American generosity.

Protracted, Undeclared Wars

The U. S. engaged war against the Taliban Muslim radicals in January of 2002. After six long years of waging war, the Taliban is still surging in the provinces along the Pakistan border. The U. S. entered war against Saddam Hussein in Iraq in March of 2003. After five long years of fighting, Iraq continues to be in and out of civil war with Shi's and Sunnis at each other's throats and a corrupt government that is mostly impotent and paralyzed. American military forces are wearing thin as some recruits have seen as many as two or more extended stays in Iraq. Syria and Iran are both sending freshly trained terrorists in an ongoing basis to keep the chaos alive.

The Islamic policy in the Middle East is to keep the U.S. involved in these protracted wars so that they can bleed America financially, exhaust our armies, and break the will of the American public. After ten years, the Taliban in Afghanistan bankrupted the armies of the Soviet Union; finally, by 1989, the Berlin Wall came crumbling down, and the Soviet Empire collapsed. The Islamic world believes that America, like the Soviet Union, will ultimately be bankrupt, its military demoralized, and the American nation ripe for conquest from Islamic terrorists planted and operating within U.S. borders.

The sons of Ishmael are relentless in their hatred for Isaac, his faith, and his culture. America's military is active in Afghanistan, Iraq, and Pakistan. Iran is flexing its potential nuclear muscles, knowing full well that the U.S. is already spread thin in the Middle East. A large terrorist strike at a major oil field in Saudi Arabia or elsewhere in the Middle East could quickly escalate into a major world war. China, Japan, and India are already competing for oil with America and other Western nations. The quest for oil may be the catalyst that triggers another massive world war.

Is America Ripe for Attack?

Since 9/11/01, with the destruction of the Twin Towers and the bombing of the Pentagon, Islamic extremists have been patiently biding their time for the next assault against America. Open and porous borders have allowed thousands of militant Muslims to enter the U.S. form guerilla training cells. They await a signal to strike another blow against America. This could be in the form of a small, fast, underwater submarine capable of inflicting untold damage to an American port.

Terrorists could strike at any one of the many soft spots in America including nuclear power plants, water systems, electric grids, or at a mass gathering of people, as in a sporting coliseum. Islamic terrorists have the potential of obtaining a nuclear bomb from any number of places including the Soviet Union and even from our own stockpile of weapons. God-fearing Americans need to know that any terrorist strike against America will result in further erosion and loss of long cherished liberties under the **Bill of Rights**. Remember those?

Our Spiritual Crisis

America's political, economic, social, and domestic ills stem from its broken covenant with God. The people who settled and built America did so under a conditional covenant relationship with Jehovah. Obedience to His covenant Law would insure blessings, and disobedience would invite curses.

The covenant people, the preamble people who were founders of this Republic and who wrote our U. S. Constitution, are all gone. Their successors and beneficiaries have betrayed this covenantal contract, broken covenant, and worshipped other gods. They have allowed other cultures, gods, religions, languages, and moral codes to fill a land that was once dedicated to Jesus Christ, the Bible, and God's Law. In the quest for material abundance, the pleasures of sin, and the love for other gods and cultures, they have lost the knowledge of the one, true, and living God, Jehovah, and suffer from a spiritual famine that engulfs the entire nation!

The Moral Free-Fall of America

All of American society is in a moral free fall from the absolutes of God's eternal Law. Preachers have long declared the Ten Commandments, Statutes, and Judgments of the Bible void, and our politicians, news pundits, and journalists followed them in a complete divorce from God and His Law. Having discarded the moral absolutes of God's Law, the country is now in a moral free fall. We murder our unborn children and call it freedom of choice. We swap wives and call the sin of adultery an extra-marital affair. We allow sodomites to ply their vile evil in broad daylight and call it an alternative life style. We encourage interracial mixing and call it racial reconciliation.

Everything the Bible calls sin is now given a place of honor in America. What God hates, America loves. The moral carnage in our land is reaping a harvest of pain, suffering, and death as millions follow the pathway of alcohol, drugs, and free love, reveling in the pleasures of sin. The country is awash in pornography, prostitution, gambling, binge drinking, and an obsession for the erotic. Interracial mixing, homosexuality, same-sex marriage, and perversion are the prevailing moral theme. Like Sodom and Gomorrah of ancient history, America is ripe for judgment. It will come as surely as night follows day.

The Time of Jacob's Trouble

The problems facing the United States of America, the single greatest nation to ever grace this earth, can be understood only when we know its biblical, historical, and prophetic context. America is the great birthright nation of Joseph, fulfilled in his son, Manasseh. The people who settled this land and until about 1890 were Israelites descended from ancient Israel. These are the covenant people of Scripture, descended from Abraham, Isaac, and Jacob, and Scripture declares that in the latter days of their history, they would fall away from Jehovah, their covenant God, and enter a time called **Jacob's Trouble.**

This time of unprecedented trouble would become so intense that in every nation where these biblical Israelites were in dispersion—including America, Great Britain, Scandinavia, Europe, Australia, New Zealand, South Africa and elsewhere—they would come to a political, economic, and military end in preparation for the arrival of Jesus Christ and the inauguration of His Kingdom rule in this earth. The end of all these nations is called *"the full end of all nations" (Jeremiah 30:11).*

This time of trouble in the nations of the Christian West is described in Jeremiah 30:7: *"Alas! For that day is great, so that none is like it: it is even the time of Jacob's trouble; but he shall be saved out of it" (Jeremiah 30:7)*. Daniel voiced this same prophetic announcement (Dan. 12:1): *". . . there shall be a time of trouble, such as never was since there was a nation even to that same time: and at that time thy people shall be delivered, every one that shall be found written in the book."* Jesus Christ Himself reaffirmed these warnings when He declared, *"For then shall be great tribulation, such as was not since the beginning of the world to this time, no, nor ever shall be. And except those days should be shortened, there should no flesh be saved: but for the elect's sake those days shall be shortened"* *(Matt. 24:21-22— emphasis added)*.

The English word *trouble,* appearing in the text of Jeremiah and Daniel, is from the Hebrew root word *tsaw-raw'* and *tsawr* and means *a tight place, tightness, narrow, adversity, affliction, anguish, distress, tribulation.* In the latter days, Israel was to find herself in a tight place, a tight spot with no way out. Their back was to be against the wall. Their plight was to be very much like the trouble that Israel faced as bondslaves in Egypt when they cried out in their trouble and Jehovah heard them (Exodus 3:23-24). The trouble facing Israelites in America is very much like ancient Israel in the Exodus from the Egypt. Israel was caught between Pharaoh's army and the Red Sea, with no way out (Exodus 14:8-15).

This great tribulation is also reminiscent of the day when Israel withered before the Philistine armies that had invaded the land, and their captain and leader (Goliath) challenged the armies of the Israelites (I Samuel 17). This time of *Jacob's Trouble* was prefigured in the days of Gideon when the Midianites had swarmed the land and threatened the very existence of the nation of Israel (Judges 6). It is the kind of trouble Hezekiah and the nation of Judah faced when 185,000 Assyrian soldiers were camped around the city of Jerusalem (Isa. 37:36-38). Jacob's time of trouble is like that facing Asa when a million-man army under Zerah, the Ethiopian, came against the Israelites, and there seemed to be no way out (II Chr. 14:9-12). The same kind of trouble came upon the nation of Judah when Jehoshaphat was on the throne, and the combined armies of Moab and Ammon threatened annihilation (II Chr. 20:1-4).

In the midst of trouble never before known, the nations of modern Israel were to come to their full political, economic, and military end. The covenant people would receive their much-deserved correction and punishment but be delivered out of this time of unprecedented trouble. *" . . . though I make a full end of all nations whither I have scattered thee, yet will I not make a full end of thee: but I will correct thee in measure, and will not leave thee altogether unpunished"* *(Jeremiah 30:11).* Punishment upon Israel was always remedial, corrective, and not to the destruction of the race. This is not to say that great suffering and pain will not come upon the unrepentant and unsaved in Israel. The Time of Jacob's Trouble will bring the cry of ancient Israel, when in their affliction *"they cried unto the LORD in their trouble, and he delivered them out of their distresses"* *(Psalm 107:6).*

All of the trouble that was to come upon biblical Israel, identified on the world stage in modern history as the Celtic, Anglo, Saxon, Germanic and kindred peoples, is trouble that either God sent or God used. In this case, God's covenant people have brought this evil upon themselves through disobedience to Jehovah. The divine covenants, charters, and guarantees that issue from the unconditional covenant Jehovah made with Abraham will not fail His people. A remnant in every Anglo-Saxon nation under heaven will be spared in the time of Jacob's trouble. In the meantime, Israelites need to pray, live a righteous life, and focus on the Lord Jesus Christ and His Kingdom.

The trouble compounding on every hand will be the impetus for the covenant people to find their way back to Jehovah God.

The gathering political, economic, social, racial, and military problems will drive God's people into His arms. There will be no other option for them. They will have to repent or perish. There will be no neutral ground. We will find deliverance in Jehovah God and His mercy, or we will suffer pain in the fire and brimstone of God's impending wrath upon an ungodly, reprobate, and perverse generation.

For many years, the words of II Chronicles 7:14 have been used to call for national repentance: *"If my people, which are called by my name, shall humble themselves, and pray, and seek my face, and turn from their wicked ways; then will I hear from heaven, and will forgive their sin, and will heal their land."* At long last, this call for repentance will be heard by a God-fearing remnant of covenant people living in America and elsewhere among the nations of modern Israel. The economic deprivation that is coming upon this land, with third-world poverty abounding, will bring Israel to her knees. Repentance may be the only silver lining in the storm clouds gathering over America.

We are on living on the edge, approaching the precipice of catastrophe! Only God knows what lies ahead for America. You can be sure it is big trouble! No arm of the flesh can save us. Nothing less than intervention from heaven will save the blood-bought children of Jehovah. America is on the verge of national political, economic, social, and racial upheaval that will eclipse everything in our previous history. Fasten your seatbelts, for the turbulence is already beginning, and the wildest ride of history is under way.

8

AMERICA IN CRISIS: IS THERE A WAY BACK TO GOD?

Fall 2008

America is a nation in crisis. Tens of thousands of silver-haired, God-fearing Americans cling tenaciously to the traditional, historic, and biblical ideals upon which America was founded. They helplessly watch as the country they love drifts rapidly into socialism, multiculturalism, racial diversity, humanism, and moral reprobation. For millions of Anglo-Saxons, particularly those born just before and shortly after World War II (1939-1945), the country of their childhood has vanished. The America of the 21st Century is unrecognizable as the same country for Americans with a reference point of 1950. We have slipped over the precipice into the abyss of spiritual, moral, political, social, and economic chaos. America is in crisis, and in the face of spiritual, moral, political, and economic chaos, not one single person on the national stage has the spiritual and moral courage to call America to national repentance! As a nation, we have stumbled from one catastrophe to another. There is barely time to process one event before another happens. This country cannot catch its breath from one upheaval until another one is on the way. Like a drunken sailor, we stumble from one national emergency to another. We may have become so spiritually calloused that we cannot see or hear the God Who gave this nation its birth.

Is God Speaking to America?

Millions of Americans have apparently forgotten that Jehovah *"is the governor among the nations"* (Psa. 22:28) and that from His throne in the heavens, *"His kingdom ruleth over all"* (Psa. 103:19). The civil rulers of America have apparently forgotten the warning issued from Jehovah when He declared, *"Be wise now therefore, O ye kings: be instructed, ye judges of the earth. Serve the LORD with fear, and rejoice with trembling"* (Psa. 2:10-11). Tens of thousands of American clergy have apparently forgotten that Jehovah said, *"Woe be unto the pastors that destroy and scatter the sheep of my pasture! . . . behold I will visit upon you the evil of your doings, saith the LORD"* (Jer. 23:1-2). The God of Scripture is clearly speaking to those who have eyes to see and ears to hear in America!

Political Chaos

The two major political parties have tied the nation up in gridlock, with Congress in a state of abject paralysis. Congress is filled with the best men and women money can buy. The voice of biblical and historical truth is mute in the White House, the halls of Congress, and in the U. S. Supreme Court. A radical liberal reared in extremist Islamic theology in Jakarta, with deep racial and cultural roots in Kenya and for the past twenty years in black liberation communist theology in Chicago, is making steady gains for the White House, cheered on by left-wing television networks, communist-infested university and college professors, and socialist theologians. If the Obomination that maketh desolate does come into office, it will happen because Americans deserve nothing better.

Devastating Weather Patterns

America has been sorely tested in 2008. Devastating floods in Iowa and the entire Mississippi flood plain wrought havoc in the heartland. Much of Iowa and the Midwest corn belt was baptized in flood waters. Devastating fires ravaged much of California. Hurricanes ravaged our coastline from Florida to Texas. Earthquakes rattled California, and the earthquake along the New Madrid fault rattled windows and shook more than half a dozen states in the heartland. A record-setting number of tornadoes ripped across the country, leaving in their wake a path of devastation, loss of life, and property damage beyond calculation. Disaster officials working at FEMA could not bring relief to one catastrophic event before another one was under way. Still . . . did anyone connect the dots and realize that a sovereign God might be speaking to this country?

Foreign Entanglements

American military units are engaged in combat in Afghanistan, since 2002, in Iraq since 2003, and US military units stand guard in South Korea, Kosovo, Germany, and elsewhere around the world. The old KGB Guard in power in Russia, swimming in oil revenues, is trying to reassemble the former Soviet Union. The Russian strike into Georgia was the first step in the growing Russian imperialism. Overflowing with oil revenues, Russia is arming to the teeth. Awash in money garnered under liberal free trade with the United States, China is in the middle of a massive military buildup.

Many of the NATO countries, including Great Britain, France, and Germany, are being overrun with young, militant Muslims who crowd the streets of London, Paris, and Berlin. The Islamic oil-producing nations are becoming super rich from the billions of dollars worth of oil Americans use. The super rich oil sheiks in the Middle East are busy buying up property and corporations all over America. Pakistan already has nuclear weapons, and Iran is moving in that direction. With all of its generous foreign aid to more than one hundred countries, America is the most despised and hated nation under heaven.

Economic Chaos

In the face of the current global economic crisis, economic, political, and social infrastructure is crumbling into chaos. The monetary policies of the privately owned Federal Reserve System, government's surrender to greedy corporate bankers and Wall Street financiers, social engineering for home loans to the minorities and indigent welfare classes, the enormous debts piled up with credit card buying, run away entitlements, government subsidized aid to illegal aliens, billions in foreign aid to more than 100 countries around the world, hundreds of billions poured into the wars waged in Iraq and Afghanistan, and a free-for-all spending binge by both Democratic and Republican Congress—these failed policies have brought the nation to bankruptcy! Economic judgment is upon America, and my fear is that we have witnessed only the tip of the iceberg.

Since 1980, America has undergone profound economic change. The manufacturing base that supported the Middle Class has been off-shored to Asia, thanks to Free Trade policies of the US Government. Millions of jobs have been outsourced to India and the Far East, leaving U.S. workers who once lived the American dream to find themselves working minimum wage jobs and paying $4.00 per gallon for gasoline. The great American Middle Class is emptying as America moves forward, where only the rich and the very rich or the poor or moderately poor fill the landscape.

Wall Street Meltdown

The rich, the super-rich, the powerful, and the movers and shakers of high finance have presided over the meltdown of some of the largest and oldest financial institutions on Wall Street. Bear/ Stearns, Lehmann Brothers, Merrill-Lynch, Freddie Mac, Fannie Mae, Wachovia, AIG, and others have undergone a financial meltdown. The largest drop in the 112-year history of the DOW occurred in the week ending October 10, 2008, when hard-working Americans lost 2.4 trillion dollars in the process. The only winners were the fat cat CEO's who harvested multiplied millions just ahead of the financial collapse of these major financial giants.

The buy-now/pay-later credit addiction of Americas has come to harvest. The insatiable credit binge of the Federal Government, state and local governments, and the American public has come to an end. The artificial credit financial system is dissolving into oblivion as Babylon shakes, rattles, and heaves. The enormous public and private debts that have piled higher and higher in the last forty years have catapulted the financial system of America into the abyss. The 750-billion dollar bail out from the Federal Government is only a temporary band-aid. The financial future of the Babylonian system is described in Revelation 18. The big earthquake has yet to come. When it comes, millions of Americans will literally witness the saga of "riches to rags in one hour" (Revelation 18) come true.

Demographic Armageddon

Even far more ominous than the political and economic peril is the changing racial face of America. Since 1950, America has undergone a radical change in demographics. A tsunami of non-whites, most of them from the third world and upwards of fifty million of them without proper documentation, have entered the US since 1970. The arrival of more than fifty million Latinos combined with millions of Asians, Hindus, blacks from Africa, and Central and South Americans has forever changed the racial composition of this country. The plunging birth rate of Anglo-Saxons, combined with the tidal wave of non-white immigration, precludes any long-term resurgence of the nation that existed from Jamestown 1607 to the year 1950.

The loss of Caucasian blood and intelligence from America is irreversible. Examine Brazil and other South American countries to see where America is rapidly moving. No Caucasian nation in recorded history has ever recovered from the dilution of its blood with the non-white races. Certified, pedigreed Caucasians are already on the endangered species list according to those who study demographics.

The Moral Free Fall

Since 1950, America has repudiated biblical morality from the scene of this nation. The moral meltdown of biblical values began in the churches, quickly spread to the cinema, television, and the media, and soon found widespread support in all layers of civil government. The U. S. Supreme Court followed this moral collapse with a spate of historic decisions that completely reversed the foundations of biblical morality. Long standing racial segregation was replaced by integration of the races in every aspect of American society.

The cultural revolution of the 1960s, including rock music, drugs, God is dead theology, and a socialist/communist agenda on college and university campuses across the nation, shook the foundations of biblical Christianity. Supreme Court edict removed God, prayer, and the Bible from public schools in 1962 and 1963. The Civil Rights Act of 1964 cemented enforced integration upon America. The Supreme Court decision of *Loving v. Virginia* in 1967 overturned statutory laws that banned interracial marriage. This was the final nail in the coffin of preserving the racial integrity of America.

The flower children of the '60s are the current decision makers across America. A spate of US Supreme Court decisions beginning in the early '70s (*Row v. Wade,* 1973, endorsed the murder of unborn children) removed the Ten Commandments from public venues in the country. Homosexuality received government endorsement and protection under Federal law in 2003. America is now in a moral free fall. Nothing sacred remains standing. The county is plunging toward the big, black hole of moral anarchy. Only God knows where it will end.

The Root of the Problem

All of America's problems can be traced to one root cause. All of our national problems have a spiritual cause. The cure? Nothing less than spiritual reformation of our covenant people. There is no political, economic, social, or military solution to our problems. We are afflicted with a catastrophic illness that has infected every part of our national body. We have disconnected from the one, true, and ever-living God, the authority of His Word, and from Jesus Christ, the Son of God Who came to save His people from their sin. Having discarded Jesus Christ, the Bible, and our Christian cultural values, we now love, serve, and follow the gods of this world.

The blood, tears, and Christian values of former generations have been squandered by a people who have forgotten the Living God and created new gods to worship. We have invited all the religions of the world with their heathen gods to America. We worship at the golden calf of multiculturalism. Racial diversity is a revered tenet of most mainline churches. Having disconnected from God and His Word, we are left with no moral compass, no north star to guide us. Leadership from the pulpits is a thing of the past. The American clergy have refused to take a stand in the moral freefall of our country.

Is There A Way Back?

Can America recover from the spiritual, moral, social, political, economic, and cultural plunge into darkness? Are there any significant signs of repentances in the land? Do you hear any movement among the American clergy to call the nation to repentance? Are civil leaders calling the nation to a state of sackcloth and ashes? Is there any indication *Roe v Wade* will be reversed and the bloody carnage of the abortion clinics ceased?

Is anyone calling for the repeal of the U.S. Supreme Court decisions that have endorsed and mandated government protection of interracial marriage, sodomy, and same-gender marriage? How about the return of prayer, Bible reading, and the Ten Commandments to our schools?

Have you heard any call for America's disconnect from billions in foreign aid to the Israeli Government in Tel Aviv? Has anyone called for the return of segregation to American public schools, colleges, and university campuses? Is there any attempt to allow the name of Jesus Christ to be allowed in public prayers in the U. S. Congress, the U.S. Military, and other venues? Have you heard any outcries for the removal of the multicultural, multiracial moral standards from this land? Have you heard of any national outcry for the U. S. to get out of the United Nations and cut off all foreign aid, particularly to those nations that hate the United States?

Has America Moved Into Reprobation?

Once a nation moves into apostasy, there is no hope for spiritual and moral recovery. Apostasy is the willful and deliberate departure from God, the authority of His Word, and the immutable moral standards of His divine Law. Spiritual apostasy is the deliberate and wholesale departure from the one, true, and Living God. When Jonah was sent to preach repentance to the Caucasian Assyrians at Nineveh, a Semitic people, around 862 BC, Nineveh's people repented (Jonah 3). About 150 years later in 713 BC, Nahum was sent yet again to preach judgment upon Nineveh. You see that within 150 years of Jonah's preaching, the nation had moved into total apostasy, from which there is **no** return. Romans 1:24-32 records the state of a people whom God gives up to total reprobation.

A nation on the road to apostasy and total reprobation is characterized by these three conditions:

1)   The people have lost all desire for repentance and are content to deliberately and willfully walk in sin.

2)   The people reject the message of repentance when it is plainly proclaimed.

3)   The people reject the messengers who call them to repentance.

The **judgment** of God will soon visit a nation that has moved into apostasy and been given over to reprobation. Has America reached this point? This watchman reports; you decide. For a more complete biblical analysis of this subject, send for our tape or CD titled "The Parable of the Potter's House." You will not be disappointed with this lesson even though this message and the messenger have largely been rejected by the people of this land.

9

THE LIVING CHURCH: YOUR ARK IN JACOB'S TROUBLED TIME

Winter 2009

A re you building an ark of safety for the time of trouble soon to visit America? Visionary souls clearly see the U.S. government floundering out of control. Many families are fleeing the United States in anticipation of a complete breakdown of society. Others believe that financial collapse and social upheaval will force the U.S. Government to put a security force on the streets of America to enforce order. *The Army Times*, Sept. 8, 2008, reported that the 3rd Infantry Division's 1st Brigade is being trained to use against American civilians for "civil unrest" and "crowd control." Many believe the Wall Street meltdown will eventually bring "Main Street USA" to her knees, causing people to take to the streets and look for politicians' heads. Will the non-white ghettos of America explode in racial upheaval should food shortages begin? Are you prepared for the unraveling of our American society? What about your children? Have you thought about an ark of safety?

There is clear evidence that the United States of America is very much like the great *Titanic* that floundered in the North Sea after hitting a massive iceberg in 1912. The unsinkable *Titanic,* filled with numerous wealthy, well-educated people (many of them believers) suddenly did what everyone thought was impossible. The *Titanic* sank in a very short time. Hundreds aboard that ship sank into the cold, watery grave. America is very much like the Titanic. We have been floundering on the sea of spiritual, moral, political, economic, and social confusion, with every indication that the America we once knew and loved can never recover from the tidal waves dashing against our national shores.

A Candid look at Where We Are

A long succession of government policies that both the Democratic and Republican parties fostered with their Jewish financier/counselors has placed our nation in economic, social, and demographic jeopardy. With only minor differences, both major political parties have taken us toward moral and economic bankruptcy. And that is not all! Without a whimper of protest, politicians and their parties have supinely watched the invasion of the United States by upwards of sixty million **third-world non-white** immigrants since 1965. They have led us into costly, protracted wars of "democratic liberation" in Iraq and Afghanistan, while leaving the United States unprotected and under massive invasion from Mexican nationals who colonized the American Southwest, with roots running to all corners of America, while no one was looking.

A succession of American politicians—Democratic and Republican—have engineered, participated, and/or acquiesced in removing biblical, statutory laws that banned abortion, sodomy, race-mixing, and other heinous crimes. Activist judges sitting on the US Supreme Court and at Appellate and Federal District Courts have made a shambles of the United States Constitution and have used their office to destroy the moral and spiritual foundations of America to the ground.

Insatiable greed and debts owed to powerful lobby groups have caused average Americans to completely question, disregard, and mistrust politicians. Most of those elected to public office on the national level ultimately sell their political souls to gain re-election. The confidence we place in our public officials at the national level has reached the lowest approval rating in our nation's history.

The arrival of millions of third-world non-whites onto American soil poses a clear danger for not only this generation, but especially for future generations of Caucasian Americans. These third-world souls share none of the moral and Christian values long-standing with other Americans, but instead bring with them an assortment of heathen gods, cultures, languages, and mores in direct conflict with historic, American, biblical values. Our nation is faced with increasing social unrest, massive unemployment, failing government entitlements, and a welfare class that will take to the streets and set American cities on fire at a moment's notice. Only a thin veneer of civilization prevents this non-white, third-world population from exploding in the face of our politicians.

If the United States moves toward economic depression, massive unemployment, food shortages, and a curtailment of utilities including electricity, gas, and water, our urban centers will become tinder for social unrest, rioting, violence, and unparalleled civil disorder. Heavily populated areas of the United States will become extremely dangerous. Electricity, water, and gas may become non-existent. Major highways may become heavily policed and difficult to navigate. Worst of all, our politicians may have already confiscated guns from law-abiding Americans—leaving only criminals and thugs with the guns and ammunition. Think about that!

Do You Have an Ark?

Visionary people must have the spiritual insight and presence of mind to look ahead and anticipate what must be done before it becomes too late.   One does not need to be all that bright to sense some very difficult days ahead in our beloved America. Most Americans, at least those living in this generation, have not faced truly tough times.   However, those who lived through the Great Depression (1929-1939) and through World War II have vivid memories of the hard times into which people were thrust. Americans born since 1960 have seldom faced truly difficult conditions, such as food shortages, gasoline rationing, no electricity, and a third-world existence.   We are indeed a spoiled generation.   If all of the amenities and luxuries we take for granted were suddenly gone, we would soon see another side of America that few today can imagine.

So, I ask this question: are you trying to build an ark of safety?   What is your plan?   Where is life taking you?   Are you moving in the will of God?   Are you reading your Bible faithfully and prayerfully, seeking the wisdom and leading of the Holy Spirit? Do you have good counselors?   Do you talk with wise people? Do you have a circle of trusted friends for fellowship?   Do you have a church family?   Better still, do you have a church community?   Do you know your neighbors?   Do they share your ethnicity, heritage, faith, and worldview?   How protected are you and the children you love?

More than four millennia ago, a faithful member of our ethnic heritage and faith could foresee a time of trouble coming. He was a man who cherished his family and set about to provide for them before impending disaster and judgment came. This man walked in justification before a Holy God with his sin debt settled in sacrifice before his Creator. He had maintained his genetic bank so his offspring, by not participating in the race mixing of his generation, would remain in covenant with their Creator. Finally, this man walked with God in daily communion. Through prayer and worship, Noah became a visionary man who found grace in the eyes of his Lord. This gift of grace enabled Noah to have the vision to build an ark to the saving of himself, his family, and their seed, as well as that of other life forms, to continue life after the Flood of judgment. The Bible tells us, ***"By faith Noah, being warned of God of things not seen as yet, moved with fear, prepared an ark to the saving of his house; by the which he condemned the world, and became heir of the righteousness which is by faith"*** *(Hebrews 11:7).*

These questions seem appropriate: do you believe you are being warned of things not yet seen? Do you have a certain amount of the wholesome fear of God within you? And, do you believe that you have some responsibility to build or find an ark to survive the deluge of evil and judgment coming upon America? Have you answered the hard questions that may need to be asked if American society comes unraveled? Will you be able to manage the most basic necessities of life? What about your children and other extended family members? Will you go down like the Titanic, or will you seek the refuge of a lifeboat? This is a Mayday call! Are you listening?

The Historic Ark

The church of which Jesus Christ is the Savior and Head has been the ark for Christians during the last two thousand years. This church survived the collapse of the Imperial Roman Empire. After 476 A.D. when Rome fell to the invading Gothic (Israelitish) tribes, the church of Jesus Christ became the ark around which civilization continued. The invading armies that brought Roman civilization to dust eventually were converted to Christianity. Thus, the church survived the fall of Rome.

When life became intolerable in England in the early years of the 17th Century, visionary Christians formed themselves into a church built upon Jesus Christ, the Rock, boarded a ship, and sailed for the New World. They had a vision! That vision was to plant the church of Jesus Christ in the New World and build a Christian nation. Their immediate goal necessitated that they board ship and get to the New World to plant a colony. Their plan upon arrival was to worship God, build houses, plant gardens, multiply children, and take dominion of this New World. The Pilgrims and the thousands of Puritans that followed them in the early 1600s laid the foundations for everything that turned out to be biblical and Christian in America to this very day.

Three Potential Scenarios

One of three scenarios is likely to unfold in America in the near future:

One: America will undergo the effect of **Brazilification,** where this nation will become a melting pot of every race under heaven. The white race will be swallowed in the surging, non-white population, and the whole country will be dumbed-down and become much like modern Brazil. Study modern Brazil closely, and you may see the future of America. You have to know that Brazil has been blessed with abundant natural resources; but ethnic bankruptcy has kept the nation from doing what the Caucasians did in North America.

Brazil is the fifth largest country in the world, just slightly smaller than the United States, and is larger than the entire continent of Europe. It contains some of the greatest continuous forestland in the world, has huge deposits of iron and other minerals, and one of the largest river systems of the entire world. It is one of the largest producers of corn, soybeans, and cotton in the whole world, yet with all of its abundant resources, Brazil has never been a world power! Why? Check out the racial composition of this country, and you will find the answer! Brazil contains hues of many different races and has no genetic bank of Caucasian DNA to make it what the USA is (or, should I say, was!). Many biblically oriented anthropologists see America as the second Brazil in the Western Hemisphere, with the original, homogenous, Caucasian race simply being absorbed into the non-white races filling our landscape.

Two: We could witness the **Balkanization** of America, where the nation divides into racial, cultural, religious, and linguistic political states rife with hostility and given to radical forms of ethnic cleansing. This racial balkanization may follow the pattern set in Yugoslavia, where the country divided into different ethnic and religious groups. Yugoslavia, just a little larger than Wyoming, includes Slovenia, Croatia, Bosnia-Hercegovnia, Serbia (including Kosovo), Montenegro, and Macedonia. The country is nothing more than a boiling pot of ethnic and religious stew. Is that what multiculturalism will bring to America?

This country has several different languages and three different religious faiths. As you know, American troops are now garrisoned there to keep peace between the warring Christian Serbs and the Muslims who occupy much of this country. There is always the possibility that America could be carved into many ethnic countries—Black, Mexican, Asian, Muslim, American Indian, and Hindu, with the White minority left to wander as nomads without any corner to call their own. Discrimination against Whites in America is already a fixed social pattern.

Three: America could drift into anarchy, an all-out **Civil War,** with race wars, ethnic cleansing, religious and cultural wars, and even foreign invasion from the Chinese. Have Mexicans not already invaded and overrun us? What foreign invader is next? Will the millions of Muslims already on our soil run a guerilla-style offence of terror against the US? Will the "hate America" militants of every dark race on the planet invade this country?

Build the Ark Now, not Later!

Now is the time for spiritual and visionary thinking! Without a vision, the people perish (Proverbs 29:18). What is your vision? Once you establish a clear vision, write it down plainly on a tablet (Habakkuk 2:2-3). Then move forward with your goal! What is the most immediate goal you need to meet? Put legs under your vision. Suppose the historic ark, the living church, is your vision. The goal then is to gather folks of like ethnic heritage, faith, and worldview into one spiritual body of which Christ is the Head. You then have a church! Having established a **vision** and then a **goal**, you are ready to build a **plan**. The plan must contain all the essential details of how this vision can be fulfilled.

The Vision, the Goal, the Plan

Let Nehemiah be your guide to a vision, a goal, and a plan. Nehemiah had a vision of securing the defenseless and run-down city of Jerusalem. His goal was to rebuild the walls around Jerusalem. His plan was to divide all willing Hebrew/Israelites into work details, each assigned to a particular section of the wall, and build it with great speed before his distracters could organiz and destroy his vision, his goal, and his plan. Guess what! They completed this incredible project in fifty-two days! A man with a vision, a specific goal, and a plan can!

What about you? Are you ready to build your own ark? Are you ready to join others already working on the ark? Or do you have a vision that is better than the church as an ark of survival? If so, would you share that vision with us and others as soon as possible? The titanic of nations is floundering on the high seas of spiritual apathy, moral decadence, political paralysis, economic meltdown, and racial genocide! Will you board the lifeboat or go down with the ship? We report! You decide! May Jehovah God help us all to hold on to Jesus Christ, our faith, our ethnic heritage, and our moral values and remain steadfast, anchored in the Word of God, in one of the wildest rides in the history of our covenant people!

10

AMERICA'S OBITUARY

Spring 2009

The Republic of the United States of America passed away on November 4, 2008, after a protracted disease of spiritual apathy, moral decadence, racial genocide, social disintegration, multiculturalism, and after the ingestion of millions of Latinos, Central and South Americans, Hindus, Asians, Muslims, and assorted other third world aliens. Death came as the polls closed on November 4, 2008, and a coalition of white liberals, Christian evangelicals, Latinos, and a solid, Black voting block elected the first non-white, foreign-born, Muslim-educated, Marxist, Socialist, Liberal as President of the United States of America. The America we once knew is no more. This nation has been hijacked and conquered. The children and youth growing up in America will never know the country that was once the shining city upon a hill. How tragic that these children will never experience the blessings of what it meant to be an American!

That day has passed and will never come again! The day of repentance has passed in America. **The true prophets of God will preach judgment upon the nation and repentance for the remnant that our sovereign God chooses to call into His Kingdom and truth.**

The United States of America was born on July 4, 1776, when a Caucasian delegation of mostly Christian landowners, planters, businessmen, and Statesmen were engaged in a horrific war against the English Parliament and its army garrisoned on American soil. The fledgling Republic of the United States was born amid unbearable suffering of the American Continental Army under the command of General George Washington. The birth pangs were so acute and the suffering so great that there were times when the birth of the country appeared to be stillborn. In the end, America's rag-tag army, deprived of most of the ordinary food, clothing, and ammunition necessary to sustain an army, were protected by divine providence and allowed to gain victory over the largest and most powerful military power then in existence.

America was conceived amid the growing religious unrest in the British Isles and elsewhere in Europe in the early 1600s. A group of adventuresome Englishmen planted the first colony of settlers along the James River in Virginia in 1607. The first English settlement at Jamestown was followed by the arrival of the Puritan delegation at Plymouth, Massachusetts in 1620. The American Republic was in gestation from Jamestown, 1607, until its birth some 169 nine years later in 1776.

During its gestation period, America was nourished in the womb of divine providence and was rooted in a very biblical and Christian culture established by successive waves of devout English Colonists who followed the Puritans to the shores of North America. In the 1500s, the Spanish had come to the New World looking for gold. The French followed in the 1600s, looking for riches in fur trade. The English arrived in the 1600s, seeking a place where religious freedom could be a way of life. America was not conceived amid a desire for gold or for worldly riches, but with an intense love for Jehovah God and personal freedom.

The spiritual and moral nourishment provided America during the **gestation period** of development enabled biblical statutes to become the foundation upon which America would rest. Statutory laws reflecting Bible Law prohibited abortion, sodomy, miscegenation, murder, rape, and assorted heinous crimes. These statutory guidelines were to the foundation of each of the succeeding States to join the Union in the course of history. The homogenous, Caucasian population, mostly Protestant Christian, was united in God, Scripture, and all things Christian. This spiritual, moral, and racial atmosphere in the womb of divine providence prepared the birth of the most spectacular nation in the history of the world to come forth on July 4, 1776.

The most Caucasian, Christian, and biblical culture ever to flourish on the planet unfolded in the conception, gestation, birth, and youth phase of the United States of America. Successive waves of English, Scotch, Irish, Welsh, German, Dutch, French, Swedes, Danes, Norwegians and other kindred people arrived at intervals beginning in the early 1600s and continuing to fill the landscape into the early years of the 20th Century. Aside from a small Black and Native American Indian population, the entire nation was homogenous, filled with Caucasians who flowered into a pro-White, Bible-oriented culture that valued Jesus Christ, biblical morality, industry, and a strong work ethic.

The **Republic of the United States of America** leaves behind a great legacy of national and world accomplishments. No nation in the annals of history ever rose to such greatness in so short a time. From thirteen struggling, independent English Colonies along the Eastern seaboard of the Atlantic in the 1600s, America rose to greatness and world fame by the end of the 1800s. The successful waging of the Spanish-American War in our own Western hemisphere in 1898 solidified our national pride.

The American Republic of many states in one union nearly dissolved in the tragic war between the North and the South waged between 1860-1865. This fratricidal war of Caucasian father against son, brother against brother, was a blood letting from which America never fully recovered. The results of this war bore bitter fruit.

The U. S. Constitution was forever altered with the passage of the 13th, 14th, and 15th Amendments, which insured America's loss of its homogenous, Caucasian population in favor of a multiracial, heterogeneous population. Moreover, the population displacement created by the casualties in this tragic Civil War eventually paved the way for the immigration of large numbers of Jews from Easter Europe beginning in 1890 and into the early 1900s. These Jewish immigrants quickly seized positions of influence in American Universities, the media, entertainment, finance, and as counselors to American Presidents.

The early 1900s brought major developments to America. At home, the passage of the Federal Reserve Act of 1913 transferred the nation's printing presses to a privately owned banking cartel. The 16th Amendment, added to the U. S. Constitution in 1913, paved the way for a Federal Income Tax, the first in American history, to fund the cost of operating the U. S. Government under auspices of the Federal Reserve System.

American armies brought an end to World War I in 1918 and became a formal contender for leadership among the nations of the world. By 1930, America had survived the roaring '20s, only to plunge into the depths of financial depression in 1929, a financial crash that lasted until the opening of World War II in Europe in 1939. The Great Depression of the 1930s was exacerbated by the great drought that turned the Midwestern United States into a howling dust bowl. Then, against the advice of some of the greatest Americans then alive (including Charles Lindberg, Henry Ford Sr, and a legion of other national giants), American armies invaded Germany following the Japanese's bombing of Pearl Harbor on December 7, 1941.

The United States of America emerged from World War II in 1945 as the undisputed political and military power of the world. No other country owned the atomic bomb. And, America's military power was the most revered force on earth. American armies and the U. S. Navy dominated both land and sea. The industry, ingenuity, and work ethic of the American people had turned the entire nation into a war machine as civilians and soldiers united in the war effort. The American public was tired of war when it finally ended in 1945 following the bombing of Hiroshima, Japan on August 6, 1945, and three days later of Nagasaki. The use of the atom bomb ended World War II and moved war to a new, lethal killing field.

After World War II, the nation pursued the American dream of private enterprise. GIs returned from the battlefield and joined the American civilian population in an explosion of business, agriculture, and industry. The baby boom commenced with a huge population explosion that began in 1946 and continued through 1964. The hard working, Bible believing, mostly Protestant, Caucasian population of America were busy turning the American dream into a reality as home building, business, agriculture, and industry surged.

While Americans were focused almost exclusively on rebuilding their war-torn lives in the late 40s and early 50s, sinister forces were gathering as dark clouds over the grand old Republic. The Soviet Union, aided and abetted by billions of American lend-lease dollars, was given an open door to gobble up most of Eastern Europe and a portion of Germany at the end of World War II. The Soviet Communist machine in Russia, pretending to be a close friend during the war, began flexing its muscles and becoming a contender for world dominance. The Cold War era began as soon as World War II had ended and broke out into open conflict when the United States engaged the North Koreans in a war that raged from 1950-1953. This was the first undeclared war that the U. S. Government waged under the auspices of the United Nations and ended without our victory.

The birth of the Jewish Israeli State on May 14, 1948, again under the auspices of the United Nations with the support and approval of the United States Government, marked a significant turning point in American history. The United States' marriage to the Zionist Jewish State in 1948 catapulted this foreign government into a place of honor that continues right up to the current death of the American Republic. Since 1948, the Israeli Government has captivated American Middle East policy. Billions of American taxpayer dollars have flowed into building, preserving, and maintaining this antichristian State. Without American aid, the Israeli State would have been stillborn! America's war against Iraq was largely engineered by Jewish neo-cons within the U.S. Government.

During the 1950s, European powers began to surrender their African colonial holdings as the French, Germans, Dutch, and other European powers retreated from Africa. Black rule returned to much of Africa and with it the collapse of the political, social, and economic infrastructure that Europeans had built. The void created by the breakup of Colonialism in Africa paved the way for Russian aggression and Marxist-style Communism to take root in much of Africa. Soviet aggression in Africa caused a surge in the Cold War between the United States and the Soviet Communist Nation.

Communist aggression continued throughout the 1950s; the launching of Sputnik in 1957 gave the Russians a jumpstart into the space race. By the early 1960s, the French had grown weary in Vietnam, and American armies followed their retreat in defense of South Vietnam by 1963. This ten-year war ended in American defeat in 1973. A communist surge followed the retreat of American armies that left millions of Vietnamese dead. This tragic war waged under United Nation rules of military engagement left America demoralized and lost as a nation. To our everlasting shame, our own American soldiers returned from the scourge of war only to suffer ostracism and abandonment by their own nation.

The clouds of the Cold War Era that rained fire and brimstone in Korea (1950-1953) and in Vietnam (1963-1973) were the outward and visible toxicity that existed between the United States and the Soviet Communist Regime. Inwardly, the United States was suffering great spiritual and moral convulsions that were as devastating to the country as any war could ever be.

Movement toward full racial integration began in the 1950s. It began with the forced integration of the American military in 1946. Pentecostal churches, along with a few other denominations, had become multi-racial in the early 1900s. In 1954, the U.S. Supreme Court in *Brown vs. Board of Topeka* ordered the full integration of American public schools, colleges, and universities. President Eisenhower ordered thousands of armed soldiers to push government-mandated racial amalgamation in public schools, colleges, and universities throughout the South. The Civil Rights Act of 1964 further cemented the national will to integrate the races. The 1967 U.S. Supreme Court decision in *Loving vs. Virginia* struck down all bans against interracial marriage in the United States. Race mixing was made legal under government edict in the 1950s and 60s. America would never be the same!

The 1960s marked the most significant cultural revolution ever to occur within the borders of the United States. Millions of young people on college and university campuses became infected with rock music, hard drugs, and communist ideology. The flower children from the baby boomer generation were content to abandon long-held spiritual and moral values in preference for free love, drugs, rock music, and a hippie lifestyle. Many liberal theologians and educators announced the **"God is dead"** theology that began to grip the soul of America, ripping it from historic Christianity. These ideologues and progressive liberals now fill the pulpits, university chairs, Congress, our state houses, and our courts and legislative halls.

The homogenous Caucasian population of America came under assault with the passage of the **1965 Immigration Legislation,** which opened the floodgates to non-white, third-world immigration and simultaneously restricted immigration from Europe, Scandinavia, and the British Isles. By 1986, the floodtide of immigration had swelled into the millions, and President Reagan and the U.S. Congress granted amnesty to millions of Latinos and other illegals living in the U.S. The restrictions placed upon illegals entering the United States in 1986 were never enforced; consequently, upwards of forty million Latinos have squatted on American soil to date and essentially have colonized California, Arizona, New Mexico, Texas, and portions of Colorado and other states.

Then in 1973, for the first time in her history, our government endorsed the barbaric practice of infanticide. In *Roe vs. Wade,* 1973, the U. S. Supreme Court, with the support of many liberal theologians, granted to women the legal right to abort children. This barbaric practice has continued unabated and allows full-term babies to be aborted at the discretion of the physician. In 2003, Federal Judges in New York and California issued restraining orders blocking enforcement of the Partial-Birth Abortion Ban Act that previously the U. S. Congress passed and President George W. Bush signed into law. Some fifty million children have been murdered in the abortion killing fields in America since 1973. While Presiden

The 1980s and 1990s witnessed the dismantling of what little else the cultural revolution of the 1960s had left standing. God, prayer, and the Bible had been removed from the public schools by Government edict in the 1960s. In the 1980s, the Government assaulted the Ten Commandments when the U. S. Supreme Court in *Stone vs. Graham,* 1980, struck down a Kentucky statute requiring the display of the Ten Commandments in public schools. Following this historic decision, the Ten Commandments became a target of scorn by liberal ideologues across the land. A spate of Court decisions forced the Ten Commandments, the cross, the nativity scene, and all things Christian out of public venues throughout the country.

Systematically, America has been purged of any signs and symbols that represent its historic, Christian origin.

The closing years of the 20th Century and the first decade of the 21st Century have witnessed the moral freefall of America. Sodomy and every form of sexual perversion are commonplace. On June 26, 2002, the U.S. Supreme Court stuck down a Texas law prohibiting sodomy. Sodomy is now practiced and protected under color of law and protected by the U. S. Government. On November 18, 2003, in *Goodridge vs. Dept. of Public Health,* the Massachusetts Supreme Court ruled that same-sex couples could marry in that state. With encouragement from liberal clergy, activist judges, liberal politicians, and university professors, homosexuals are pushing for nothing less than national acceptance of same-sex marriage and the trashing of the biblical, historic definition of marriage being that holy state entered by one man and one woman. That the two be required to be of the same race, as was initially intended, is beyond consideration.

The 21st Century is witnessing the continued freefall of the United States of America. Following the lead of many clergy, educators, politicians, judges, news media, and entertainment venues, the public continues to condone abortion, sodomy, race mixing, fornication, drugs, alcoholism, rock and rap music, and crimes of violence. Escalating rates of murder, rape, and armed violence have resulted in the largest prison population in the civilized world. Half of all couples live in cohabitation without marriage. Divorce claims one of every two marriages. One-third of newborns arrive in the world without a declared father. The historic, Christian family is rapidly disappearing from our landscape as dysfunctional families become the new norm. Where is our shame?

American armies are now garrisoned in South Korea, Germany, Iraq, Afghanistan, and in other corners of the world. Some 30,000 American military personnel have been engaged on the ground in Afghanistan since 2002, yet the Taliban is stronger today than it was three years ago! Some 140,000 American military in Iraq have been on the ground since March of 2003. Hundreds of billions of borrowed dollars have been poured into these pro-tracted wars. American involvement in the Middle East wars, financing the Israeli State, and working with North Korea, Iran, and other rogue nations seeking nuclear weapons presents a clear challenge for America. American foreign aid outlays to more than one hundred nations of the earth are one of the most significant expenditures in the budget of the United States Government!

In the past two fiscal years (2007 and 2008), our economy has undergone a complete meltdown. The U. S. Government essentially has nationalized the largest banking cartels in the nation on the backs of the American taxpayer. The initial 750-*billion*-dollar bailout in 2008 has failed to yield any help to an economy that is now in the tank. Three of the five oldest Wall Street banking firms in the nation have failed, while the remaining two are teetering on collapse. Two of the three largest automobile manufacturers in America essentially have been nationalized to keep them from going bankrupt.

American free trade policies have resulted in the dismantling of our manufacturing base as companies have moved their operations to Mexico, India, China, and other places where cheap labor is abundant. The great American industrial machine has been off-shored, sending millions of jobs elsewhere. While America allows the free flow of imports from all over the world, U. S. exports have been denied the same benefits. This surge in imports combined with the decline in exports has resulted in the largest trade deficits ever to accrue in our history. America is moving irreversibly, day by day, toward a third-world economy. Slums and ghettos containing millions of Blacks living on the welfare dole are all that is left in the urban areas of the United States. Even thousands of small rural towns are fast becoming ghettos inhabited by low-class whites living on government entitlements.

The Republic of the United States of America has passed away! There will be no revival of this nation. The plunging birthrates of the Caucasian population plus the surging immigration of non-whites have permanently changed the racial face of America. **One hundred million non-whites live in America!**

By 2040, the Caucasian population of the United States will be the minority race. The surging, non-white population into the Democratic Party will ultimately turn the nation into a one-party, Socialist/Marxist State. The Caucasian people have already become disenfranchised, and there is little chance that a conservative, Christian, Caucasian will ever live in the White House again.

With other native, Caucasian Americans, we mourn the passing of the United States of America! The America we knew is forever gone! The gravediggers and morticians now occupy the White House, the Congress, and the Supreme Court. America is now dead and being placed on life supports in a vain hope to keep it alive. We are borrowing billions of dollars from China, Japan, and other nations to keep our nation on life support. All is vanity!

America is clinically dead, and no amount of repentance will bring our beloved nation back. Preachers can cry out for repentance, and well-meaning souls can quote II Chronicles until they run out of oxygen, but the God of Heaven will not hear them. **The day for repentance has passed, and the hour of judgment has come!**

The Republic of the United States of America has joined the graveyard of nations. Life will continue as the physicians, gravediggers, and morticians try to keep us on life support. **Know this: the God of Israel will save a remnant from the rotting spiritual and moral corpse that was once the greatest nation on earth!** Every American will be forced to find a niche in the political, economic, social, and racial chaos that will characterize the new America. God will surely save a remnant for His glory and honor, and I pray you will want to be numbered in that family!

Survivors Plan

The prudent among the covenant population of America will seek geographical locations in this country where others of their own race, faith, and moral standards can guarantee the spiritual, moral, and racial standards of by-gone generations. These enclaves will require a vibrant, Christ-centered, Bible-oriented church community who likewise seek to preserve some semblance of a free enterprise economy among themselves and the fringe population where they live. They will fiercely defend the historic, Christian marriage, family, morals, and racial standards of God's Word.

The new, third-world America will emerge into a far different country than we have ever known. Catastrophic events lie ahead for this nation as America is vexed within and from without! There will be no security or peace in the America crafted by the New World Order. Wise people, especially those with children and youth, should exercise prudence in staking out a future for their children.

We encourage you to seek others who share a common heritage of faith, race, morals, and biblical worldview. You need to be rooted in a community of homogenous people sharing the same vision and understanding of where we are moving in this country. You will need the mutual protection that one neighbor will share with another. No one is going to look out for you! You must become rooted in a church community where Jesus Christ, the Bible, and a biblical culture prevail.

To the best of their ability, these communities need to exercise Christian dominion of their land, talents, and resources. They must live by faith in Jesus Christ, be empowered by the Holy Spirit, multiply children, build strong families, plant gardens and orchards, work the land, exercise their minds with witty inventions, and like Abraham and Sarah, ***"Look for a city which hath foundations, whose builder and maker is God"*** *(Heb. 11:10).*

These God-fearing, blood-washed, Bible-believing, Spirit-filled Christians must *"Occupy till Jesus Christ Comes"* *(Luke 19:13).*

11

FINDING A
NEW GOSHEN

Summer 2009

With all that is going on in the world, you might wonder if it is time to find or perhaps build a new land of Goshen. To the visionary Christian Israelites scattered across the hinterlands of the United States of America, greetings! Where should Israelites make their stand for spiritual, moral, racial, and cultural preservation? Is this not a good time for Biblicist Christians to contemplate their circumstances and weigh carefully the options available to them? Do you need to chart a course of action for you, your children, and future posterity? We know what the Bible says: *"without vision the people perish" (Pro. 29:18)*. Is finding or building a new land of Goshen within your scope for the 21st Century?

Most Christians discern the handwriting on the political walls of contemporary America. The United States Government has been hijacked by an alien, foreign, global cartel of Wall Street Bankers, financiers, media-moguls, and behind-the-scene operatives in the shadows of the Bilderbergers, Trilateralists, the Council on Foreign Relations, and assorted clandestine organizations. These operatives have placed a black face on the Jewish controlled government of the United States of America. Their goal seems to be to deliver America into the hands of a global, one-world government.

Consider This

Our sovereign God is being faithful to His covenant Law. God warned us time and time again in Scripture that if His covenant people fail to keep His commandments, statutes, and judgments, they would forfeit their land, possessions, prosperity, and blessings. Strangers would then rise to high positions of power, and God's people would end up as the tail—fleeced, robbed, taxed, and oppressed by their new masters. This is precisely what has occurred in America and other nations of the Christian West. America has abandoned God, so we are reaping the covenant curses and sanctions God promised. Bible-believing Christians can confirm that God is keeping His promises. Leviticus 26 and Deuteronomy 28, plus a multitude of other Scriptures, contain the penalty for forsaking Jehovah and His Law!

We are only in the beginning of sorrows as the covenant people of this land harden their hearts and worship other gods, replacing God's Law with the tenets of Humanism, Socialism, and rank Communism. The election of Barak Hussein Obama on November 4, 2008 marked a watershed moment in America's history. We shall never be the same again. Events shaping the future of this country are irreversible. The non-white under class from the third world now massing across the hinterlands of America will insure the ultimate disenfranchisement of the Caucasian, American population. The rapidly changing demographic composition has irrevocably altered the future racial state of America.

Galloping Socialism and creeping Communism have been coming to America by degrees for many decades. The basic tenets of Socialism and several of the major planks of the Marks and Engel's *Communist Manifesto,* published in 1848 have been operating in the United States for many years. The progressive, graduated income tax and government-mandated public education of all children are striking examples and underscore how long we have been moving down this road. Government nationalization of American banks and automobile manufacturing are glaring examples of the expansion of socialism in America.

It makes little difference whether the face on the Federal Government is white or black: the policy decisions remain the same. Political parties come and go, but the policies remain unchanged at their core. Wall Street bankers, financiers, and corporate and media moguls—all from the left side of Genesis 3:15—run the Federal Government. What can we expect when generations of covenant people reject Jehovah and His Law for the gods of their own creation and impose laws carved from the depraved, sinful minds of man? Does Jehovah not declare that *"The LORD hath made all things for himself: yea, even the wicked for the day of evil" (Pro. 16:4)?*

Take Courage, Remnant Christians

Bible-believing Christians should take great courage in knowing that a sovereign God is in full control of the Socialist/Communist demolition crew now camped out in D.C. Reflect on the promises in Psalm 37 and related passages throughout Old and New Testament Scripture. Consider a sampling of the powerful words of Psalm 37:

1) "Fret not thyself because of evildoers, neither be thou envious against the workers of iniquity." Why would Jehovah not want you to fret about the evildoers now camped out in D.C.?

2) "For they shall soon be cut down like the grass, and wither as the green herb." In the mean time, what must remnant Christians do?

3) "Trust in the LORD, and do good; so shalt thou dwell in the land, and verily thou shalt be fed." But this is not all. Continue to read verse 4.

4) "Delight thyself also in the LORD; and he shall give thee the desires of thine heart." If we do our part, notice what Jehovah promises to those who walk in obedience.

5) "Commit thy way unto the LORD; trust also in him; and he shall bring it to pass." If you read on, the blessings following obedience to His command Word just keep multiplying.

6) "And he shall bring forth thy righteousness as the light, and thy judgment as the noonday."

Continue to read to the end of Psalm 37. Make a list of what Jehovah requests of His children and the promised blessings that follow. We live in dark, difficult days; but these can be days of tremendous blessing and prosperity if we really believe God and obey His Command Word. Whom do you believe? Do not allow yourselves to grow weary of the multitude of media counselors, astrologers, stargazers, and monthly prognosticators? Read your Bible, pray, walk with wise men, and follow the commands of your God, and you will continue to occupy and take dominion as the children of the most high God.

What Does History Tell Us?

Remnant Christians living in America during the 21st Century are not the first to ponder their future when political oppression rises. History affords many examples of remnant Christians who have been forced to make watershed decisions about their future in a given country. In the 1500s, all of Europe was awash in great religious conflict between Roman Catholic and Protestant factions. When a strong leader emerged in a given country and was passionate in his religious persuasion, the people in their realm were forced to conform to their leader's affiliation. Those who refused suffered persecution. Strong Roman Catholic rulers in England in the mid 1500s forced Protestant believers into exile in Geneva, Switzerland. It was here that the Geneva Bible, printed in 1560 and the forerunner of the **King James Bible**, was translated.

The Pilgrims fled to Holland and escaped the jurisdiction of the English king in search of religious freedom. They later returned to America and opted to seek a new jurisdiction where there was religious freedom. Successive waves of Protestant Puritans fled the jurisdiction of England and came to the New World in the years that followed the arrival of the Pilgrims in 1620. History is replete with persecuted Christians fleeing the jurisdiction of one country to find freedom in another.

Historically, persecuted Christians have resorted to three steps in seeking a redress of their grievances. First, they appealed to government leaders in charge for clemency in seeking religious freedom (Daniel 1:8-12). Second, if no relief was found, they fled the jurisdiction. Joseph and Mary fled the jurisdiction of Herod (Matt. 2:13-15). Third, if they chose not to flee, they could remain in their locality and suffer persecution for doing well. The Word of God gives the context for this step in I Peter 3:13-17.

Growing numbers of Christians in contemporary America believe this country is becoming increasingly hostile to Christians and will have zero toleration for passionate, convicted Christians committed to belief in Jesus Christ, the Holy Scriptures, and a code of biblical absolutes. Liberal humanists, awash in Socialism and with a bent toward Communism, are pushing for strong hate crime legislation, gun control (including registration, ammunition control, and taxation), universal socialized health care, national security police force, the elimination of home schooling, and the general dismantling of historic freedoms that Americans have enjoyed for many generations.

A small, zealous, committed left-wing Communist/Humanist movement wrested the control of the Federal Government in D. C. These people are foot soldiers for Wall Street bankers, financiers, media moguls, and behind-the-scene policy makers who seized control of the White House, Congress, and the courts. They view zealous Christians who uphold the moral absolutes of the Bible and the U.S. Constitution, keep their children out of government schools, cherish free enterprise, and seek religious freedom apart from the 501-C3, government-endorsed religious bodies as a clear danger to their plans for merging America and its citizens into a one-world, global government. These Christians are in the crosshairs of those who run **Home Land Security.**

In the face of this continuous threat to personal and religious liberty in America, many remnant Christians are seeking a new land of Goshen or perhaps planning to build one in this country. We all must trust God to defend them from the strong arm of the emerging police state or simply suffer persecution for doing well (I Peter 3:13-17).

Remnant Christians, Do Not Despair!

Those who are committed to the Lord Jesus Christ, the absolutes of the Bible, and the principles that have guided the founding of this nation should not become overly discouraged. History is always in the hands of a dedicated, zealous, convicted, and well-disciplined minority. A small minority of dedicated, zealous Bolsheviks overpowered the established order in Christian Russia between 1905 and 1917 and established a full-blown Communist state. The monarchy in France was overthrown beginning in 1789 by a zealous and fanatical band of revolutionary thugs. In both of these examples, a small, dedicated minority enabled evil to be triumphant over good.

Quite to the contrary, the American War for Independence received the support of only a small percentage of the total population. Most Americans were fearful of committing to the cause lest they lose and be placed in the hands of British soldiers. George Washington and his rag-tag army, with fearless members of the Continental Congress, was able to subdue the vastly superior British Army and Navy and free colonial America from the British.

A sovereign God always keeps His faithful eye on the remnant that seeks to do His will. Remember: God always has a remnant! Elijah was convinced that because the Israelites of his generation had forsaken the covenant, thrown down the altars, and slain the prophets that he was the only one left. It remained for a sovereign God to remind Elijah that He had a remnant of seven thousand in Israel who had not bowed the knee to Baal. Through the pen of St. Paul, the Holy Spirit reminds us that *"Even so then at this present time also there is a remnant according to the election of grace" (Rom. 11:5).* By His sworn oath, Jehovah entered an unconditional covenant to preserve His people for all of time (Jeremiah 31:35-37).

A Look Back in History

The history of our people gives many examples of how a surviving remnant became the next great move in God's unfolding plan. For the record, let us briefly pull one historic model from the archives. Examine the historic model of the Israelites who went down into Egypt about 1706 BC following a famine in the land of Canaan. Jacob had taken his family, including all of his sons and their wives and children (except for Joseph, who had been marvelously taken to Egypt some thirteen earlier). Jacob's family numbered only seventy souls when they arrived in Egypt around the year 1706 BC. This one man's family had grown exponentially to number about three million souls by the time of the Exodus in 1491 BC.

Joseph invited the Israelites, with the consent of the ruling Pharaoh, to settle in Goshen in the very best area of Egypt (Genesis 45:10; Genesis 46:26-28; Genesis 47:5-6). Scripture declares, *"Israel dwelt in the land of Egypt, in the country of Goshen; and they had possessions therein, and grew, and multiplied exceedingly" (Genesis 47:27).* Goshen was situated in the most eastern province of Southern Egypt, not far from the Arabian Gulf, lying next to Canaan. In this favorable land, which may have been watered by rain from heaven, the Israelites flourished and multiplied children.

This is the question remnant Christians today must answer: how did a single family numbering seventy souls survive the next 215 years to become a population of three million, make their exodus from Egypt, and establish a great political, economic, and military power under David and Solomon? Within less than one hundred years after their arrival in Egypt, the Israelites had fallen into conflict with the Egyptian government. Exodus 1:1-22 contains the full story. The Israelites were very fruitful, used **no** birth control, had large families, and multiplied exponentially in the land.

In time, Joseph died, all his brothers passed on, and a new Pharaoh arrived who did not know Joseph. Fearing the Israelites might become a major threat to the security of Egypt, the new Pharaoh launched an oppressive program of forced enslavement against the Israelites, forcing them to build treasure cities for his pleasure, including Pithom and Raamses (Exodus 1:11).

In spite of this forced labor and oppression, the Bible says that *"the more they* (the Egyptians) *afflicted them, the more they* (the Israelites) *multiplied and grew. And they were grieved because of the children of Israel" (Exodus 1:12).* In the face of this ever-increasing Israelite population, the Egyptian government issued new and oppressive laws. All of the male children born to Israelite women were to be put to death. Infanticide became the law of the land for male Israelite children. In an effort to shut down the ever-growing quest for freedom to worship Jehovah and celebrate His feasts, the Egyptian government became even more oppressive.

The Pharaohs who occupied the throne of government as kings and priests and whom the Egyptian population worshipped placed the Israelites under extremely harsh work sanctions, as confirmed in Exodus 5:1-23. This increasing oppression of the Israelites ultimately forced them to try to flee the jurisdiction of their Egyptian homeland and petition Pharaoh to leave the country. The Bible shows that emancipation from Egyptian bondage came only after a series of plagues befell Egypt, each affecting something sacred to one or more of the gods whom the Egyptians worshipped. Finally, in 1491 BC, Moses led three million Israelites out of Egypt under the light of a paschal full moon. This historic Passover marked the birth of the nation of Israel and was mandated as a festival to be observed by Israelites throughout all succeeding generations (Exodus 12:14).

These Questions Deserve an Answer

1) How did the Israelites manage to maintain their spiritual, moral, and racial integrity for more than two hundred years— living in such proximity to non-Israelites and in a land where heathen gods abounded?

2) How did the Israelites survive one of the political power centers of history for more than two centuries?

3) How did the Israelites allow a sovereign God to determine **when** and **how many** children they should have at the very time that the birth rate among the Egyptian population was in decline?

4) How did the Israelites manage to encourage succeeding generations of Israelites born in Egypt to remain in the land of Goshen?

5) How was it that all the Israelites living in Goshen at the time of the Exodus were supernaturally protected from an infestation of flies (Exodus 8:22-23)? The plague of hail that fell upon Egypt did not touch the land of Goshen. Why? Read Exodus 9:22-26. And, when pitch- blackness covered Egypt by means of a solar eclipse, the Israelite dwellings in Goshen all had light. (Exodus 10:21-23). How can you explain this?

6) If a sovereign God severed the Israelite population of Goshen from the Egyptians and protected them from the plagues that devastated Egypt, providing refuge, can He not do it in a new land of Goshen? Read also Isaiah 4:5-6.

7) Is it not time to either **find** or **build** another Goshen similar to the first model in Egypt?

Remnant Israelites in America would do well to ponder these questions as they seek to preserve a Christian remnant amid a country rife with heathen gods, religions, cultures, languages, and races of every kind. And that is only the beginning of our concerns! How about gun controls and ultimately gun confiscation? How about the complete dismantling of the Bill of Rights and curtailing of free speech? What is the purpose behind a **National Security Force** to control domestic unrest? What about proposed **Hate Crime Legislation** that could imperil a public discussion of the Bible's perspective on abortion, homosexuality, and race mixing?

No Christian Israelite in America lacks serious concerns regarding how the children and youth of this generation are going to survive the 21st Century and beyond without some prayerful consideration! Moreover, it is imperative that these same Christians move and act upon a vision! **It is time to find or build another Goshen!**

We Have Limited Options

Christians living in the 21st Century have few available to them. In previous eras, there was always another jurisdiction that might be favorable to those fleeing religious persecution and political oppression. These options are becoming extinct! A few folks have opted to move north to Alaska, somewhat separated from the Lower Forty-eight down under. Alaska is huge—with almost as much land area as the entire Western USA. Some Americans have fled to places in Central and South America, but at great risk because of the political instability and racial composition of that part of the world.

Most remnant Christians in America will opt to remain in this country and either join or build a **new land of Goshen** and trust a sovereign God to preserve them and their children from the curses that without question are plaguing America. Let us all pray that God-fearing families with children will make the sacrifices necessary to become deeply rooted in a church/community that is spiritually centered in Jesus Christ, a church/community that rests upon the moral absolutes of the **King James Bible,** preserving the racial integrity and ethnic heritage of the Celtic, Anglo, Saxon race, and working on a new **land of Goshen** in our beloved but imperiled America.

If you share this vision, may Jesus Christ be praised and you be blessed! Above all, may Christ give you spiritual discernment and understanding in building or finding another land of Goshen where you can plant your spiritual and racial feet for this and future generations, or until the King returns to claim the nations and kingdoms of this world as His very own (Revelation 11:15).

12

FINANCIAL ARMAGEDDON

Fall 2009

Along with the rest of the world, America is moving irreversibly toward financial Armageddon. The foundations of economic Babylon are shaking; the reverberations are felt in financial capitals throughout the world. Out of this monetary crisis, a one-world global economy, complete with a one-world currency and banking system, is emerging. America is caught in the vortex of this global crisis, so every citizen eventually will feel the financial pain. The ninety-five-year history of the privately owned international banking cartel—the Federal Reserve System—has brought America to the precipice of bankruptcy.

The international banking cartel and special interest groups (including the Trilateralist, Bilderbergers, Council on Foreign Relations, and other clandestine groups) have placed a black face on the Jewish Government that has gained control of the U. S.

Government. Both the Democratic and Republican Party are owned by these inside operatives. The President, his cabinet, the U. S. Senate, and House of Representatives are showcased for the public while the real power in government is unseen. Under Obama's administration, some thirty-two czars operate as front men in the shadows of the executive branch of government and are accountable only to the faces hidden behind the curtains.

The American public is being conditioned for entry into a third world economy as the treasure and resources of our country are reallocated and siphoned into the pockets of the money barons and foreign capitals. The balance of wealth will be spread to the rest of the population under the auspices of socialism. The Caucasian population of the United States is now disenfranchised as the non-white masses surge and proliferate from two factors: high birth rates and a tidal wave of non-white immigration. The homogenous white stock that once occupied America is rapidly disappearing as their birthrate drops to an average of about 1.6 children per family.

Out of economic meltdown and the ensuring chaos, deprivation, and insecurity, people begin to seek financial hope, security, and stability no matter the cost—even the loss of their many freedoms. History affords many examples of the economic chaos that produces tyranny and gives rise to powerful dictators. Only two options are possible for America's financial future: complete economic collapse or the creation of more debt-bearing, unsecured printing press money, which will create a mountain of debt and bring hyper-inflation.

God-fearing Americans may be well served to examine a case in point. Consider the case of the Weimar Republic in Germany: it affords an excellent example of what economic chaos can mean for the future of any country. At the end of World War I (1918), the victorious Allied leaders gathered at the Versailles Conference to forge a treaty under which the war was concluded and Germany was punished. President Woodrow Wilson and Premiers David

Lloyd George of Great Britain and Georges Clemenceau of France were known as the "Big Three" at this conference. They signed a treaty on June 28, 1919, but the U. S. Senate never ratified it. This treaty became the seedbed for World War II. Germany was stripped of much of its long-established territory, including Alsace and Lorraine, much of Schleswig, the districts of Eupen and Malmedy, Southeastern Silesia, Posen, a strip of West Prussia, the mouth of the Memel River, and the surrounding territory. It was ceded to the Allies, the city of Danzig, all of its overseas colonies, and its rights in Turkey and China. The Saar Valley, with its valuable coalfields, was placed under control of the League of Nations, the Rhineland was demilitarized, and livestock in Germany surrendered. In addition, Germany was assessed reparations of $33,000,000,000!

The seedbed for a dictatorship in Germany after World War I was sown by the terms of the Treaty of Versailles (1918-1921). The victorious Allies were determined that reparations were to be paid at a time when the German government simply could not meet these demands. The Weimar Republic arose out of the chaos and unrest of World War I and the ensuing Treaty of Versailles. Three opposing political forces were operating in Germany at this time: monarchists, who wanted a restoration of the German empire, the Communists, who sought a dictatorship patterned in the style of the Bolshevik Revolution, and the National Socialists (Nazi party) that demanded a dictatorship, the re-arming of Germany, and the tearing-up of the Treaty of Versailles. Adolf Hitler, an Austrian war veteran, headed the National Socialists.

In the midst of this chaos, Germany suffered from incredible hyper-inflation of their currency, placing the whole financial structure of the nation in peril. Prices would skyrocket in a matter of hours, and people found the paper currency all but worthless in the midst of this chaos. Hunger and deprivation gripped the population, causing people to give almost anything for food. Money became worthless! Various leaders made several attempts to solve the widespread depression that had afflicted Germany and most of Europe. In the midst of this chaos after World War I ended, the Germans were desperate and hence ready to follow Hitler and the Nazis. President von Hindenburg was re-elected in 1932; then, in 1933, he appointed Adolf Hitler as Chancellor (Prime Minister) of Germany. In 1934, President von Hindenburg died, and Hitler abolished the presidency and seized complete power. Creating the title of leader or fuehrer, Hitler then began rebuilding the nation.

The point here is that Americans today are not unlike the German population of the 1920s and 30s. The enormous billions, yea, trillions of printing press dollars being placed into circulation are increasing the velocity of money to a point where hyperinflation will be inevitable. As the U.S. Government pumps trillions of printing press money, anchored to nothing but thin air, into the economy, the collapse of the dollar is inevitable. People will lose personal fortunes. Like Germany, food could be too expensive to buy if it is even available.

If our economy should continue to falter, this could trigger massive domestic problems in the United States. Hyperinflation could encourage unrest among the public. The millions packed into the urban ghettos might plunder, riot, and turn American cities into burning infernos. The U. S. Government will then send federal troops to keep these urban populations under control.   Food could become scarce as the transportation system necessary to keep the supermarket shelves stocked falters. When people are hungry, widespread panic often besets the general population, who them become eager to accept the strong arm of a dictator who will "save the country."

In the election of 2008, a coalition of white Liberals, mainstream Christians, Latinos, and a solid wall of Black voters placed a Black face onto a predominately Jewish dominated Federal Government. Now, this President and sitting U. S. Congress have spent more money than the combined total of Bush

2, Clinton, Bush 1, Reagan, Carter, Ford, Nixon, Johnson, Kennedy, Eisenhower, and Truman. Make no mistake about it: many of these former Presidents were not afraid to roll up federal deficits!

Socialism has become rooted in contemporary America. Communism may be creeping around the corner. The U. S. Government has nationalized GM and large banking cartels and is moving toward nationalized health care. The country is facing bankruptcy. As the titanic of nations struggles in the waters of debt, immorality, spiritual apathy, political gridlock, and economic paralysis, our government continues to spend money like a drunken sailor. It is difficult to find a more irresponsible government than the one endorsed in the election of 2008. The titanic is sinking, the band keeps playing, and the party spirit continues, but no one in government is calling for national prayer, fasting, and turning from the wicked state of the nation.

A veritable financial Armageddon now faces America. California is bankrupt, and several other states are competing for financial insolvency. It is therefore urgent that God-fearing Americans put their spiritual, moral, and financial houses in order. America has rejected God, the Bible, and the moral absolutes of God's Law. Now what? Jehovah has given the nation free rein to self-destruct. **The Obomination that maketh desolate is our sovereign God's response to our wickedness. America has abandoned God and His Law, and yes, God has abandoned America!**

The U. S. Government has but two options left: with an eleven-trillion-dollar debt, it can wait for the burdened economy to collapse and bring on the greatest economic crash the world has ever known, or it can continue to print more unsecured paper currency, inflate the dollar, and prolong the inevitable. This will bring on hyperinflation that ultimately will weaken the dollar until it is worthless.

Our entire economy is built around debt. Every dollar in circulation has a lien against it. Americans no longer know how to function without credit cards and bank loans. Medicare is bankrupt. Medicaid is bankrupt. Social Security is approaching bankruptcy! California is bankrupt, and several other state governments are perilously close to it. Millions of Americans are hopelessly in debt.

Do not be fooled by those who look to the future with rose-colored glasses. Get out your Bible, man! Read Isaiah, Jeremiah, Ezekiel, and the Prophets. While these spiritual giants gave great hope for the remnant, they sounded the alarm to the nations of Israel and Judah. The long-term forecast for America is not good. God will save a Christian remnant, but judgment will come to the nation at large. God's Word does not lie; neither does the historical record of nations.

Remnant Christians will do well to prepare for financial Armageddon. Get out of debt! At the crash, cash will be king! Get out of the cities. Go to the land, man, go to the land! Choose your friends wisely. Invest in rural farm areas away from the urban sprawl, livestock, tools, precious metals, and without fail the Kingdom of God. The only treasure you will take with you beyond the grave will be what you gave for the cause of Jesus Christ and the advancement of His Kingdom. Everything remaining will end up as wood, hay, and stubble in the emerging new America. Above all, do not despair and lose hope! After all, if we indeed are facing the time of Jacob's trouble, God's Kingdom is near!

Under God's plan, the minority (those others called fools) end up being the majority. Noah entered the ark as the minority and exited as the majority. Lot was the minority in Sodom but ended up being the majority. Israel in Egypt was the minority but ended up being the majority. Out of the ashes of the 21st Century, Jehovah Elohim, Whom we know as the Lord and Savior Jesus Christ, will build His Kingdom. *"And the seventh angel sounded and there were great voices in heaven saying, The kingdoms of this world are become the kingdoms of our Lord, and of his Christ; and he shall reign for ever and ever"* *(Rev. 11:15).*

13

JOSEPH'S EMERGENCY STOREHOUSE

Winter 2010

With the precarious, undependable economy, there is every reason to believe that families need a **Joseph's Emergency Storehouse**. **When other plans fail, you will need it.** As the Federal Government of the United States moves toward financial bankruptcy and insolvency, any number of events could trigger perilous days. Whether the emergency is man-made or the act of a sovereign God Who obviously has lifted His blessing of grace from this land, you may need to be spiritually and physically prepared. It does not take a prophet to recognize that perilous days lie ahead.

We have millions of belligerent, sub-culture people demanding more and more handouts and subsidies from the U.S. Government. The diminishing Middle Class in America is growing angry and may take to the streets at some point. Emerging totalitarianism at the national level tries to control every aspect of our lives. The 12-trillion-dollar unsustainable debt mounted by the Federal Government can only mean a future of financial collapse or at the very least hyperinflation, surging to the point of financial collapse. This emergency may witness the collapse of the dollar and its replacement with a global currency.

The town hall and tea party gatherings across America during recent months indicate a political awakening among Middle Class Whites. However, only if these gatherings are motivated by more than political and economic interests will we witness a return to the moral and spiritual foundations of Bible truth. Any genuine repentance has yet to emerge at these gatherings. What is apparent is that there is an increasing surge of people who are absolutely fed up with the liberal elitists in both major political parties, which have worked consistently to destroy the United States for the past forty years.

The future of the United States appears to one of a nation under Almighty God's judgment. America has been spiritually and morally disconnected from the Bible for many decades. Having abandoned God's Word and found other gods to love and serve, Jehovah has granted us our national request and has turned His back upon this nation. We have broken covenant with Him and now have no spiritual or moral compass to guide us out of the darkness. We are trying to fight our way out of the current economic meltdown by borrowing and spending. Economists actually believe that by digging the hole deeper, we shall eventually emerge out of the financial pit. The transfer of America's manufacturing base to the Far East, where cheap labor abounds, has filled America with cheap junk made in China and elsewhere in Asia. Americans have hired the masses of Asia to manufacture their wares, leaving approximately fifteen million Americans without a job. The economic showcase of the world has been transferred from a producer nation to consumer nation. The millions of jobs that we have lost to Asia may never come this way again. The American dream has turned into a nightmare as millions of Americans tighten their belts and pray for their future.

The eight-year war in Afghanistan waged on borrowed dollars from foreign governments, combined with another protracted, seven-year war in Iraq, also fought with borrowed money, have pressed both the U. S. Treasury and Armed Forces to the limits. Additionally, the United States has allowed itself to be invaded and colonized by Mexican nationals for the past twenty-five years, leaving us with some forty million Latinos who have squatted, settled, and fastened themselves upon the American Fatherland.

The population demographics of the United States have radically altered, and the American Fatherland of White people has disappeared behind the tidal wave of third-world immigrants. In the face of this calamity, the time has come to encourage remnant Christians to look ahead, plan ahead, and make provisions for those you love, including family members who presently malign and vilify you for your Christian beliefs.

In the face of uncertain national and international times, every family should give immediate attention to building an **emergency storehouse**. Consider the following developments.

1.   WorldNetDaily cites strong evidence that some government agencies are stockpiling huge amounts of canned food.

2.   Jim Randas, former U.S. Intelligence officer, appeared on ABC news and told Americans to start stockpiling food.

3.   Grocery store prices are rising faster than any time in U.S. history.

4.   Worldwide grain stocks are dropping precipitously as biofuels consume inventories.

Your spiritual discernment and foresight in preparing **Joseph's Emergency Storehouse** could be a powerful witness to unbelievers, especially to family members that presently shun you. However, you must be discreet and quiet as you build your storehouse. Do not give the local loons any indication of what you are doing, and you must be prepared to defend your castle from intruders.

Can We Open Our Bibles?

A little more than four full chapters in Genesis detail the importance of Joseph's storehouse. Genesis 41, 42, 43, 44, and a part of 45 chronicle the record of Joseph gathering all the food of Egypt into a storehouse in preparation for a seven-year famine that was to come upon the land. Joseph not only saved the citizens of Egypt, but also the divine favor of Jehovah had placed Joseph in a position to preserve his father, all of his brothers, and their wives and children—a family that numbered seventy souls total.

When Joseph's brothers placed the young lad of seventeen years of age into a pit and later sold him into slavery, it appeared as if his life were destined to suffer the worst of all misfortunes. Being kidnapped and carried into a foreign land, sold at a slave auction, and enslaved by some wealthy Egyptian—this was a fate that no Hebrew ever wanted to face! Little did Joseph know that slavery was not the only fate that destiny had in store for him. After serving several years as a slave in the house of Potiphar, an officer and captain of the Pharaoh's palace guard, Joseph was falsely accused, charged, and jailed for a rape he did not commit. Confined indefinitely to the dank, dark, and primitive Egyptian dungeon, Joseph made the best of prison life; his behavior and demeanor soon got him favor with the keeper of the prison, who placed Joseph in charge of the other inmates.

During his time in prison, Joseph became acquainted with two of Pharaoh's servants, his chief butler and chief over all the bakers, when he accurately interpreted a dream that each of the servants had. Shortly thereafter, according to Joseph's interpretation of their dreams, the chief baker was hanged and the chief butler was released and returned to the palace to serve the Pharaoh. Unfortunately, the chief butler forgot to keep his promise to speak a word of favor to Pharaoh about Joseph. Thus, Joseph continued to languish in prison. After two full years passed, some dramatic circumstances unfolded in the palace of the king. The Pharaoh had also dreamed a dream that baffled all the magicians of Egypt. It was then that the chief butler remembered Joseph, a Hebrew in the prison who could interpret dreams.

In very short order, Joseph was ordered to be shaved, his prison clothes changed, and to be brought before the Pharaoh. Joseph correctly interpreted the Pharaoh's dream and predicted seven years of great plenty, with food in abundance, to be followed by seven years of drought and severe famine. Joseph instructed Pharaoh to *"look out a man discreet and wise, and set him over the land of Egypt . . . and let him appoint officers over the land, and take up the fifth part of the land of Egypt in the seven plenteous years. And let them gather all the food of those good years that come, and lay up corn And that food shall be for store to the land against the seven years of famine . . ." (Genesis 41:33-36).*

The rest is history. Joseph was immediately elevated to the office of Prime Minister, in command of all of Egypt; only the Pharaoh was greater in authority and power. Under Joseph's leadership, they gathered one-fifth of the harvest during the seven years of plenty and built storehouses in all the cities of Egypt. In thirteen years, Joseph moved from the pit and the lowest in the land to the palace, where he was now the second most powerful man in all of Egypt.

Joseph changed his drab prison garb for the finest linen in Egypt, a gold chain of immense value around his neck, the ring of the great Pharaoh upon his finger, and the second chariot in Egypt. The greater purpose for his collection of grain into storehouses was to meet the needs of Joseph's own family.

The famine became so sore in the land that ultimately, Joseph's own family of long-lost brothers, the very ones who had sold him into slavery, were forced to come to Egypt to buy food during the famine. In due time, Joseph discovered himself to his brothers—much to the joy of his aged father Jacob! It was not long before the entire family of Jacob-Israel then moved from Canaan to Egypt and settled in Goshen, the best land in all of Egypt. In true form to his great character, Joseph humbly explained to his brothers why they had sold him into slavery, all within the providence of God: *"And God sent me before you to preserve you a posterity in the earth, and to save your lives by a great deliverance. So now it was not you that sent me hither, but God: and he hath made me a father to Pharaoh, and lord of all his house, and a ruler throughout all the land of Egypt"* (Genesis 45:7-8).

The far-sighted vision of a caring God set in motion a plan to save all Jacob's family. He turned the wicked, evil scheme of Jacob's sons to effect a plan to prevent the starvation of this family. Joseph, the birthright son, was placed in a position of remarkable authority to achieve the goal of preserving life in a future famine. By building great storehouses throughout the land of Egypt during the seven years of plenty, the family of Jacob-Israel and all of Egypt were spared death by starvation. The evil that Joseph's wicked brother's intended for him God purposed for good. As Joseph said to his brothers following the death of Jacob, *" ...ye thought evil against me; but God meant it unto good, to bring to pass, as it is this day, to save much people alive"* (Genesis 50:20).

Joseph's Emergency Storehouse

We do not need a great interpreter of dreams to let us know that very perilous times lie ahead. The spiritual famine that grips the covenant people of America and other white homelands across the globe is becoming acute. Our rejection of God, the authority of His Word, and the foundations of Christian moral and spiritual laws have turned America upside down. Every indication is that this spiritual famine will increase in intensity as socialism, communism, and fascism become rooted in the leadership of the United States of America.

The ceiling on the national debt now stands at 12-trillion dollars. There is absolutely no possibility of this country servicing this debt owed to the private international banking cartel known as the Federal Reserve Banking System. At some point, the collapse of the dollar and the dissolution of the American economy will be irreversible. Exactly when that time is: that is the million-dollar question! This country is headed for financial Armageddon. Can you imagine what might happen to the welfare population, packed like sardines into the large cities, if they should suddenly lose their government checks, food stamps, and housing? Rioting, plunder, and burning will send plumes of smoke high over every urban area of America. Of course this would precipitate a state of national emergency and a declaration of martial law. This spiritual and moral famine will ultimately witness the transformation of America into a third world country. The disconnect from God and the utter rejection of His Law, complete with willful breaking of all covenants, will usher in an era of secular, progressive humanism that difficult to imagine.

Every indicator points to a time of spiritual, moral, and literal famine in this land! America is on the precipice of national calamity and catastrophic danger. Prophetically, this is called the "Time of Jacob's Trouble" (Jeremiah 30:7). To the praise and glory of God, however, Scripture declares, *"he shall be saved out of it"* (referring to the elect).

Islamic terrorists waging jihad in the form of nuclear and biological warfare is not the only danger that lurks in our future. The original, homogenous Caucasian population that settled and developed America and turned it into the showcase nation of the earth has been diluted with foreign and alien races that have injected false gods, religions, ideologies, and genes into the racial make-up of the Caucasian people.

Racial polarization and a deepening hatred of Whites on the part of liberals, who are ashamed they were born White, combined with the masses of non-Caucasians pose clear danger for the Anglo-Saxon population of America. Hate crime legislation, gun controls, and socialized legislation governing life from the cradle to the grave are all poised against Middle Class Whites. Caucasians are rapidly becoming the minority race in America as races of every hue gather in a floodtide of color. Whites are essentially a disenfranchised people and are in increasing danger of losing all political control at the ballot box.

The spiritually discerning sense terrible dangers lurking in the shadows of the socialist/communist government now trashing all remaining elements of the U. S. Constitution and the former Republic of the United States of America. The wise and prudent people are taking steps to be prepared for whatever may visit America. The United States Government itself has taken steps to bury food, water, and other essentials deep into top secret underground caverns. Mainstream people are urging citizens to take steps to be prepared in the event of a national state of emergency or enactment of martial law. This emergency could be one created by our own government, by home grown Islamic terrorists, or foreign armies. Our political correctness has given cover and immunity to Islamic terrorists, Black Panthers, and assorted other groups that are part of this country. There is even the possibility that the sleeping Anglo-Saxon giant could be awakened, and, realizing what has happened to his country, take to the streets. Open civil war is not an unthinkable possibility should sufficient numbers of Americans discover that they and their children are being sold out to the Wall Street Bankers and one-world ideologues. Many thoughtful Americans believe that the nation is simply too far-gone for any return to the Republic established under the U. S. Constitution.

When All Plans Fail!

Every family needs a Joseph Storehouse that contains the most essential items necessary to sustain the family during a time of national or community emergency. This storehouse might become extremely important in the event of any kind of emergency, including national disasters. If the transportation system of the nation were to be shut down, it would be a matter of hours until the shelves at the supermarket would be bare. Wal-Mart would soon be empty, and food and other shortages would immediately be apparent.

Think for a moment. What if electricity were to be cut off? Or highways would be closed and barricaded? Imagine having no water! No flushing of the toilets, no showers, simply no water—then what? What if the only food you had available for one month or more is what you could presently find in your home? How prepared are you for a national disaster or a man-created emergency? Consider how complicated life might be if you were suddenly, in a matter of minutes, pushed into a lifestyle of rural America 1900. When all other plans fail, you will need Joseph's Storehouse!

Consider This

Joseph was sent ahead to prepare for those he loved! Granted, he did not have any understanding of what Jehovah was doing by sending him into a foreign land. How can you be certain that your storehouse is not being put together to assist those you love at some time? How can Joseph's Storehouse become a life saving event for those you love? How could your storehouse become a witness for God in a time of great need?

Basic Storehouse Plans

1) Be spiritually prepared and in communion with the Living God at all times by faith in Jesus Christ, having daily altar calls in your home, daily reading from the Bible, regular Sabbath worship services, and observing the holy days.

2) Be in spiritual and physical communion with a church family that shares close theological, racial, and geographical ties.

3) Water is critical: prepare a source of water independent from public utilities. Perhaps consider a hand-pumped, private well. A natural water filtration system, AquaRain, is available and is one of the best on the market. You may wish to google aquarain.com on the internet and talk to these good people or contact them by telephone. Ask for Cindy Cutler or Robert Burney if you wish to call them at 1-800-572-2051.

4) Food is also essential in your Joseph's Storehouse. Most food reserves include hard red winter wheat, oats, millet, brown rice, and assorted beans. Grains can be sprouted, ground into flour, or soaked and used as cereal. A store of spices, sauces, and soups is desirable (six-ounce cans of tomato paste, canned cream of chicken, celery soups are good possibilities) as are any other items necessary to make grains more appetizing. Your canned foods can be rotated so that you are constantly re-supplying your shelves with new items as you use the old.

5) Purchase heirloom seeds; having access to garden seed could be extremely beneficial in a time of great uncertainty. It is extremely important to find a source of good seed for gardens and perhaps feed for livestock. For starters, you may wish to go on line at http://www.survivalseedbank.com. This website offers a survival seed pack that will plant a full acre of non-hybrid, open-pollinated seeds. Do not wait to plant a garden until the emergency arises. You need experience, so take your sons and daughters and head for the garden when spring comes.

6) Make a list of items that you feel are really important to you and your family. Include flashlights, emergency radios that will operate without electricity, first-aid supplies, medicines, herbs, and essentials for typical forms of injury and illness, a means of defending life and property, essential clothing (including footwear, cold weather clothing, and other clothing essentials). Do you have a store of soap, lotions, toilet paper, and other essentials?

Procrastinating is not something you want to do when it comes to preparing Joseph's Storehouse. Be pro-active! Be prepared!

If you have prepared before and no need arose, praise God! The fact is that you were prepared if the crisis came!

The America of 2010 is a different country than any of us have ever known. The America that we all once knew is no more. In the midst of this chaos, it is important to remember this: *"God is our refuge and strength, a very present help in trouble. Therefore will not we fear, though the earth be removed, and though the mountains be carried into the midst of the sea" (Psalm 46:1-2).* It is better to be prepared than sorry! The foolish virgins forgot to take oil in their lamps. Remember to keep the oil of the Holy Spirit burning and in your spare time, turn off the television, Internet, cell phone, or I-pod and prepare Joseph's Storehouse!

14

AMERICA: YOU HAVE BROKEN THE COVENANT OF YOUR FATHERS

Spring 2010

America, you have broken the covenant of your ancestors who plied the waters of the Atlantic almost four hundred years ago to plant a nation, a shining city on a hill for the glory of God and the advancement of the Christian faith. Oh, how God smiled upon those first European Americans, honored their love and commitment to His Word, and blessed them like no nation under heaven has ever been blessed! The first great wave of Caucasian Pioneers to settle this country in the early 17th Century took possession of this country in covenant with God. That covenant is still in force, and we are in dire trouble as a nation because we have lived in willful violation of this covenant made between the Founding Fathers and the God they loved and served.

Today, tens of millions throughout America languish in debt, under excessive taxation, and live in homes that are worth less than the mortgage owed on them. They are jobless, have maxed out their credit cards, and are without hope of realizing the American dream. We have lost our way and are losing our country because we have broken the covenant of our ancestors. The United States faces imminent financial collapse, potential civil war, and even worse, a declaration of martial law with the guns of our own military ordered to turn on us as we face a totalitarian dictatorship, perhaps even Stalin style. We cannot save our country without a return to the faith of our Founding Ancestors, and we are spiritual light years away from their biblical commitment.

We suffer from an abundance of hireling, predator preachers; greedy, self-serving politicians; humanist educators; and successive generations of absentee fathers. We are in the midst of an economic meltdown, protracted, no-win foreign wars, Latino invasion from our southern border, staggering deficits owed to foreign bankers, a Federal Government in total paralysis, massive joblessness, and a fourteen-trillion-dollar national debt. Plagues, natural disasters, and catastrophic weather patterns also visit our land because we have broken the covenant of our ancestors and have rejected, scorned, and even mocked the God we once loved, served, and obeyed.

America's Greatness

America became the showcase nation for the glory of God, the oppressed, and the enslaved of every country on the planet. In just a few short generations, the vast, primitive wilderness of our American fatherland was turned into a thriving, bustling nation of private homes, churches, farms, factories, schools, colleges, universities, and charitable institutions that opened their hearts and pocket books to the whole world. America became a land filled with churches as hymns of praise and the Word of God resounded from the Atlantic to the Pacific! The statutes and laws that governed America were the same as those found in the Holy Bible. The America dream became the envy of the world as those who lived in this land enjoyed all the bounties that heaven could possibly bestow upon a people. America became a great nation because the ancestors who laid the political, spiritual, and moral foundation for this country honored God, revered the Bible, and loved one another.

America was a nation of homogenous people who shared a very close racial and ethnic heritage from Europe, a faith in the one and only true God, Jesus Christ, belief in the Bible, and adherence to the statutory law that reflected biblical absolutes. Heaven smiled upon this land, and the America dream was the envy of the world. That nation that was bustling with a Christian, European cultural mandate has been transformed into a multicultural, racially diverse, pluralistic society that worships every god under heaven, honors every religious view on the planet, and is on the verge of criminalizing Christianity and those who live by biblical absolutes.

The 21st Century America

Fast forward to the 21st Century—if you dare! Millions of Americans wake up every morning and in stark bewilderment wonder how they lost their country. Americans languish with tens of thousands of their sons volunteering to fight in international wars, financed by foreign dollars and led by politicians who have neither the intention nor the will to win. And, while our sons are dying in Iraq and Afghanistan, millions of Mexican nationals are invading the country from the South every year. What do our leaders do but turn a blind eye and pretend to wage a war on Islam?

Millions of Americans are unemployed and spend their idle time plying the isles of Wal-Mart, looking for sale prices on goods made in China and Mexico. America, once the manufacturing capital of the world, now finds its factories transported overseas and American workers without jobs, financial security, or any future. Millions of jobs that once belonged to Americans are now done in India, China, and elsewhere in the world as struggling

American companies seek cheap labor in the third world countries. For tens of millions of Americans whose homes are now vacated, with foreclosures abounding and homelessness a growing phenomenon, the American dream has become a nightmare. The very descendants of the Founding Fathers who entered a covenant to love, obey, and serve Jehovah God are now in the process of losing their country. Foreign dollars and alien races are buying farmland, factories, town houses, and real estate up and down the land. Foreigners occupy homes and land once owned by the descendants of those who built this country. America has become the largest debtor nation in the world. Our national debt, at fourteen trillion dollars, is unsustainable. The interest on this debt for one month is approaching one hundred billion dollars. Our children and untold generations have been mortgaged by the secular progressive minds running the country.

The America built upon a covenantal theology has been lost and is being delivered into the hands of a global cabal of international bankers and elitists who are determined to reduce the great Middle Class into a herd of bleating, defenseless sheep. Hireling preaches seal their lips in cowardly silence while predator wolves devour their sheep.

The bells of judgment are tolling in this land! All the warning signs of heaven are flashing bright and clear! The titanic of nations is sinking, with the lifeboats hard to find! The pulpits of this great nation are busy proclaiming a cotton candy theology and filling the minds of their parishioners with marshmallow fluff while the nation slips into the spiritual and moral abyss. But America did not break loose from its covenantal moorings overnight.

A Look Back

Beginning with the Civil War (1860-1865), America began to lose its spiritual anchor in the covenant God and His Word that had guided this nation for 250 years. The decline was subtle and gradual, but ever inching away from the covenant laid by

America's founding fathers and the God Whom they loved and served. With the advent of Woodrow Wilson (1913-1921), World War I (1914-1918), and events thereafter, the departure from the ancestral covenant laid in the early 1600s accelerated consistently.

The 1930s was a decade of widespread economic suffering in the Great Depression beginning in 1929 and did not end until America became engulfed in World War II (1941-1945). The break with our Christian Fathers and the covenant they made with God continued through the Cold War era from 1946 until the collapse of the Berlin Wall and the dismantling of the Soviet Union in 1989. At times, this Cold War erupted into red hot flames: Korea (1950-1953), the Cuban Missile Crisis (1961-62), and the Vietnam War (1963-1973) spring to mind. In all of these bloody engagements, American armies left the battlefield without a victory because those leading them in Washington D.C. lacked the political will to win and sacrificed their native sons on the altar of treason!

In the late 1950s and throughout the 60s, America was baptized in the filth of a moral revolution that left the nation seriously wounded and spiritually emaciated. The covenant of America's ancestors was bruised, tattered, and bloodied in the cultural, moral, and spiritual revolution of the 60s. A whole generation of flower children reared on pot, rock and roll, free love, and Marxist theology became the poster children for America. The God of America's ancestors was declared dead by a generation of wimpy, powder puff preachers who joined the flower children in their rejection of the covenant law and morals of former generations.

Very soon, the fruits of this wicked and apostate generation from the 50s and early 60s could be seen. Prayer in public schools was restricted in *Engel v. Vitale* in 1962. Interracial marriage, long forbidden by covenantal law, became legal in *Loving v Virginia*, 1967. The murder of unborn children was legalized in *Rose v Wade*, 1973. The Ten Commandments were removed from public schools in *Stone v. Graham*, 1980. The sin of sodomy was declared legal in *Lawrence v. Texas*, 2003. The Ten Commandments, the very heart of our covenantal ancestors' belief system, was removed from the public's eyes in *Glassroth v Moore*, 2003. The very first state-recognized homosexual marriages were legalized in *Goodridge v Dept. of Public Health* by the Massachusetts Supreme Court in 2003. By the end of the 20th Century, America virtually had been stripped of the covenantal foundation laid by the Christian Fathers of the 17th Century.

The Covenant of Our Ancestors

The faithful, God-fearing Puritans who flocked to the shores of North America by the thousands in the Great Migration of 1630-1641 established church communities built upon a covenantal contract with Jehovah God. This covenant embraced four basic presuppositions.

First: Jehovah placed a special call on this people and the country they were to inhabit. They envisioned themselves as God's New Israel, walking in the model as the ancient Israelites who had fled Egypt and established themselves as the covenant people of Jehovah. They believed that the call of God required them to create a new Israel, living in obedience to the covenant law of God and by faith in Jesus Christ trusting Him to bless the work of their hands. These early Puritans desired to build a New Jerusalem, a shining city on a hill that would reflect the glory of God and His covenantal law to the whole world.

Establishing a New Jerusalem was the goal for the Puritan fathers as they endeavored to follow the model of ancient Israel and the covenant law given to Moses at Mt. Sinai. The special call that was upon their lives was nothing less than the call placed upon ancient Israel as the special and peculiar treasure of Jehovah God in the earth (Deuteronomy 7:1-9). This call required the original settlers to place God and others ahead of self (Luke 9:23-26) and to love one another (John 13:34-35).

Second: This call was to be actualized in terms of the covenant made between the settlers with Jehovah God and each other. This covenant required the settlers to honor and obey the Commandments, Statutes, and Judgments of the covenant; in return, the work of their hands would be blessed. These original Americans believed in the one God Who wrote a continuum of truth in the Old and New Covenants of Scripture. The blood of Jesus Christ had made reconciliation for sin, so the redeemed in Jesus Christ were now called into a life of discipline, selfless love, and obedience to the laws of Jehovah. The New Covenant required a vertical obedience to the covenant, giving Jehovah honor and obedience. The horizontal aspects of the covenant required each settler to deny himself, love his neighbor, and live in daily commitment to his fellow man.

The original Americans envisioned the covenant made with Abraham, Isaac, and Jacob, and then with national Israel to be a direct continuation with them as they planted their church communities in the New World. The covenantal words given the Patriarchs and the nation of Israel became the model for God's New Israel attempting to take root in New England. Not only did the covenant require undivided honor, love, and obedience to Jehovah, but also a complete sacrifice of self-love and self-will in order to obey God and love one another.

As these church-communities grew in vertical and horizontal obedience to the covenant, these settlements became towns; thus, the first civil governments in the New World were formed. From these humble beginnings, church-communities in New England would become much of the inspiration, intellect, and leadership for what became the United States of America.

Third: A sovereign God would keep His promise and honor the settlers' obedience to the covenant with blessings, prosperity, and security on an individual and corporate basis. The "right heart attitude" of the people would compel them to honor God and obey His covenant law. The state of the people's hearts and loyalty to God and the covenant was measured by the blessings or the curses that would befall them.

The covenant called the American settlers to remember this: *"Behold, I set before you this day a blessing a curse; A blessing, if ye obey the commandments of the LORD your God, which command you this day: And a curse, if ye will not obey the commandments of the LORD your God, but turn aside out of the way which I command you this day, to go after other gods, which ye have not known . . . And ye shall observe to do all the statutes and judgments which I set before this day"* (Deuteronomy 11:26-32).

When a searing drought would come, the lack of rain indicated the removal of God's approval on the people's activities. If the crops blistered and withered, the settlers would humble themselves in repentance and amid fasting and prayer seek the face of God, Whom they may have taken for granted. A "right heart attitude" toward God and the covenant contract would mean that one settlement might be spared from Indian attack, while another church-community, whose hearts were hardened in sin and disobedience to the covenant, was wiped out. Any misfortune would invite personal or corporate examination and a search for sin that would offend God and cause Him to withdraw His blessings. A "right heart attitude" could mean plentiful rain and abundant harvests, while "hardened hearts and dishonor to God and the covenant" might mean drought, famine, disastrous storms, pestilence, or a visit from the Indians was imminent.

In any case, a "right heart attitude" in the face of a smallpox epidemic, hail storm, Indian attack, drought, or some other disaster would invite the settlers to humble themselves from pride, complacency, self-righteousness, or other sins, and cause them to seek the face of God in fasting and prayer. The Puritan settlers believed that since they were sinners, all had an urgent need for personal and corporate examination for sin. Heartfelt prayers, fasting, and self-examination would merit the favor of God and lift the curse from their personal or collective lives. Repentance toward God and faith in Jesus Christ were regarded as the only means of insuring the vertical terms of the covenant. And, only at the cross in repentance before God could the settlers be united in selfless love one to another and maintain the horizontal aspects of the covenant.

Fourth: The original Americans in covenant with God believed that a cycle of repentance would usher in God's grace, and that out of this death to self and in the midst of personal and corporate humility, repentance, and turning from wickedness, a new era of heartfelt, enduring blessing would come. For the Puritans, godly repentance meant a change of mind in respect to sin, God, and self. This repentance had to be preceded by sorrow (II Cor. 7:8-11). However, sorrow that may initiate repentance is not to be mistaken for repentance. A change of mind and direction had to occur, along with the putting away of sin or iniquity. This is the end of true remorse for sin.

Keeping a "right heart attitude" was the key to maintaining the vertical terms of the covenant and insuring generational blessings in personal and corporate lives. A life that was in right relationship with God by faith in Jesus Christ would motivate and bring forth a body of people that would inspire a daily commitment to dying out of self-love, self-will, and self-gratification and would in turn guide believers to love God and one another in covenant life.

The original settlers believed that obedience to the covenant would give unlimited, enduring blessings to all future generations: *"And it shall come to pass, if thou shalt hearken diligently unto the voice of the LORD thy God, to observe and to do all his commandments which I command thee this day, that the LORD thy God will set thee on high above all nations of the earth: And all these blessings shall come on thee, and <u>overtake thee</u>, if thou shalt hearken unto the voice of the LORD thy God"* *(Deut. 28:1-2).* Disobedience to the covenant would insure the curses would fall (Deuteronomy

28:15-68), whereas repentance called the people to periodic renewal and rekindling of the covenant with God (vertical relationship) and with their neighbor (horizontal relationship) in dying to self-love and self-will and a daily commitment of sacrificial living and loving one's neighbor. Each generation, and often multiple times within the life of each generation, a renewed commitment followed a time of repentance and turning from apathy, complacency, pride, and worldliness.

The Painful Road to Repentance

Fast forward to America in the 21st Century. All the Tea Party events and town hall meetings that can be assembled in America will never appease the wrath of the God, Whose name and covenant Law has been dishonored in this land. Successive generations of hireling preachers have abandoned God, forsaken His Law, fleeced the sheep, and refused to call the nation back to God and the covenant of our ancestors. Only when we renew and establish both the vertical and horizontal aspects of the covenant of our ancestors can the curses be lifted from this land.

A stink rises all the way to heaven from the hireling preachers, antinomian Christians (?), U.S. Congress, White House, Supreme Court, many State Houses, and even most local Court Houses across America. As horrible and despicable as many of our civil leaders are, they are not the primary problem in this country. America's political, economic, foreign policy, and military disasters are not the greatest problems this country faces. The greatest problem lies in the unrepentant American clergy and their unrepentant followers who live in wanton disobedience to the covenant of their ancestors and love to have it so.

Breaking the covenant between our Founding Fathers and the Living God is the problem. This ancestral covenant was the basis for the church communities that laid the foundations for this nation. These church communities became towns, then cities, and transitioned into colonies, states, and a nation ending up under the *Articles of Confederation and Perpetual Union* in 1781 when the War of Independence had ended. The Christian foundations of the early 17th Century were the basis for the Republic that was established following the War of Independence (1775-1781).

We cannot reclaim our country until we reclaim our faith! Our faith lives in the truth, heritage, and biblical foundations of the covenant laid by God-fearing Americans in the early 17th Century. If we do not repent and make this 180-degree course correction, this country will remain under the covenantal curses of Leviticus 26 and Deuteronomy 28! America's entire future rests on a covenant with God. America cannot be saved with Tea Parties and the ballot box! America cannot be saved in revolution! This country will be saved only if and when we repent and mend the broken covenant with Jehovah, the only God of this nation.

15

THE FALL OF THE AMERICAN EMPIRE

Summer 2010

Is the world's largest nation-empire in danger of collapse? Are we witnessing the fall of the single greatest nation ever to grace the planet? Will America have the shortest lifespan of all the empires in history? Has any empire in history ever risen and fallen again so swiftly, as America appears to be doing? Can Christians discern that the fall of America is imminent? Is the collapse of America by God's design or man's? Who orchestrated the collapse of the world's greatest nation? Are we as a nation simply in decline, or are we facing America's demise? Is the impending collapse preventable, or is it already too late? And, if America does go over the cliff, is your family prepared for the consequences? We report! You decide!

Americans born before our country's 1941 entry into World War II may be bewildered as they contemplate the state of the native land into which they were born. Silver-haired Americans must be in total shock as they witness the political, economic, military, and racial demise of the nation that has provided their life-long home. Apprehension is gripping millions of Americans as they watch their homeland stagger from one calamity to another, with hardly any reprieve before another disaster strikes. America is like a drunken man staggering from one colossal crisis to another. Before the people can process one calamity, another is on its way.

Nations and empires do not always decline over extended periods of time. History shows that empires can suddenly go into free fall and expire. Consider the warning of Niall Ferguson, professor at Harvard University and Harvard Business School and a fellow at Jesus College, Oxford. Professor Ferguson argues that not all empires rise and fall in a predictable way, as Rome did. Some, like the U.S., are vulnerable to sudden catastrophic shocks that can bring about the demise of an empire. Professor Ferguson made the following observations in the *Vancouver Sun,* British Columbia, Canada, March 8, 2010: "The most recent and familiar example of precipitous decline is the collapse of the Soviet Union . . . less than five years after Mikhail Gorbachev took power, the Soviet Imperium in central and Eastern Europe had fallen apart, followed by the Soviet Union itself in 1991. If ever an empire fell off a cliff, rather than gently declining, it was the one founded by Lenin.

"If empires are complex systems that sooner or later succumb to sudden and catastrophic malfunctions, what are the implications for the United States Today? First, debating the stages of decline may be a waste of time—it is a precipitous and unexpected fall that should most concern policy-makers and citizens. Second, most imperial falls are associated with fiscal crises.

"Alarm bells should therefore be ringing very loudly indeed as the United States contemplates a deficit for 2010 of more than **$1.5 trillion**—about 11 percent of GDP, the biggest since World War . . . .

"These numbers are bad, but in the realm of political entities, the role of perception is just as crucial. In imperial crises, it is not the material underpinnings of power that really matter, but expectations about future power . . . One day, a seemingly random piece of bad news . . . Suddenly, it will be not just a few policy wonks who worry about the sustainability of U. S. fiscal policy but the public at large, not to mention investors abroad. It is this shift that is crucial . . . .

"Neither zero percent interest rates nor fiscal stimulus packages can achieve a sustainable recovery if people in the United States and abroad collectively decide, overnight, that such measures will ultimately lead to much higher inflation rates or outright default. Bond yields can shoot up if expectations change about future government solvency, intensifying an already bad fiscal crisis by driving up the cost of interest payments on new debt. Just ask Greece.

"Ask Russia, too. Fighting a losing battle in the mountains of the Hindu Kush has long been a harbinger of imperial fall. What happened 20 years ago is a reminder that empires do not in fact appear, rise, reign, decline and fall according to some recurrent and predictable life cycle . . . .

"Rather, empires behave like all complex adaptive systems. They function in apparent equilibrium for some unknowable period. And then, quite abruptly, they collapse. Washington, you have been warned."

Without question, this is an alarm bell. Does anyone in government have the sense to listen? How many people actually sense that something catastrophic in the financial status of the country could be the preverbal straw that breaks the camel's back? Any number of events could trigger complete unrest in the already jittery American public and send overseas investors scrambling to disconnect from trusting their financial fortunes in American investments. American armies, like the Soviet Union, are in a protracted war in the Hindu Kush Mountains of Afghanistan, and who knows what this bottomless pit could precipitate? The American population is fully capable of coming unglued, and if it does, millions will take to the streets if government welfare programs and entitlement programs disappear by default.

There is no lack of prognosticators and journalists to give their projections of where the American empire is headed. The underground presses are working overtime with dire predictions of what may lie ahead for this country. The Internet is crammed with websites that reveal how conspirators are orchestrating the demise of America's empire. An unending stream of printed newsletters, newspapers, radio talk shows, short-wave broadcasts, and neighbor-to-neighbor conversations are abuzz with how fast the American empire is moving toward insolvency.

Americans who work for a living, run a business, or are engaged in something that fits into the free enterprise system are in panic mode. They are witnessing the Federal Government orchestrating the financial collapse of the free enterprise system. Successive leaders in both political parties have run up unsustainable debt, each one trying to surpass their predecessor.

Republicans in office from 2000 to 2008 eclipsed all previous spending records, and since 2008, Democrats led by the stranger in the White House have increased the national debt to such astronomical levels that few economists alive believe that America can long survive. The current debt of **fourteen trillion dollars** is growing at the rate of **four billion each day** (as per Fox News clip on June 9, 2010). At this rate, the national debt will reach **19.6 trillion by 2015.** The interest on this debt will be **unsustainable**, with the collapse of the American economic system eminent.

Many Christian conservatives believe that there is an orchestrated plan to commence the collapse of the America's free enterprise system and merge the United States into a global, one-world government, the demise of the dollar, and the emergence of a new international currency. At this point, having been divested of most of its wealth and treasure, America would quickly be reduced to a third world nation with squalor and poverty becoming commonplace. Simultaneously with this new economic order would come a totalitarian dictatorship in the United States with National Socialism and even Communist ideology backed by military force.

Time for Serious Talk

There are several crucial reasons why God-fearing Americans need to know that the American Empire is moving toward a catastrophic plunge into the graveyard of nations. Christians deserve answers from their spiritual shepherds. Stewards and ministers of God's Word ought to know what is happening and be able to provide biblical insight and encouragement to the Christian remnant within the folds of this country.

In reverence for God and the truth of His Word and with deepest love and affection for the covenant people, the following thoughts are placed before our reading audience for their consideration. It is certain that this list could be elongated by a number of other factors that support the potential collapse of the American Empire. The points made here in this order appear, from our window to the world, to be the reasons why the fall of the American Empire is underway.

1) The loss of spiritual dependence upon and direction from our Sovereign God and Lord Jesus Christ. History confirms that men cannot govern nations without faith in a sovereign God, the Governor of nations. Ultimately, nations will fail, regardless of the system of government. All man-made governments eventually fail. There is no form of government that can endure without dependence upon and direction from God. America lost all sense of her need for God and has gone so far as to break the covenant made between Jehovah and her ancestors of the 17th Century, leaving us adrift without a compass or North Star to guide us.

The American clergy has failed this nation. Both the pulpits and the pews have disconnected from the covenantal faith of our fathers. America is adrift on the ocean without vision or any sense of national destiny. **Our spiritual separation and alienation from our sovereign God is at the root of all our problems.** We have forsaken God, thrown down altars to His name, and failed to preach His Law; we need to bring our nation to the Cross of Jesus Christ as the only remedy for our guilt of sin. We have vilified God-fearing men who dared to tell the truth to an unbelieving, unsaved generation.

2) Having discarded the Holy Bible as the rule of truth, America has no absolute moral code to guide our footsteps in the 21st Century. Without an absolute moral system of values, America is a nation awash in pluralism. Without God's Law as the model for all legislation, we have no check upon wickedness, leaving moral anarchy to prevail throughout the land. Statutory laws once modeled after the moral truth of Scripture have been discarded in favor of man's laws. The source of law determines the god who will be worshipped. Government has become the god of America. Situation ethics govern the moral habits of the nation. Having abandoned the absolute truth of Scripture and lacking any clergy to call this nation back to God and His Law, the people are running wild. Wickedness of every kind is rampant.

Everything that God hates and calls sin is labeled "good" and protected under statutory law and court decree by American legislators, activist judges, and humanist educators. This list includes abortion, sodomy, miscegenation, and other heinous crimes against God and His created order. Creationism has been replaced with evolution in the public schools and in much of mainstream Christianity. America is a land with many competing moral standards. Jesus Christ as the only way, truth, and life has become one among many pathways to eternal life. Absolute truth found in Jesus Christ and His Word, and no place else, was the guiding compass for the 17th Century Americans who settled this land in covenant with God. Where are we now?

3) The disintegration of the historic, nuclear family of one man and woman united for life for the multiplication of children and the godly dominion of God's earth has simply crashed and burned. About 70% of America's children live in single-parent homes or in foster homes. Career moms, adultery, and no-fault divorce have shattered the sanctity of the Christian family in America. More than 50% of married couples admit to extra-marital affairs. 50% of couples live together outside the covenant of marriage. The redefining of the biblical, historic institution of marriage to include practicing homosexuals is an affront to God and turns six thousand years of history upside down!

More than one third of children in America are born out of wedlock. The historic Christian family has been trashed; the resulting carnage has created a nightmare as this country seeks to grapple with the subsequent social upheaval. The historic, biblical family is the anchor of any nation. Without this foundation, the American empire cannot survive. The church, public schools, community, state, and nation are dependent upon the institution of the family to survive. The American Empire is in peril with the disintegration of the family.

4) The loss of personal ambition, initiative, reliance, responsibility, and self-government has swelled the ranks of the American public with incompetents, sluggards, derelicts, drug addicts, and welfare abusers. The free enterprise system that fueled the greatest nation building in the annals of history catapulted America toward the stars with the highest standard of living ever. As America prepares to go over the cliff, it is afflicted with a shrinking population of competent, ambitious, and responsible workers. Government welfare, excessive regulation of business, high taxes, and a movement toward socialism have stifled personal ambition, leaving fewer people willing to risk opening a business.

The U.S. government is now the largest employer on the planet, so private business must compete with a socialist government that rewards the lazy and punishes the zealous who place their talents and initiative on the line for the fruits that come from a free market. With one of the highest tax rates on business among the nations of the world, and crippled with overly zealous unions, excessive regulations, millions of illegal workers competing for jobs, and government entitlements that stifle and compete for the need to go to work and earn a living, the American Empire is on the precipice—ready to free fall into the economic abyss.

5) The ingestion of more than 100 million non-Caucasian people into our nation has made a radical demographic shift from which we shall never recover. As America was transformed from Republic to Empire following World War II, the racial face of America has been altered beyond recognition. From Jamestown (1607) through to about 1965, the United States was, with some exceptions, an homogenous population of Caucasian people, with Christianity the predominate religious faith and with a law system modeled after the Bible. The American Empire now spreads its mighty wings to encompass every race, religion, and ideology on the planet and in the process has lost most of its original Christian savor. The first major flood of non-Christian and mostly Eastern European Jews arrived in this country beginning in 1890. This tiny minority of people has become the majority at the highest echelons of banking, finance, government, news media, television, cinema, and other highly profiled areas of our culture.

The immigration bill passed in 1965 opened the floodgates to third world, non-white immigration. This continuous tsunami of people, together with the hordes from Asia and the thirty million Latinos from Mexico, has literally transformed the racial face of

America. The Brazilification of the Empire is underway as America essentially becomes a non-white nation. The country that was once Caucasian, Christian, and modeled after Bible Law seems lost forever.

6) The American population has become a nation of far too many indulgent, self-gratifying consumers rather than producers. A major character transformation of our nation has been underway: this deficiency in character has greatly accelerated as the generation that weathered the Great Depression and World War II pass on to their reward. The Baby Boomers born between 1946 and 1964 are in general far less hardened, less frugal, less ambitious, less diligent, and less spiritually and morally equipped than the generation that lived through sixteen years of depression and war. The grandchildren of this Great Generation are far less capable of sustaining what is left of the American free enterprise system of capitalism. The generation now making policy decisions for our America is spoiled with indulgence in materialism; they are morally deficient, have a poor work ethic, and are awash in character deficiencies.

America has become a nation with more and more of its citizens dependent upon government. The ever-expanding nature of welfare and entitlement programs has encouraged less and less personal initiative, ambition, and creativity. Americans have become consumers rather than producers. Almost everything that can be purchased in a typical Wal-Mart or Target will have been made in China or someplace outside of the USA. This country would be in crisis if it became necessary to wage a war with materials manufactured in the United States. The great American industrial manufacturing complex has been diminished to a point where alarm bells should be ringing everywhere!

7) The American Empire has an unsustainable military presence in more than 100 nations of the world and is engaged in costly, protracted, no-win wars that are moving the America Empire toward financial collapse. America wages undeclared wars on borrowed dollars and with a mercenary army. These wars are waged without personal sacrifice to the American_public: no rationing, no war bonds, and no national will to win these wars. Policy strategists in both major political parties wage these wars without a clear mission or even intent to win. American military forces have been engaged in the Hindu Kush Mountains in Afghanistan since December of 2001. In just months, the U.S. Military will have been engaged against the Islamic Jihad forces for ten long years—without any victory in sight.

American forces have been on the ground in Iraq since March of 2003. U.S. troops remain garrisoned in Germany (since 1945), South Korea (since 1953), and Kosovo since (1999). The military forces of the American Empire are stretched thin in multiple continents waging war with mercenary forces—and all on borrowed money! Much like ancient Rome, with its far-flung empire, and unable to halt the Gothic hordes invading their homeland, America appears incapable of guarding its southern border from an invasion of millions of Latinos. At the same time, American armies are on the ground in Iraq and Afghanistan waging protracted wars on foreign soil without victory. While the U. S. seeks to contain the Islamic threat by waging protracted wars in Central Asia, its homeland is being invaded and colonized by Mexican illegals who are bleeding America of its treasure and resources.

8) By 2015, the national debt will skyrocket to 19.6 trillion, and the cost of servicing this debt will far exceed the combined wealth of all goods and services produced in the country. The debasement of America's fiat currency is underway, leaving the collapse of the dollar inevitable. The tax and spend policies of the past fifty years, on the part of both political parties, has America approaching bankruptcy.

The U.S. Congress surrendered its constitutional authority to control the nation's currency into the hands of the privately owned

Federal Reserve Bank in 1913. The current President is presiding over a bankrupt empire, and individual states will eventually default as the financial demands are place upon them by socialized healthcare and cap and trade energy taxes. The international banking cartel and corporate CEOs are orchestrating the economic collapse of America's existing economic system and the merger of the nation into a world government complete with a global currency, world court, police force, and taxing authority.

Sobering Conclusions

The fall of the American Empire is not slow moving. The collapse of America appears to be accelerating like a racecar speeding down the tract. All that remains for financial Armageddon and the collapse of the empire to be complete is the loss of all confidence by the American public and overseas investors. It will be most fortunate if civil war does not follow this collapse. The potential for martial law, nationalization of industry, and full-blown socialism to be ushered in is high. America is headed for third world poverty and squalor unknown in our history. Plunging standards of living will bring the American population to a level of poverty that few would want to consider. Life will continue in America, but it will be a far different country than anyone living ever could have imagined.

The collapse of the economic system will end entitlements, including welfare programs, social security, and most pension funds. The America that will emerge from this collapse will be unlike anything that people have ever experienced.

Think and Plan Ahead

Failure to plan is a plan to fail. Establish your priorities carefully as you contemplate the future. Without trying to sound redundant, this writer has been sounding alarm bells since the early 1960s. Our message essentially has remained unchanged throughout the decades. Those who have heeded the warning are spiritual light years ahead of those who have disregarded this call to spiritual, moral, and economic preparedness. I urge you to prioritize your life around these immediate goals.

1) Set your spiritual house in order. A personal relationship with Jesus Christ that includes daily prayer, devotions, Bible reading is imperative. Becoming pro-active in a Christ-centered, Bible believing church community is also imperative. You will need not only a church family, but a community of neighbors sharing the same racial heritage, faith, and worldview. Do not attempt to survive this impending storm without God, your church family (good neighbors who love God and one another), and a close attention to biblical truth and standards.

2) Divorce proof your marriage, multiply godly children, and train, discipline, and educate them in biblical Christianity. Purpose to build a strong Christian family. The godly multiplication of children is key to the future dominion of the Christian remnant, no matter what happens in America. Do not allow your children and youth to attend a public school. Provide home schooling, Christian schooling, or private tutoring.

3) Geography is also very important. Avoid urban centers, heavy concentrations of people, nuclear and military facilities, and non-white population centers. Be prepared to defend your castle from vagabond intruders and both wild and domesticated beasts.

4) Get out of debt and stay out. Avoid debt like th plague. Do not fall prey to credit buying. Remove yourselves from credit addiction's buy now and pay later syndrome.

5) Make wise investments with your capital if you have any to work with. Abraham invested in gold, silver, livestock, and land. Four millennia later, this is still a good investment strategy.

6) Think about providing good water, food, and affordable shelter in the days ahead. These are basic necessities of life; it is imperative that we not look to government to supply these needs in a time of crisis.

7) Judgment proof your lives by living close to God. By faith in Jesus Christ, plead the blood and righteousness of Jesus Christ every day and recite the 91st Psalm as your hedge of protection. America is a nation under covenantal sanctions (curses); only by His grace will we avoid the catastrophic events that God will turn loose to judge this nation in days to come. God is looking for repentance from His people (II Chronicles 7:14)—not the non-Israelite hordes that have pitched their tents in this land.

Hope for the Future

Remnant Christians who seek the face of their God, multiply children, and walk with a generational theology have nothing to fear from the future. God will not forsake His covenant family. The unconditional promise made to Abraham by a covenant keeping God will not fail the remnant tucked away in the folds of America or any other White homeland now marching over the cliff into the graveyard of nations. There is hope and a future for the remnant, for by the election of grace (Romans 11:5; Isaiah 1:9; Jeremiah 29:11-13), there will never be a day when Jehovah God will not preserve His remnant.

Notice: If you would like a more full biblical explanation of why the American Republic (now an empire) is in freefall, you may wish to hear on CD or cassette our three-hour series entitled "The Fullness of Nations" (ask for Series #79), delivered from this pulpit in 1993. The present state of America was carefully predicted in that series of Bible lessons given seventeen years ago.

16

WHEN BABYLON FALLS: THEN WHAT?

Fall 2010

When Babylon collapses, will you stand and shout "Glory"? Or, will you weep and wail? One thing is certain: Babylon the Great, that vast city of power, commerce, banking, and trade that was destined to ensnare the world, is shaking like never before! The foundations of Babylon the Great are in turmoil. America is the head nation of this Babylonian city of global finance. Babylon the Great is approaching the end of her reign, and we can all be sure that we have partaken of her delicacies ourselves. *"For all nations have drunk of the wine of the wrath of her fornication, and the kings of the earth have committed fornication with her, and the merchants of the earth are waxed rich through the abundance of her delicacies" (Rev. 18:3).* We all are guilty of contributing to and drinking from her pleasures. But rest assured that she will fall. Amidst all the suffering, the question is this: will you beg for a quick, painless death, or will you shout "Hallelujah"?

Are you prepared to survive the inevitable financial Armageddon that is knocking at America's door? How many Americans live in denial of the catastrophic financial crash that looms ahead? You can bet the front men leading us down the primrose path of economic oblivion will not sound the alarm! We, the American electorate, entrusted our destiny to a Jewish government with a black face. European Americans stand disenfranchised in the country their forbears bled and died to give them. Now, consider these questions:

Have you considered the awesome consequences of what a financial crash could mean to this country, or more particularly, for your family? How would you cope with the consequences of a complete financial collapse? Are you prepared to survive without money? If every electronic bank account were suddenly worth zero and all the Federal Reserve notes you could pack in your wallet would not buy a loaf of bread, what would you do? If every major city and urban area of America were burning in riots, what would you do?

The current economic meltdown began in earnest in December of 2007 and continues unabated in November of 2010. Government-paid economists, liberal news pundits, and suave politicians mimic the oft-repeated phrase that the economy is reviving, and that America's economic engine is firing again. "Jobs are coming back," they say. "Consumer confidence is rising!" Financial stoplights might be shifting from red to amber where "they" live, but I certainly do not see any green lights here! Financial experts point out that corporate profits are up and that the stock market is healthy. Washington politicians keep saying that the jobs are re-bounding, yet unemployment figures (based on real figures—not political surveys) are more than double the number official government sources give. In late 2010, housing statistics released by the U. S. Government point to the sharpest decline in new housing since records first began. Foreclosures on both newer and older homes continued to reach new levels this past summer.

Public confidence in the financial status of America continues to decline. As the unsustainable national debt soars and the U. S. Government continues to print more currency, people are beginning to lose all confidence in our future. Panic-stricken Americans are beginning to convert paper assets into gold (now above $1300 an ounce) and silver (now above $23.00). Once public confidence reaches critical mass, the American financial system will tank, and the country will plunge into the darkest economic abyss of its history.

Financial Armageddon!

The **Great Depression of 2007** continues to witness the unraveling of the American dream for millions who witnessed their pension funds and stock market investments vaporize in the economic meltdown. More than fifteen million Americans are still unemployed. More than 50% of America's population is surviving through some form of government subsidy. The U. S. Government is pumping billions of borrowed dollars into the economy to revive what is left of the glory days of this country. Hundreds of billions have been injected into the banking, automobile, and lending institutions of this country to keep America solvent. The U. S. Government, in a frantic effort to keep the country from plunging into the depths of depression, has continued to pump billions (even trillions) into the economy.

Suffocating taxes, government regulation, sky-high health insurance mandates, and other government controls are killing American manufacturing. Millions of jobs lost in the second Great Depression (2007) have been shipped overseas and will never return to America. Government policies have forced American business to leave the U. S. and move their operations to other more tax friendly, less regulated nations. There has been a hemorrhage of jobs out of the U. S. for the past twenty years. The Free Trade policies of the U. S. Government has flooded America with cheap, foreign-made goods while American exports have been forced to battle high tariffs and other obstacles imposed upon them by foreign governments. Free Trade has forced the great American manufacturing machine overseas; foreigners are now filling millions of jobs once held by Americans.

Financial Armageddon is knocking at America's door. Following are three potential scenarios that some far-sighted economists believe could come to America's financial future. To forestall immediate collapse and financial crash unprecedented in all of America's history, any one of the following events could play out:

1) Massive cuts in social security, medicare, medicaid, welfare programs, food stamps, and other federal financial ties to the general populace: This type of financial austerity would usher in civil unrest. Millions would take to the streets (as they recently did in Greece and in Atlanta, GA, when more than 25,000 angry, violence-prone Blacks showed up for 400 openings in government-sponsored housing. This event in late summer 2010 demonstrated that only a thin veil of civility holds back the millions of Blacks packed into the ghettos). With about 50% of the American public dependent upon the government for economic sustenance, you can only imagine what might happen if these programs ended. America could go up in flames with civil unrest, rioting, and fires in every major urban area. Martial law, military forces on the streets, and a suspension of the U. S. Constitution would follow in the wake of this disruption.

2) The U.S. Government could impose astronomical tax increases that would suffocate all business and kill what is left of the Free American Enterprise System. The results could be economic meltdown, complete with massive unemployment, civil unrest, martial law, the suspension of the U.S. Constitution, and totalitarian dictatorship.

3) The third scenario is that the U.S. Government would print more money, inflate the money supply, and flood the nation with cheap dollars. The result would be the same: hyper-inflation would send consumer prices through the roof, the dollar would become worthless, the monetary system would fail, civil unrest would follow along with martial law, the Constitution would be suspended, and a strong-arm dictator would take over, complete with military enforcing the demands of the totalitarian regime.

The Day of Reckoning Has Come!

Since the end of World War II in 1945, both political parties and the Presidents and Congresses leading them—with very few exceptions—have been taxing and spending on an unprecedented scale. The last few successive Presidents were big spenders, and both political parties piled up deficits and the debt owed to international banking cartels; in fact, the debt owed the Federal Reserve System stands at **14.3 trillion**! The interest on this debt is unsustainable, as you can imagine. By 2015, it will have mushroomed to such astronomical figures that it will be the major budgetary item facing our government.

The American public has lived in a fairytale world of over-indulgence for more than half a century. We have become addicted to a lifestyle that includes palatial homes, expensive furniture, new cars, designer clothes, exotic vacations, high-tech communications, tanning beds, and a spirit of opulence that far exceeds any previous generation. This fantasy world has been made possible by easy credit and a buy now/pay later attitude unknown to former generations. We are addicted to swiping a credit card and thus paving the way to economic prosperity. But it is a false front. The day of reckoning has come. The party is over. The day of economic inebriation has ended!

As millions of Americans sober up from their extended flirtation with artificial wealth and credit buying, we are about to be hit with the most stunning economic news yet. The U. S. Government is about to default not only on its own fifteen-trillion-dollar public debt, but even more startling, on Medicare, Medicaid, food stamps, government subsidized housing, welfare, and—hold on to your seat—the Social Security fund! In fact, the U. S. Government in Washington DC is bankrupt! The present Congress is presiding over the bankruptcy proceedings of the United States of America. California is bankrupt! New York and several other states are approaching financial insolvency. Governments have simply spent themselves into oblivion. With massive welfare doles, free hospital care, free education, subsidized housing, and massive entitlements to millions of illegal aliens pouring into this country, America has gone broke! The U. S. has funneled hundreds of billions in foreign aid to scores of countries all over the world. We are currently waging a nine-year war in Afghanistan on borrowed dollars, while the seven-year war in Iraq was funded with borrowed money.

The day of reckoning has come! America is broken, and not a single politician or statesman can fix it. No arm of flesh can save America. God and God alone can save us at this point. The sin debt and corresponding curses that have befallen us are far greater than would ordinarily bring a nation to repentance. The covenant people living in America are guilty of apostasy. **When a people apostatize, they willfully and deliberately reject God, the authority of His Word, and the way to repentance. This deliberate rejection and mocking of God can only mean that judgment lies ahead for America.**

From apostasy there is generally no turning back. The window of repentance is fast closing. Judgment from God is the sentence upon such a nation. We may never witness a day of national repentance in this country. If not, we will surely witness catastrophic and sudden judgment on a scale unknown before. Even though we as a nation never repent, it is never too late for a godly remnant to repent!

The Only Cure

Americans should flock to their respective churches and cry out in repentance to God! An urgent, compelling cry to heaven must reach Jesus Christ. Heartfelt steps of repentance must be accompanied with acts of contrition that include but are not limited to the following action:

1)   Covenant people who call themselves Christian must flock to their respective churches and repent for allowing heathen gods and religions to be honored in this land. We should demand that America return to the Christian faith of our fathers and to the laws that issue from the Bible.

2)   Professing Christians must renew and commit to the covenant our Pilgrim and Puritan fathers and mothers who settled this country in the early 17th Century established. This covenant renewal would recognize the Lord Jesus Christ as the one and only Sovereign of this nation!

3)   Professing Christians must demand that all legislative statutes and judicial decrees that have legalized abortion, sodomy, and miscegenation be rescinded immediately. Biblical statutes that call for the death penalty should be re-imposed.

4)   The Federal Reserve Act of 1913 should be immediately repealed.

5)   The 14.3-trillion-dollar debt owed to the private international Banking Cartel should be cancelled.

6)   The Internal Revenue Service should be rescinded and the 16th Amendment to the U.S. Constitution repealed.

7)   Capital gains, death, and inheritance taxes must be repealed and all Free Trade agreements renegotiated to give American businesses equal footing in global markets.

8)   All foreign aid to other countries must be terminated, with George Washington's policy of friendship with all nations and entangling alliances with none immediately reinstated.

9)   The U.S. border with Mexico should be sealed and placed under National Guard protection with orders to shoot to kill. All persons convicted of employing illegal aliens should be given ten-year, mandatory jail sentences and crippling fines. All medical, educational, and welfare aid to illegals should be suspended immediately throughout the U. S.

10)   All American forces should be immediately withdrawn from Afghanistan, Iraq, S. Korea, Germany, and Kosovo. A two-year military training program should be instituted for all American men who reach their 20th birthday, unless they suffer from physical and/or mental disability.   Women should be prohibited from serving in any branch of the U.S. Military. No Muslim should be allowed to enter the ranks of the U.S. Military Service.

What If We Do Not Accept the Cure?

If we fail to take the painful steps necessary to cure the spiritual, moral, political, economic, and cultural sickness upon America, the patient will ultimately perish. Remnant Christians must move with all dispatch to judgment-proof their lives. Hope and a future for remnant Christians lies with God and God alone! Man cannot and will not save us! The arm of flesh has brought us to the precipice of spiritual, moral, and economic Armageddon! Our hope, trust, and very future must be vested by faith in Jesus Christ, the very Son of God, and in the Church of which He is the Head!

As redundant as it may seem, this **watchman in Israel** urges you to set your spiritual house in order, live with a conscience that is without offence toward God and man (Acts 24:16), become pro-active as a Christian warrior for the cause of Jesus Christ, His Word, and His Kingdom, and affiliate yourselves with a Christ-centered, Bible-based church body that shares a common worldview, the same values toward God and Scripture, and a common racial heritage with those with whom you worship and interact socially. Get out of debt and stay out of debt. Learn to live frugally.

Give careful consideration to emergency provision for clean water, food, shelter, financial security, medical needs, and utilities when the lights go out in America.

Hope for the best, but prepare for the worst! Envision yourselves aboard the great *Titanic* that set sail from Liverpool, England in 1912. Not a soul on earth believed the *Titanic* would ever sink. It was dubbed the "Unsinkable *Titanic.*" Yet it did sink on April 12, 1912, and in the span of just two hours, met its fate in a watery grave at the bottom of the ocean. Those who did not manage to get aboard a **lifeboat** perished. The English-speaking world was stunned. The unbelievable happened! Death, pain, sorrow, and tears flowed across England and America.

America is that Titanic of Nations. We are about to hit an iceberg! Only a few lifeboats are available for those who can even in this late hour manage to find one. Find your lifeboat! It is marked Jesus Christ, His Church, His covenant people, and dominion under His headship! If you have no geographical ties to a remnant church, identify with a church you find compatible even if you are not able to personally participate with this covenant body of believers on a regular basis.

Your lifeboat is a body of people sharing the same worldview, faith, theology, morality, racial heritage, and understanding of where we are in history. Join them and become pro-active Christian warriors in the culture war to save our children and grandchildren from the insanity that prevails throughout our land. The goal is to multiply godly children to grow the ranks of the Christian remnant (the family and the church) and meet the enemy at the gates. We simply must keep on until our King of kings and Lord of lords returns (Luke 19:13)! End of story.

17

THE INESCAPABLE
REALITY OF RACE

Winter 2011

Stop and consider: where do you weigh in on the single most important issue on this planet beyond your personal salvation in Jesus Christ? What is the one topic that most people dare not talk about beyond the walls of their home—a subject that immediately invites scorn, ridicule, and the charge of bigotry? What is the one issue that must we must avoid and around which we must tiptoe? No matter how conservative a politician may appear, **this is one area he will not touch!** What is that one issue considered so divisive that it cannot, dare not be mentioned in any public venue in America? Yet, this very subject is a foundational truth that impacts every other point of truth. Consider this an appeal to every husband, father, pastor, and educator in the: for the sake of truth, the honor of God's Word, and the very future of your children, remove the cloak of silence, come out of the closet, and face the reality of race!

Except for accepting and applying the blood of Jesus Christ to our lives, no other subject has more impact on the important choices we make in life! The reality of race is foundational to every major truth that holds western European Christian civilization together. If you deny the truth about race, you will forfeit the birthright that former generations bled and died to give their people. If you deny the reality of this indisputable part of life, you risk the survival of every species on this planet. Every important decision you make in life is impacted by this dirty little four-letter word: race.

Race impacts where you worship and praise Jesus Christ! Race has a profound role in your decision of who to marry. Even when you elect people to public office, this subject is front and center. When you choose a place to live, race is a factor. When you apply for a job or ask for a promotion, race is a factor. When you step onto an airplane, you subconsciously check out the racial composition of the passengers. Race is an important factor in the demographics of every ghetto in America. Race is a major factor in assessing the birth rate within any diverse population. You can no more ignore the importance of race than you can deny the reality of day and night, summer and winter, and sexual orientation.

The differences our Creator God placed on every race in His original design are unmistakable. Diversity of race goes much deeper than skin or eye or hair color, far deeper than the hair follicle, cranial structure, brain convolutions, brain weight, skeleton formation, blood composition, or a multitude of other distinct physical, physiological, psychological, and other differences. There are also major cultural, religious, and social differences among the various races God created to be unique.

There is no equality of race! Such an idea is as absurd as saying that any two individuals within a given race are created equal. Every race may have its own superior and distinctive edge over another. After all, God created every race to be distinct.

By its definition, that implies each race may have advantages that others do not. And, equally important is the fact that each race was created within the constraints of the law of kind after his kind, established ten times in Genesis one. Each kind or species was created to procreate within its own kind alone. Any flower in the garden possesses a variety of color and endless design differences. How much more so is it in the various races God created! The world, His garden, possesses a wide variety of races, each of which has its own special purpose to fulfill. Our marvelous God created every kind of fauna, flora, and race very good (Genesis 1:31); He genetically engineered each to reproduce after its own kind.

God Has A Plan for Every Race

Many have noticed that every race has a natural tendency to cluster and segregate itself. That is why Chinese, Japanese, Vietnamese, Cambodian, and other races from Asia cluster in their respective communities in America. The White Flight out of the inner cities into the suburbs is one of the most distinct social phenomena in post-World War II America. White flight remains an ongoing phenomenon as Caucasians inherently seek to cluster with their own kind. Exclusive Jewish enclaves in New York, Chicago, and other major American cities are well known. Hispanic communities thrive in California and increasingly elsewhere in response to the Latino invasion of America during the past forty years.

Every time an election is held in America, television news pundits do not avoid the subject of how the race card is played. 95% of the Black population of America voted for Barak Hussein Obama in the election of 2008. It is no secret that during the past century the Republican Party has been dubbed the party of White Americans (notwithstanding the Republican politicians that have in recent elections been begging for votes from the non-white masses). The acceleration of the non-white races in America is now reaching critical mass. The future of American politics is with the surging non-white masses—and this to the exclusion of the ever-diminishing White race. But that is another subject.

The fact of race can be ignored and circumvented, but its impact upon America cannot be denied. White people ignore the issue of race at great peril to themselves and their children. Jewish children are taught from childhood to uphold the distinctive character and racial factors that make up their community. Likewise, Asians are taught an awareness of their racial differences. They are proud of them! Only one race in America seeks relentlessly to prove its non-racial prejudice through interracial marriage: the White race. White liberals cast aside all too willingly their racial heritage to integrate and amalgamate their seed with the non-white races, especially Blacks.

America is reaching a racial crisis as the land now swarms with millions of Blacks, Asians, Latinos, Hindus, Muslims, and other non-white third world people. The skyrocketing fertility rate of third world peoples combined with massive non-white immigration into America has placed the entire future of this country at risk. Racial demographics are irreversible! You can reclaim the foundations of a tattered and broken constitution. You can reverse statutory laws that war against God and Scripture. You can repair the broken pledges and covenants of former generations. What you cannot do is reverse the racial amalgamation of America! The tide of color cannot be turned back! America is becoming a third world, non-white nation of surging "have nots" who believe that they are entitled to the benefits of free food stamps, medical care, education, Social Security. This surging mass of non-whites will insure the bankruptcy of the nation as politicians seeking their votes cater to their growing economic demands. Each and every succeeding election in 21st Century America will witness the gradual decline and loss of Caucasian political clout.

Because the surging non-white masses believe that the government owes them a living, you find them standing in line at every election to insure the advance of politicians who will let them feed from the trough of government largess. The US Government will not be able to meet the ever-increasing demands of this sub-culture. Those who work and pay taxes will simply not be able to sustain the socialist demands of those who will not work and must depend upon government. By the year 2020, White people essentially will be disenfranchised in the very same country their ancestors bled and died to give them.

Political Correctness

We live in a time when people fall all over themselves trying to be politically correct. News reporters use every means possible to avoid racial profiling when reporting on a crime, unless it is a White on Black crime. They have no problem spitting out the words "White male," especially if the victim is Black. If a White man is charged with a hate crime, it is splashed on the newsreel for all to hear; but if a Black is accused of a hate crime, it will go unreported in the newspaper and television reports. America is awash in political correctness. Only White people are profiled for wrongdoing. It is not politically correct to name a Black, Muslim, Hindu, Latino, Asian, or some other non-White for a particular crime.

White people are increasingly vulnerable to racial profiling, while non-whites are given a pass. Political correctness is a one-way street that always seems to run south for a White. Racial discrimination has become systemic for White people. Affirmative action has elevated Blacks and demoted Whites throughout the workplace. A White will suffer racial discrimination at almost every turn in the work place or on the college campus. If you want a green light for government approval at any agency from A to Z, you had better not be White. If a Black and White go up for promotion in any branch of the U.S. Military, guess who will get the appointment? And it will not make any difference how much more qualified the White person might be. That person must go to the back of the new racial bus.

Time for a Reality Check

It is time for White Americans to come out of the shadows and speak truth in all matters regarding race. Living in denial of racial truth only increases the level of frustration and misery for those wallowing in political correctness. It is past time for the plain truth to be told. The Bible is a racial book! Every writer of the sacred Scriptures, Genesis to Revelation, was from the Caucasian (Hebrew-Israelite) race. Not a single Asian is listed in any biblical genealogical record! The Bible is the family history of one people on this planet. The Word of God is the record of the posterity of Adam kind alone. Limited mention is given other peoples and races—but only as they influenced the primary point of the Bible as it unfolds the history of one family: Abraham, Isaac, Jacob-Israel, and the millions of Celtic, Anglo, Saxon Caucasians descending from them.

All races have a particular affinity to the religion out of which they sprang. Buddhism, Shintoism, Taoism, all belong to the Asians. Hinduism belongs to the Hindus. Allah and Muhammad to the Arabs. Voodooism in its various forms belongs to the Blacks of Africa. Historically, Christianity has been the religion of the White man. Beginning with the Adamites and by whatever name may have been applied to them throughout history (Shemites, Hebrews, Israelites, etc...), they are one homogeneous people with common racial genes dating back to Adam and Eve, who were the parents of just one race: White, Adamic, Caucasian stock. One of the most profound errors attributed to the White man is their proclivity to want all races to fit into the mold of Christianity. Five hundred years of aborted, stillborn evangelism of the other races should be sufficient evidence that Christianity is not and never will be a faith that has any universal appeal outside of the White race, where it originated.

Every effort to plant Christianity with the non-white world has resulted in one of two developments. First, Christianity in its historic and biblical sense will only survive as long as it is White-orchestrated, funded, and organized. Second, Christianity as a faith always will morph into the image of the religious proclivities of the non-white people where it is planted. If one travels into Africa where Christianity has alleged to have widespread conversions (I have been there and observed first hand such Negro religious services), one is appalled to witness the complete makeover of Christianity into the religious proclivities of the non-whites alleged to be born again (?) Christians.

A brief excursion into the life of Albert Schweitzer (1875-1965) is most revealing for those who are not afraid to look racial truth straight in the face. Schweitzer was a renowned Franco-German (Alsatian) theologian, organist, philosopher, and physician. He rose to prominence in every one of the foregoing fields of endeavor; his brilliance was recognized in every respective field that he busied himself to master. After spending his early years in music, theology, and philosophy, Schweitzer became a medical doctor and devoted himself to improving the health of the Africans in Gabon, West Central Africa (then French Equatorial Africa). There he founded and sustained the Albert Schweitzer Hospital in Lambarene, now in Gabon. He received the 1952 *Nobel Peace Prize* for his philosophy of *Reverence for Life.*

Toward the end of his long life, Schweitzer came to some rather unpopular conclusions about his long years devoted to the Blacks in Gabon. Among other noteworthy statements, he made this deduction near the end of his life about his investment in trying to bring Christian civilization to Africa through his endless and benevolent acts and tireless work in caring for the sick:

"I have given my life to alleviate the sufferings of Africa. There is something that all white men who have lived here, must learn and know; that these individuals are a sub-race; they have neither the intellectual, mental or emotional abilities to equate or share in any of the functions of our civilization.

"I have given my life to try to bring unto them the advantages which our civilization must offer, but I have

become well aware that we must retain this status; white, the superior, and they the inferior, for whenever a white man seeks to live among them as their equal, they will either destroy him or devour him, and they will destroy all his work; and so for any existing relationship or for any benefit to this people let white men from anywhere in the world who would come to help Africa remember that you must continually retain this status; you the master, and they the inferior, like children that you would help or teach. Never fraternize with them as equals, never accept them as your social equals; or they will devour you; they will destroy you." The above quotes are from Dr. Albert Schweitzer's 1961 book *From My African Notebook*. Again, he was winner of the 1952 Nobel Peace Prize.

A Final Thought

May I appeal to the good reason of the Christian remnant wherever you may reside in the Christian West. In this age of multiculturalism and racial diversity, the Christian remnant must become racially conscious and live as **convicted separatists** in the family, church, and community where they reside; otherwise, our children will be swallowed whole, and the blood and treasure of God's most precious species on earth will be lost forever. We must be polite and courteous to people of every race, but we must fraternize with none. We see them in the shopping malls, the grocery store, and other venues, but we must pass them as ships in the night. We may find them in the work place or in university and college classrooms, but again, we can have absolutely no social ties and no fraternal relationships with people of another race. Any attempt to do so will force compromises that you will regret to the last day of your life on this earth.

White pastors, come out of your spiritual caves, dens, and closets! Teach your congregations the racial truth of Scripture! Open your Bible and be a shepherd to the sheep people God has given you. Teach them what they need to know about race. And fathers, hear this well: teach your sons and daughters what they need to know about race. Keep your family, your castle, free from multiculturalism and racial diversity. Do not allow your children to fraternize with other races. Establish the Doctrine of Separatism as more than just a preference. Be certain that separatism is a conviction that all members of your family share to the very marrow of your bones.

The reality of race can be denied, but only at the peril and forfeiture of the future of White children being born in America. Remnant Christians should set the multiplication of White children, now an endangered species, as a priority. Those who shy away from taking a bold stand on racial realities are kissing up to Baal and stand reprehensible before the court of God, His honor, and the racial integrity of their own offspring. What will you do with this issue? Run and hide, or stand for truth?

18

ABRAHAM'S CHILDREN: THE FOCAL POINT OF POLITICAL DRAMA

Spring 2011

Students of the Bible are scrambling to dust off and restudy the Book of Genesis. The world is pulsing with activity linked to the children of Abraham, who are the principal players in the unfolding, geo-political drama of the world. Without knowledge of the Bible, the leaders and potentates of our present world are much like the proverbial blind leading the blind. God's Word is the only antidote for the ignorance that pervades the political, educational, and religious institutions and those leading them.

Ishmael-Islam

Ishmael and the Arabs descending from him represent the sand seed (desert seed) of Abraham; they are prolific, numbering **1.82 billion** in 2009. Millions of them are radical, young, and breeding like rabbits. They have a bitter hatred for the Christian West,

America in particular. The more radical and extremist followers of Allah and his prophet Mohammad are bent on waging jihad against the West. The Wahhabi brand of terrorism, favored by the Sunnis and centered in Saudi Arabia, represents the most dangerous and radical element within Islam.

The Islamization of the Christian West is underway; unfortunately, America is not immune from this phenomenon. Mosques are appearing in almost every major city in America. Islam is more than a religion: it is a system of life that embraces religious, legal, political, economic, social, and military components—just as Christianity used to and should!

A Few Facts about Muslims

1) In the early stages of conquest within a population, Muslims may appear as a peace-loving minority. As they increase in number, however, they exercise an inordinate influence in proportion to their percentage of the population.

2) Pressure then mounts for the introduction of halal food (clean by Islamic standards); Muslims then demand that supermarket chains carry their food, thus creating jobs for Muslims.

3) They then press for Sharia law, the Islamic brand of law. When they reach 20% of a nation's population, they begin to push for jihad militia formations, sporadic killings, honor killings, and the burning of Christian churches.

4) Oil-rich sheiks control most of the oil revenues, while a majority of the Arab world lives in poverty and is illiterate. Thus, while sheiks live in luxury and splendor beyond imagination, the rest of their population lives in relative squalor.

5) The Arab world views the Israeli State as their common enemy. Further, since America is the primary defender of the Zionist State, this obviously makes America the perceived enemy of the Arab world.

6) Most of the available oil in the world comes from Muslim-owned lands. The Christian West, paralyzed by environmental

gurus, is unwilling to drill in oil rich America. Unless this changes, we will remain dependant upon the Muslims.

7) The Arabs, who descended from Abraham's first son Ishmael, were excluded from the covenant God made with Abraham. However, that does not mean they lack their share of blessings. They were to become a great multitude, a family of nations. They were to be wild and untamed, and though they are favored as the seed of Abraham through Ishmael, God excluded them from the covenant of promise made with Abraham and confirmed in his son with Sarah, Isaac.

8) Their god is Allah and the Qur'an their sacred book; to die for Allah and his prophet Mohammad is their greatest aspiration. Unlike Christianity, where God dies to save His people, in the religion of Islam, Muslims clamor to die for Allah and his prophet Muhammad.

Jacob-Israel

With these salient facts, we can proceed to look where Jacob-Israel, the covenant descendants of Ishmael's younger half-brother Isaac, is today. The covenant branch of Abraham's posterity is prophetically in the *"time of Jacob's trouble" (Jeremiah 30:7).* The Anglo-Saxon nations of Jacob-Israel live under the iron yoke of Esau-Edom, who, by way of the Federal Reserve Banking Cartel and other financial and news media monopolies, exercise a financial death grip on Jacob-Israel. At the same time, Ishmael holds Jacob-Israel hostage by exercising a monopoly on the production and cost of oil.

The Caucasian population of the United States, Great British, Europe, Canada, Australia, New Zealand, and Scandinavia are the genetic star seed of Jacob-Israel and are genetically linked to Abraham, Sarah, Isaac, and Rebekah. These are the star seed of Abraham, the people who are the blood heirs to the unconditional covenant of promise Jehovah made with His servant Abraham.

These are the nations of the historic, Western, European, Christian culture that have been the movers and shakers for the past five centuries plus. Sadly, current demographics reflect plunging birth rates and a tidal wave of third world immigration into these Caucasian homelands. Simultaneously, these nations face deep economic problems, have mounted huge deficits, live under constant threats from Islamic terrorists, and are almost completely dependent on Arab oil. This indeed seems like the time of Jacob's trouble!

The leaders of these countries find themselves in a state of paralysis and political gridlock. We, their constituents, are helpless sheep estranged from God, His righteous laws, and clueless as to our racial heritage. False shepherds are fleecing the sheep people, failing to teach Bible truth. An aura of spiritual complacency and plunging moral standards plague the nations of the Christian West.

Esau-Edom

The Khazarian, Ashkenaz, Mongol, Turkish descendants of Esau-Edom, mostly known as Jews, are the bankers, financiers, and money managers of the world. They shape public opinion through exclusive ownership and control of television and other media outlets. They have laid an iron yoke on Jacob-Israel (the Christian West) and hold America and most of the Anglo Saxon world hostage to their privately owned banking cartels. Esau-Edom is riding high on the waves of power today, but prophetically they are doomed as the people whom the Living God cursed and judged in the Old Testament.

The descendants of Esau-Edom are the power behind the throne in most governments, controlling not only the wealth of the world, but also orchestrating many of the wars and reaping terrific profits from the misery of others. In due time, the iron yoke of repression upon Jacob-Israel from Esau-Edom will be broken. Then, may God have mercy upon those who have been thorns in the side of Jacob-Israel! The iron yoke of Esau-Edom will ultimately be lifted from Jacob-Israel as Jehovah intercedes on behalf of His covenant people. The unconditional covenant of promise made with Abraham is confirmed in Jacob-Israel alone— no other branch of Abraham's family.

The impending judgment of Esau-Edom will not be pleasant! Read and consider what the Prophet Isaiah declared in chapters 34 and 63 of his book and the Prophet Ezekiel in chapters 35 and 36 of his book. The Prophet Obadiah 18 notes the final judgment of Esau-Edom: *"And the house of Jacob shall be a fire, and the house of Joseph a flame, and the house of Esau for stubble, and they shall kindle in them, and devour them; and there shall not be any remaining of the house of Esau; for the LORD (Jehovah) hath spoken it."*

The Current Geo-political Crisis

In the early portion of 2011, the eyes of the world have been fixed on the Muslim world as events have unfolded in Tunisia, Egypt, Libya, and deep in the heart of other Arab states such as Bahrain and Yemen. All at once, it appears that the repressive governments in all of these Muslim strongholds are struggling to maintain their power as their people take to the streets, demanding more freedom and an end to oppression. In Tunisia, authoritarian President Zine el-Abidine Ben Ali was forced from power in January; the country now struggles to keep anarchy at bay. In February of this year, Hosni Mubarak, dictator of Egypt, was forced into exile, leaving the army in control and the future of Egypt in question. Then, in early March, Muammar el-Qaddafi took on his countrymen, killing probably thousands of his own citizens as they sought his overthrow. That crisis is still unfolding.

The United States stands almost paralyzed, its leader afraid to open his mouth for fear of offending the Muslim world. With oil production in Libya and elsewhere now in question and the Suez Canal (a primary shipping lane) subject to the unknown, oil prices have spiked. Americans are watching gasoline prices soar, creating further panic in an already stressed economy.

American military and naval power is stretched razor thin as U.S. military forces move into their tenth year of war in Afghanistan and the eighth year in Iraq, with tens of thousands of U.S. troops garrisoned in South Korea, Germany, Kosovo, and elsewhere. American military and naval strength reaches around the globe!

Our manufacturing and industry have largely been dismantled and shipped to Mexico and the Far East. Millions of American jobs have dried up, and the United States would be hard pressed to take on another Arab state—much less mount the industrialized capacity to mass-produce war machines and equipment. Protracted wars in Central Asia have exhausted American armies and machines. Both Iran and North Korea rattle their nuclear arsenals, teasing and testing the US.

At more than **fourteen trillion dollars**, the United States faces the largest unsustainable debt in the annals of history! The interest on this debt alone is clicking away at billions every day. Financial Armageddon is knocking at the door of this country; except for the new wave of Tea Party Conservatives, the politicians of this country are in a state of paralysis, with neither the will nor the knowledge to act for the future of America. Most American politicians in both major parties are addicted to the "spend and tax" policies that have guided America since World War II ended in 1945. Our politicians spend money without a clue as to how future generations are going to pay it!

Most reprehensible of all are the thousands of America clergy with all of their mainstream, politically correct, think-a-like, lockstep theology, who have neither the desire nor the will to preach the literal Word of God to an unrepentant generation of sinners. These hireling preachers, many of them wolves parading in sheep's clothing, refuse to teach the law of God and bring a sin-laden generation to repentance. Without the preaching of the law, an entire generation of unsaved Anglo-Saxon people has no conscience for the guilt of sin. Instead of defining sin by the knowledge of the law, these false shepherds specialize in a feel good theology that allows the sheep to feel good about sin.

Remnant Christians must place their total trust in the Living God and know that He will not forsake His covenant of promise to Abraham, Isaac, and Jacob. Jehovah God: He is our only hope, our future! In Him alone should we place our trust and turn in this critical hour. It is the duty of all God-fearing shepherds in modern Israel to call their respective flocks to the prayer rail and in sackcloth and ashes confess personal and corporate sins, seeking the face of Jehovah God and crying out for deliverance in this time of Jacob's trouble.

What is the most important assignment for remnant Christians? That assignment is to seek Jesus Christ with all of our hearts and appeal to Heaven for His help. We must hold fast to the unchanging Hand of God. Never before has it been more important to teach the **Gospel of the Kingdom** truth to our brethren. God alone is our trust, our hope, and our future. *"Be strong and of good courage, fear not, nor be afraid of them: for the LORD thy God, he it is that doth go with thee; he will not fail thee; he will not forsake thee"* (Deuteronomy 31:6).

19

THE JOPLIN, MISSOURI TORNADO

Summer 2011

Sunday, May 22, 2011 arrived as just another one of those spring days filled with turbulent Midwest weather caused by the warm moist Gulf Stream air colliding with the cool air coming over the snow-capped Colorado Rockies or sometimes a blast of cold air from Canada. By late Sunday afternoon, conditions were just right to spawn tornadoes in a wide band from East Oklahoma and Texas east into Northern Arkansas and Southern Missouri. The skies over Southwest Missouri were churning with dark rotating clouds when the sirens began to sound around dinnertime in Joplin, Missouri.

Then, about 6:00 p.m. a monster tornado formed and bore down upon the heart of Joplin, a tranquil American city of some 50,000 people lying square in the heart of the Bible belt. Bearing winds in excess of 200 miles per hour, the tornado tore across the primary center of Joplin's business district and a major residential district, leveling a path nearly a mile-wide and six miles long. It denuded the area of trees and turned a huge chunk of Joplin into a war zone. The entire south side of Joplin is now an enormous junkyard, full of twisted, mangled steel and cars, trees stripped of their branches and bark, splintered building materials, and assorted other items. As of this writing, 152 bodies have been recovered, and some 900 remain injured.

Rescue efforts were greatly hampered by the fact that one of the two major hospitals in Joplin was in the direct path of the tornado. The windows were all blown out of St. John's hospital and the top floors completely obliterated. Some unfortunate patients were sucked out of the windows as, in a matter of seconds, a tranquil community was transformed into a living hell. People caught outside running to their cars were sucked into the vortex of the tornado and carried to a horrifying death. In a matter of seconds, far too many souls met their fate between paradise and hades. A doctor at St. John's Hospital who survived the tornado said that nothing could prepare anyone for this type of disaster.

This powerful tornado, rated originally as an EF-5 and later upgraded to a brand new category of EF-6, is said to have been the single deadliest in the U. S. since 1953. An estimated 8,000 buildings were turned into rubble. It may be years before Joplin recovers from the staggering losses of lives, businesses, homes, and jobs. The pain, suffering, and death that visited this community in a matter of minutes are difficult to process. Buckets of tears have been shed not only by family members, volunteers, and search and rescue personnel, but also by people who simply empathize with the souls who have suffered so much in this tragedy.

About a dozen people who live in Joplin attend our worship services. To the praise and glory of Jesus Christ, all of them escaped injury and death! One mother and her four children from our congregation hunkered down in a closet as the storm unleashed its fury over their heads. When the monster storm passed, the only thing left standing of their home was the closet and single walls of what once were their kitchen and master bedroom. The mother and her children crawled out of the closet unscathed—even though the door and ceiling of the closet were ripped away. A pile of clothing was left to protect their heads. The family cried out to God as first the monster tornado bore down upon them and then the subsequent hailstorm howled around them, continuing the terrorizing fury. But God heard their cries and prayers and delivered them. The father rushed home from work in an area of town mostly unaffected by the tornado, eager to tell his family about the terrible storm he had witnessed, only to discover that this wife and children had been in the eye of the storm. Their home was completely demolished, their possessions were blown away or ruined, but they were so fortunate to be alive and completely unharmed! What a testimony that family has, and what a miracle God performed for that family!

With approximately two-thirds of the businesses of Joplin destroyed, it will be a long time before this community recovers. In an amazing demonstration of love and compassion, people from surrounding communities, counties, and even states poured into Joplin by the hundreds to help in the search and recovery efforts in the hours that followed the storm. Food, water, blankets, water, and other creature comforts arrived from other areas of Missouri, Kansas, Arkansas, Oklahoma, and beyond. Without any help from FEMA, this community pulled together and performed the Herculean task of caring for and transporting the injured through nameless, mangled streets, recovering the dead, and assisting those left homeless, dazed, and distraught. Then FEMA came, providing more assistance.

Time to Reflect

Beginning in 1620 with the arrival of the Pilgrim Fathers at Plymouth Colony and thereafter for the next twenty years, waves of Puritan fathers arrived in North America. Beginning at Plymouth and other foundling communities along the New England coastal area, God-fearing, English-speaking Christians took the land by covenant contract with the God of Abraham, Isaac, and Jacob Israel. America was settled under a covenant contract beginning in the early 1600s. The foundations of America were laid in a covenant between the Pilgrim/Puritans and Jehovah. This covenantal foundation was established upon four principles:

1)   These people believed themselves to be Israelites, not unlike ancient Israel, a covenant people under a "divine call" from Jehovah to build a new nation and establish a "City on a Hill," whose splendor would radiate the goodness of God to the whole world.

2)   This divine calling was to be worked out in terms of a covenant contract with God. This covenant called for settlers to serve God and one another as a servant people in the same fashion that ancient Israel was called to be a special, peculiar people. They were to serve God and one another. Obedience and faithfulness to this covenant contract would yield blessings of prosperity and security, while disobedience and rejection of Jehovah and His covenant would yield curses and a loss of prosperity and security.

3)   When the blessings flowed through obedience, the settlers knew they were under God's favor; but when curses followed in the forms of Indian attacks, drought, famine, floods, plagues, and other tragedies, they knew that the covenant had been breached and there was a collective call to self-examination. In what ways had they failed to love and serve God and one another? How had they breached the covenant contract established with Jehovah?

4)   The settlers believed that the path to restoration was reconciliation in heart-felt repentance and contrition of heart. They had a collective call to repent and restore themselves under the

covenant established with Jehovah when their Christian forefathers took the land. This call to repent from sin was not a time of judgmental scrutiny upon one's neighbor, but an inward examination of one's own heart to find sin and place it under the blood of Jesus Christ in heartfelt repentance.

There is absolutely no doubt that America as a collective nation has broken covenant with Jehovah. Having severely breached the covenant contract our Christian fathers made when settled this land, our nation now suffers under the curses of disobedience. We have lost our national prosperity and security. The entire nation now suffers. The Anglo-Saxon population of America has collectively rejected the Lord Jesus Christ and broken covenant with Him; now we love, serve, and worship other gods.

The number of God-fearing Christians who desperately want to observe the covenant is small. Consequently, our judgments are severe: we suffer from joblessness, economic meltdown, staggering national and personal debt, and the living standard of former generations is rapidly fading into third-world status.

The security of the American people is long gone. Millions of alien peoples have invaded the land with their strange languages, heathen gods, and anti-Christian culture and moral standards. As if that were not enough, the security of the American people is threatened by sleeper cells of foreign peoples who seek to terrorize American civilians. America lies mostly unprotected while her armies wage protracted wars in three different countries of the world—without any victory in sight!

God Will Not Be Mocked!

The curses falling upon America must be examined through the prism of Scripture. We have rejected God and breached the covenant contract of our Christian fathers. But God will not be mocked! He has turned the blessings of former generations into a litany of curses that now plague America from the Atlantic to Pacific, from the Gulf waters all the way north to Canada.

It is in this context that we must view the catastrophic weather patterns that have produced monster killer tornadoes, hurricanes, earthquakes, floods, fires, bitter cold winters, blizzards, ice storms, sand storms in the desert, and in general wreaked havoc across America.

Moreover, we would be absolute fools not to connect the dots and know that the misfortunes of our country are related to the increasing spiritual and moral apathy amongst the Anglo-Saxon population. Except for those who take His holy name in vain, one never hears the name of Jesus Christ in public. The Bible has become a foreign book to millions of Americans. The moral standards of the Bible were once reflected in national statutes that banned abortion, sodomy, race mixing, and other heinous crimes against God; but now, apostate judges and legislative bodies have rejected this high road.

A Wake Up Call from God?

The citizens of Joplin, Missouri—not unlike the people in many other states visited by ravaging tornadoes, fires, floods, spring blizzards, and drought, were immersed in the cares and pleasures of life, some of them in pursuit of riches, others simply living with little regard for God or faith in Jesus Christ. And, like millions of other Americans, the people of Joplin, Missouri on Sunday evening, May 22, were, with few exceptions, not remotely concerned that across America, some fifty-five million innocent, helpless, unborn children have been murdered since Roe v. Wade in 1973. Joplin, Missouri is a microcosm of what is taking place all across America. Nor was there concern that sodomy now thrives in the open. Further, race mixing, adultery, fornication, drunkenness, gambling, prostitution, pornography, and other moral sins are found in Joplin, just as they are everywhere. The sodomizing of the American military by morally bankrupt politicians in December of 2010 elicited hardly a whimper from American pulpits. And, the fact that race mixing is as wholesale in Joplin, as it is across America, does not even register with most Americans.

Homosexuals, fornicators, adulterers, prostitutes, and porn stars ply their trade throughout America with no more than a passing notice from establishment churches. The fact that growing numbers of Americans of every color are willing to destroy God's original design for every race and forfeit their heritage on the altar of miscegenation does not even solicit a concern among the majority of all Americans—in or outside the church. Joplin, Missouri is not unlike the rest of America in that spiritual apathy and complacency grip the hearts of our people. The percentage of those whose hearts are right with God and intensely zealous to follow His law and commandments is decreasing. The national conscience of this land is calloused, hardened, and insensitive to sin. More than one generation of Americans has never heard the preaching of God's Law; thus, they have no knowledge of their sin. Without knowledge of God's Law, sin cannot be defined, and the sinner bears no guilt. When there is no guilt, there is no compelling need to seek a Savior to absolve a guilty conscience. Sin continues to proliferate unchecked across America.

No one with knowledge of God's Word and the unfolding of events in America and throughout the Anglo-Saxon world can deny that the covenant people of Jehovah God are under judgment. America is suffering from the curses of our covenant-keeping God. Judgment is falling upon our land. Like the plagues that fell upon ancient Egypt at the time of their Exodus, America is being plagued because sin proliferates amongst us. It is difficult to imagine how much more affliction must come upon America before the hearts and minds of God's covenant people are willing to turn to God in humble repentance.

The fact that America has been in almost continuous war since the Gulf War in 1991 receives hardly a passing notice. Moreover, the fact that America has not won a war since World War II does not elicit any response. Nor has the current economic meltdown that began in late 2007 brought this country back to their spiritual and moral senses. Prolonged joblessness in America has not brought the country to its spiritual knees. Catastrophic weather has not gained the attention of the people. Government sanction and honor of abortion, sodomy, and miscegenation has not caused even a stir from the preachers and professing Christians of this land. When will se sit up and notice that God is screaming at us?

The judgments will continue in intensity as the Living God seeks to gain the attention of His people. There is one sure thing that will capture the attention of His people. Joblessness is tolerated as long as welfare, entitlements, and government subsidizes are available. But take away food, and then you capture the attention of everyone. Joblessness plus **food shortages** will bring people to full scale alert. This is precisely where the next round of judgment may come. Catastrophic weather in the U. S. and elsewhere has severely disrupted the production of food. In April and May of 2011, the USA witnessed a record number of tornadoes, leaving death and destruction in their wake. More than 500 people have been killed, with property damage in the billions. And, fires have roared across much of the agricultural belt of Texas, denuding vast areas of productive land. Late spring blizzards in the upper plains have been devastating for livestock and agriculture. Finally, rain-soaked fields east of the Mississippi have made it nearly impossible to plant the spring corn crop.

Devastating floods along the Mississippi from Illinois south to Louisiana have flooded hundreds of thousands of acres of farmland. In an effort to save low-lying towns along the Mississippi River, the U. S. Government has allowed levies to be breached, flooding hundreds of thousands of prime farmland in Missouri.

These events in the U. S. must be further analyzed within the framework of the worldwide, catastrophic weather patterns. The volcanic eruption in Iceland in mid May was the second within the last year. The 9.0 earthquake that hit Japan in April of 2011 was one among hundreds that have shaken the tectonic plates in recent months. The subsequent tsunami that roared across Japanese cities in the wake of the big earthquake literally wiped some cities and villages off the map! Floods in Australia in recent months have been utterly devastating for them. The rain-soaked, unplanted cornfields in our mid-western flood planes are a further testimony that major weather patterns can lead to serious worldwide food shortages in the coming months.

These food shortages have already become a major factor in the civil unrest sweeping across the Arab world in Central Asia. Sharply escalating food prices have helped to fuel these uprisings. Food prices have been rising sharply in the U. S. in recent months. A large percentage of America's corn crop is being turned into ethanol, further driving up the price of food and lowering national and world food reserves.

Because of all these major developments, remnant Christians need to give immediate attention to these important goals:

1: Read Luke 13 and take to heart the twice repeated words of our Lord Jesus Christ: *"I tell you, Nay: but, except ye repent, ye shall all likewise perish."* **It is imperative that every remnant Christian live with a penitent and contrite heart before the Living God.**

2: Reach out to those you love, both believers and unbelievers, and tell them what they need to hear about God, His Word, His Kingdom, their heritage, and the state of their soul and destiny.

3: Be prepared for whatever may come, whether it be something that God ordains or man creates. Food, water, and shelter are the basics needed to sustain life. These are the commodities you must provide if unfolding events continue. We now live in a nation under the judgment of God!

I Report. You Decide.

Experts provide many reasons for the catastrophic weather patterns that have visited the U.S. in 2011 and the several years preceding this year. Again, more than 1,000 tornadoes have loosed their fury from California (May 2011) all the way east to Massachusetts (May 2011), south into Alabama, Mississippi, and Florida (April 2011), and throughout Oklahoma, Arkansas, Missouri, Illinois, Minnesota, Wisconsin, Iowa, Illinois, and Tennessee. The National Weather Service has attempted to provide a rationale that includes many factors, including the cooling of the Pacific Ocean waters. But not once have I found any reference to the possibility that a sovereign God may be a decider of such events.

Perhaps among the most bizarre and foolish attempts to rational these catastrophic weather events, including the Joplin tornado of May 22, 2011, is the idea that the U. S. Government triggered these catastrophes, or that our country has enemies conspiring to destroy the USA. Conspiracy theories abound, especially among the Christian remnant. Many have simply eliminated God from the equation and have placed earthquakes, tornadoes, hurricanes, droughts, and floods into the hands of moral man. We all need to remember this: God—not man—controls events on earth! This type of conspiratorial thinking would be laughable if people suffering a lack of intelligence purported it. Unfortunately, some supposedly very intelligent people are on the cutting edge of these theories, believing these weather events to be the work of evil minds. They have apparently disconnected from the Bible, which clearly declares that a sovereign God rules not only the heavens, but here on earth: *"And all the inhabitants of the earth are reputed as nothing: and he doeth according to his will in the army of heaven, and among the inhabitants of the earth: and none can stay his hand, or say unto him, What doest thou?"* *(Daniel 4:35)*.

I recommend you read the story from the book of St. Luke told from the lips of Jesus Christ in response to those who lost their lives in tragic circumstances (Luke 13:1-5). Jesus made it clear that those who died in the tragic events mentioned in this passage were not any more sinful than the rest of the Jerusalem population. They were in the wrong place at the wrong time. Evidently it was their time to die, but not because they were more sinful than others.

The USA is ripe for judgment because God's patience with the Anglo-Saxon population of this country is running low. I live in absolutely no fear of mortal men who conspire to do evil, including those who are alleged to make toxic chemical trails in the skies over America. I do have great reverence for the Living God Who "*. . . is slow to anger, and great in power, and will not at all acquit the wicked: the LORD hath his way in the whirlwind* (tornadoes?) *and in the storm, and the clouds are the dust of his feet*" *(Nahum 1:3).*

The poor souls who perished and who simply vanished into the vortex of the monster tornado that hit Joplin were not any more sinful than the rest of America. In fact, there were many known Christians among them. The words of Jesus Christ to Americans are some that every one of us should take to heart: *"Suppose ye that these Galilaeans were sinners above all the Galilaeans, because they suffered such things? I tell you, Nay: but, except ye repent ye shall all likewise perish."* We have an urgent need for repentance across the land. Dear God, let it begin with me and the pulpit behind which I stand!

20

THE GREAT COMMISSION: INCLUSIVE OR EXCLUSIVE?

Fall 2011

The Great Commission: what is it? Who authorized this call for evangelism? Are foreign missions relevant to the Great Commission? Does the Great Commission compel Christians to evangelize all peoples of every nation? In short, is salvation intended for all races? All Christians compelled to finance foreign missions to China, Japan, Korea, Kenya, Zimbabwe, Saudi Arabia, Libya, and other non-white nations of the world? What do you believe about the Great Commission? What are you teaching your sons and daughters about foreign missions? Sacrifice a few minutes of your valuable time and continue reading.

Dare to examine a subject that few Christians can muster the courage to explore! Foreign missions are the focus of almost all Christians—regardless of their denominational affiliation. Evangelizing the world is a passion that burns as deep as any theological issue of the 21st Century. Consider the vast sums of money spent on evangelism and the army of missionaries sent to the far corners of the world. The bulletins of almost every evangelical church depict various foreign missions and those whom the church is supporting.

Christians seem to possess a relentless passion for foreign missions. There are few church budgets that do not include money for foreign missions to Africa, Asia, Mexico, Central or South America, or some other non-white corner of the world. World evangelism holds such a sacred place in the heart of 21st Century Christians that hardly anyone would dare question the legitimacy of this call to export the Gospel. **With malice toward none of these generous and well-intentioned people, may we please consult the Word of God on this matter?**

Time for Serious Reflection

Exporting Christianity beyond the Caucasian world of Europe began about 500 years ago in the early years of the 16th Century. In the late 1400s and on into the next century, sea-faring explorers from Portugal and Spain began to navigate the Atlantic. In short order, they were plying the waters along the coast of islands in the Caribbean and along the coast of the Southeastern U. S. and Central and South America. From the beginning, these ventures into the New World included the plan to take the Gospel of Jesus Christ to the indigenous natives of the new world. Spanish explorers pursued establishing Christian missions with great vigor, and the French followed suit in the interior of the Eastern U. S. and in Northeast Canada.

This passion for taking the Gospel to the non-white peoples of the earth has continued to burn in Christians from every denomination. We are now 500 years into foreign missions, with no abatement in sight. Sadly, after five centuries of gargantuan effort expended by the Christian West, the world remains largely in the hands of other religions, including more than one billion

Muslims. Moreover, where Christianity allegedly has been established successfully in some African states, it is a far cry from authentic Christianity. The theology, morals, music, and culture of these allegedly Christianized places does not equate with the Christianity of my Bible.

Five centuries of world evangelism has produced very little enduring Christianity in Asia, Africa, and elsewhere. The efforts to export Christianity to the non-white world have not yielded much fruit at all! Five hundred years of world evangelism, and in the 21st Century the world remains largely unconverted! Perhaps the testimony of Albert Schweitzer (1875-1965), arguably one of the most highly profiled missionaries in history, summarizes the quest for taking the Great Commission to the non-white races of the earth. After spending much of his life among the Blacks of Gabon and seeking to civilize Africa through his endless, benevolent acts and tireless work in caring for the sick, Albert Schweitzer had this to say in is 1961 book *From My African Notebook:*

"I have given my life to alleviate the sufferings of Africa. There is something that all white men who have lived here, must learn and know; that these individuals are a sub-race; they have neither the intellectual, mental or emotional abilities to equate or share in any of the functions of our civilization.

"I have given my life to try to bring unto them the advantages which our civilization must offer, but I have become well aware that we must retain this status; white, the superior, and they the inferior, for whenever a white man seeks to live among them as their equal, they will either destroy him or devour him, and they will destroy all his work; and so for any existing relationship or for any benefit to this people let white men from anywhere in the world who would come to help Africa remember that you must continually retain this status; you the master, and they the inferior, like children that you would help or teach. Never fraternize with

them as equals, never accept them as your social equals; or they will devour you; they will destroy you."

On Point with Biblical and Historical Truth

Before proceeding, allow me to say this: God is the author and creator of every separate and distinct race, and He found all of them very good (Genesis 1:31). In the principle of Original Design, God has a place, a purpose, and a future for representatives of every pure race that He created. God is not the author of nor is He responsible for the hybrid races that have emerged from violating His law of Kind after His Kind, appearing *ten times* in Genesis chapter one! Every race deserves the respect, honor, and dignity that God purposed for them. But God did not place all the distinctive races of the created world under covenant and law. Only Adam Kind, per Genesis 1 and 2, was placed under covenant and law. Adam and his posterity alone—not the other races—were placed under covenant and law and charged with the liability of sin. Not having been placed under the law and with no liability for sin, the other races share **no guilt** for sin and share no complicity in the ethical fall of Adam and his posterity.

The Bible places only Adam and his posterity under covenant and law; therefore, they alone are responsible for breaking covenant and transgressing God's law. In fulfilling the Law of Kinsman Redeemer (Leviticus 25:47-49), Jesus Christ took on the seed of Abraham (Hebrews 2:16; Romans 9:5) to provide the means of **redemption** for those who were sold under the guilt of sin and under the judgment of God. The Word of God is clear! The law is applicable to those who were under the law. Jesus Christ came to redeem those who were under the law (Galatians 4:5).

The Bible defines sin as the *"transgression of the law"* (I John 3:4). *"Now we know that what things soever the law saith, it saith to them who are under the law . . ."* (Romans

3:19). Moreover, God declares this in Romans 4:15: *"... for where no law, there is no transgression."* That is not all! Scripture declares in Romans 5:13 that *"... sin is not imputed where there is no law."* In Adam's sin, all the posterity of Adam fell (Romans 5:12).

Yes, death passed upon all the other races because in Adam's fall, the whole creation fell. *"Nevertheless death reigned from Adam to Moses, <u>even over them that had not sinned after the similitude of Adam's transgression</u> ..."* (Romans 5:14— emphasis ours). Adam was given lordship over the entire world (Genesis 1:28-29). His fall occasioned the fall of the entire creation: *"For we know that the whole creation groaneth and travaileth in pain together until now" (Romans 8:22).* Adam and his posterity alone bear the judgment for breaking the covenant and transgressing the law.

The non-white races of the world do have and practice a communion with the Creator, but are not under covenant or law. They have no place for atonement for sin, and every religion non-whites endorse works with a plethora of gods. Only in Christianity did uncreated God step out of time and eternity to become man to save His people from their sin. In all other religions, mortals seek to become god. Again, *only* in Christianity did God become man in the Person of Jesus Christ to save His people from their sin.

The Bible is the record of Adam and his posterity (Genesis 5:1-2) *alone*. Other races may appear in the narrative of the Bible, but only because they influenced or in some way interacted with Adam and his posterity, and Israel in particular. The Bible is a family history of Adam Kind; beginning in Genesis 12, it becomes the history of one man: Abraham and his posterity. Trying to make the Bible applicable to all the races of the earth would be no different than taking a handbook for a Ford Focus and making that manual the handbook for every vehicle manufactured in the world. The Bible is no more applicable to all races of the world than trying to learn how to operate a Porsche by reading the manual for a Ford Focus.

The Premise Does Make A Difference

The current theological interpretation of the Great Commission found in Matthew 28:16-20 and elsewhere in the New Testament rests upon the following presuppositions. Examine these premises and remember this: if the premises are faulty, the whole foundation for world evangelism rests on the sinking sand of humanism. The idea of taking the Gospel to Asia, Africa, and the rest of the non-white world is built from these *false* premises:

1)   All races share a unity in Adam. World evangelism assumes that all races are descended from Adam and Eve. **The Bible does not teach this.**

2)   They believe that all races descended from Adam, all were under covenant, and therefore all are responsible for keeping God's law. **The Bible does not teach this.**

3)   They believe that all races suffered liability in Adam's fall and therefore all races must be saved from sin. Again, **the Bible does not teach this.**

Time for a Reality Check

After 500 years of world evangelism and taking the Great Commission to all nations of the earth, what does the record show? What is the fruit from this planting? Is it asking too much to examine the fruits of taking the Gospel to all races of the earth? What do the facts show?

1)   After five hundred years of world evangelism, not a single nation in all of Africa or Asia has truly embraced Christianity in its biblical and apostolic form. Where it has been "accepted," it has been integrated with the religion of the indigenous people, watered down, mixed thoroughly, and is hardly recognizable as the faith once delivered to the saints. Remember Christ's warning to His disciples about casting the pearls of His Kingdom to the wrong people?   (Matthew 7:6).

2)   World evangelism and foreign missions have accelerated the non-white immigration into America and all the other Anglo-Saxon nations fixated with taking the Gospel of Jesus Christ to the non-white world. Missionaries have beaten a path into Asia, Africa, Mexico, and Central and South America. The result? Millions of their *alleged* converts have followed them back to America and the rest of the Anglo Saxon world. This racial fusion is clearly against the teaching of Scripture.

3)   Exporting the Gospel to the non-white world has inspired the integration of the races as much as any other single event. The walls of segregation were torn down brick by brick as foreign missions and non-white immigration flooded America and the Christian West. The pews of many denominational churches were the very first to be fully integrated in the U. S. This social movement has fueled the passion for interracial marriage.

The Great Commission in Biblical Perspective

The Great Commission consists of the instruction given by Jesus Christ to His apostles during the forty days following His resurrection from the dead. The most complete account of the Great Commission is recorded in Matthew 28:16-20. Other accounts are found in Mark 16:14-18, Luke 24:44-49, John 20:19-23, and Acts 1:4-8. Each of these accounts should be studied in detail, and as these words are harmonized, they bring together the full and essential elements of all that Jesus intended for His disciples and those who followed them to understand about the Great Commission.

The words of instruction found in St. Matthew's Gospel are generally conceded to be the most comprehensive in regard to the Great Commission. Following His resurrection from the dead, the eleven disciples had gone to an appointed mountain in Galilee where Jesus Christ, in His own person, came and delivered these words: *"All power is given me in heaven and in earth. Go ye therefore and teach all nations, baptizing them in the name of the Father, and of the Son, and of the Holy Ghost: Teaching them to observe all things whatsoever I have commanded you: and, lo, I am with you always, even unto the end of the world. Amen" (Matthew 28:18-20).*

The context for the Great Commission found in Matthew and in all other accounts is the total Bible. The words of Jesus Christ to His disciples cannot be removed from the context of the law of Moses, the Prophets, and the Psalms, as Jesus Himself is so careful to tell us (Luke 24:24). The important question that must be decided is this: for whom did Jesus intend the Great Commission? Did Christ intend for the Great Commission to be inclusive of all races on earth, or did He intend for His instruction to be exclusive to the people chosen in election before the foundation of the world (Ephesians 1:4,5; II Timothy 1:9; Romans 9:4,5; Isaiah 45:4, 17, 25, Psalm 77:15)?

If Jesus intended for the Great Commission to be inclusive of all races, one must conclude that Jesus Christ must be very disappointed, for only a small percentage of the people in every generation for the past two thousand years has ever professed Jesus Christ as Savior. In fact, for the past two thousand years, the earth has remained a largely unconverted world, and this continues right into the 21st Century in the midst of instantaneous communication.

If, on the other hand, the Great Commission were exclusive to the people for whom Jesus Christ died, one can conclude that the sovereignty of God has been fully satisfied, for in every generation, a faithful remnant has received the good news of the Gospel of our Lord and Savior Jesus Christ. While there has never been a generation that witnessed anywhere near a complete conversion, there has not been a single generation where a faithful remnant has not been called out of darkness into the marvelous light of the Gospel. In truth, God has never been frustrated in the matter of the Great Commission. Every soul numbered in the election of God the Father has been drawn to Jesus Christ for salvation (John 6:44, 65).

Reflect upon the words of Jesus Christ in John 17:2: *"As thou has given him power over all flesh, that he should give eternal life to as many as thou hast given him."* As many souls as were ordained by God the Father to be the recipients of salvation have come to that saving grace. Every soul in the election of God the Father will be effectually called to the good news of the Gospel.

God will not be frustrated. All who are part of the elect will come to a state of salvation: *"All that the Father giveth me shall come to me; and him that cometh to me I will in no wise cast out" (John 6:37).* No soul numbered in the elect of God will be lost. *"For it is God which worketh in you both to will and to do of his good pleasure" (Philippians 2:13).* None will be lost that are drawn to Jesus Christ by God the Father. Some may come dragging their heels and resisting with all their might, but they will still come. *"So then it is not of him that willeth, nor of him that runneth, but of God that sheweth mercy" (Romans 9:16).* Of this you may be certain: *". . . as many as were ordained to eternal life believed" (Acts 13:48).*

The Great Commission has not arrived stillborn for the people for whom Jesus Christ died. The precious blood of Jesus Christ extended to the outer limits of God's election. Not one soul in the elect of God has been or will be left behind. The atonement of Jesus Christ was limited to the exact number of souls in God's elect. Our Father chose, named, and numbered the elect before the foundation of the world (Ephesians 1:4-5; II Timothy 1:9). His sheep hear His voice, and a stranger they will not follow: *"My sheep hear my voice, and I know them, and they follow me: And I give unto them eternal life; and they shall never perish, neither shall any man pluck them out of my hand. My Father which gave them me, is greater than all; and no man is able to pluck them out of my Father's hand" (John 10:27-29).*

Sadly, religious television networks, radio, and the Internet are overflowing with well-intentioned preachers who believe it is their bounden duty to fulfill the **Great Commission** and take the Gospel to every creature under heaven. With passion they fund and send missionaries into every corner of Asia, Africa, South and Central America, Mexico, and elsewhere to convert the world. Almost every church budget in the U. S. allocates the funding for foreign missions. With due respect to these highly motivated evangelists, they have simply misinterpreted Scripture. Had they followed the counsel of Jesus Christ, His apostles, and the disciples who followed them, they would have realized the Gospel is exclusive to the sheep people whom the Father chose in election (Matthew 10:5- 6; 15:24; I Peter 1:1-2; Acts 26: 6-7; James 1:1, etc.).

The following are a mere sampling of the multitude of verses that confirm the fact that the Great Commission is exclusive to those chosen in election by God the Father, redeemed by the blood of Jesus Christ, and effectually quickened and sanctified by the Holy Spirit.

1: The salvation of the elect rests upon Jehovah's covenant of promise to Abraham that He would be a God unto Abraham and his seed after him: *"And I will establish my covenant between me and thee and thy seed after thee in their generations for an everlasting covenant, to be a God unto thee, and to thy seed after thee"* (Genesis 17:7).

2: That the Abrahamic Covenant upon which salvation rests was exclusive to Isaac and not Ishmael or any other of Abraham's issue is confirmed in Genesis 17:19, 21: *"And God said, Sarah thy wife shall bear thee a son indeed; and thou shalt call his name Isaac: and I will establish my covenant with him for an everlasting covenant, and with his seed after him."* Ishmael was excluded from the covenant (Genesis 17:20, 21); at a later time, the bondwoman Hagar and her son Ishmael were cast out (Genesis 21:10, Galatians 4:30).

3: God's choice of Israel for His elect is confirmed in Deuteronomy 7:6: *"For thou art an holy people unto the LORD thy God: the LORD thy God hath chosen thee to be a special people unto himself, above all people that are upon the face of the earth."* This choice was in confirmation of the sworn oath Jehovah made with Abraham (Deuteronomy 7:8). Out of his seed would come the people who were the objects of Jehovah's unfailing love (Genesis 15:5, 17:7, Jeremiah 31:1-3).

4: Throughout Scripture, God confirms Israel to be the people chosen in election: *"For thou hast confirmed to thyself thy people Israel to be a people unto thee for ever: and thou, LORD, art become their God"* *(II Samuel 7:24)*.

5: Jehovah chose one people in the earth to receive His inheritance: *"For thou didst separate them* (Israel) *from among all the people of the earth, to be thine inheritance . . ."* *(I Kings 8:53)*.

6: Among all the peoples of the earth, God chose Israel alone to be the recipients of His covenant of salvation: *"For Jacob my servant's sake, and Israel mine elect, I have called thee by thy name . . ."* *(Isaiah 45:4)*.

7: The exclusivity of Israel is punctuated by the Prophet Amos, who speaking of Israel declared this: *"You only have I known of all the families of the earth . . ."* *(Amos 3:2)*.

8: Jehovah made Israel His exclusive choice among all the peoples of the earth: *"At the same time, saith the LORD, will I be the God of all the families of Israel, and they shall be my people . . . I have loved thee with an everlasting love . . ."* *(Jeremiah 31:1, 3)*.

9: Israel, alone among all nations of the earth has been chosen as the peculiar treasure of Jehovah: *"For the LORD hath chosen Jacob unto himself, and Israel for his peculiar treasure"* *(Psalm 135:4)*.

10: Jesus Christ declared Israel to be the exclusive object of His salvation grace: *"I am not sent but unto the lost sheep of the house of Israel"* (Matthew 15:24).

10: Jesus announced in the call of Zacchaeus that he, being a son of Abraham, was a fit vessel for salvation: *"This day is salvation come to this house, forsomuch as he also is a son of Abraham. For the Son of man is come to seek and to save that which was lost"* (Luke 19:9-10).

_11: The Lord Jesus Christ declared Himself to be the good shepherd that has come to give his life for (Israel) the sheep people of the Bible: *"I am the good shepherd: the good shepherd giveth his life for the sheep"* (John 10:11). Jesus further announced that His sheep knew His voice, and a stranger they would not follow (John 10:4-5, 27).

12: Jesus also declared that the sheep people had been given Him by the Father: *"My sheep hear my voice, and I know them, and they follow me: And I give unto them eternal life; and they shall never perish, neither shall any man pluck them out of my hand. My Father, which gave them me, is greater than all . . ."* (John 10:27-29).

13: St. Paul declares that the adoption, the glory, the covenants, the law, the service of God, the promises, and even Jesus Himself is the exclusive property of Israel: *"Who are Israelites; to whom pertaineth the adoption, and the glory, and the covenants, and the giving of the law, and the service of God, and the promises; Whose are the fathers, and of whom as concerning the flesh, Christ came . . ."* (Romans 9:4).

14: Consider this compelling announcement about Israel and the exclusivity of the salvation given them: *"Blessed be the Lord God of Israel; for he hath visited and redeemed his people . . . to perform the mercy promised to our fathers, and to remember his holy covenant; The oath which he sware to our father, Abraham . . . To give knowledge of salvlation unto his people by the remission of their sins"* *(Luke 1:68, 72-73, 77).*

The above Scriptures are but a mere introduction to the biblical literature available to confirm the <u>exclusive</u> nature of the Great Commission. For those who believe otherwise, all the Scripture in the world may not be sufficient to change their minds. But those who build their worldview from the Bible will clearly understand that the Great Commission is intended for the people chosen in election before the foundation of the world. God is not frustrated by the billions who have never been saved. Instead, God has saved the exact number of souls in every generation Whom He chose for salvation.

21

CODE OF THE WEST:
THE VALUES THAT
MADE AMERICA GREAT

Winter 2012

The 21st Century is witness to an increasing number of Americans who have lost faith in themselves and in their country. They perceive a nation in sharp decline from its former glory, a country in a moral and spiritual free fall from that of previous generations. Millions of Americans who have a point of reference from the '40s and '50s are disillusioned and despondent as they helplessly witness the country they love being transformed into a progressive, secular, humanist society with little, if any, place for God and zero respect for His Word. This millennial generation seems quite content to remove the spiritual and moral landmarks of former generations.

People between the ages of eighteen and twenty-nine have been labeled the millennial generation by sociologists, pollsters, and demographers. A high percentage of the millennial generation that did go to the ballot box in 2008 cast their vote for Obama. Roughly 50% of the millennial generation has lived in an out-of-wedlock arrangement, and from this same group, one out of every three children is born to an unwed mother. A high percentage of the homosexual population is numbered in this age group. And, from this same age group we all can attest to shocking numbers of interracially mixed couples. Finally, the millennial generation, like the previous one, is prone to favoring abortion, although data on this indicates perhaps a slight decline.

Most of the millennial generation consists of the children or grandchildren of Baby Boomers, born between 1946 and 1964. Baby Boomers themselves were cut loose in many ways from the spiritual and moral values of their parents and grandparents, who as survivors of the Great Depression (1929-1939) demonstrated even greater character and strength by going on to survive and win World War II (1941-1945). Children born to the great generation that survived the depression and war of their parents and grandparents embarked on a path quite different from their antecedents.

In fact, they rejected the spiritual and moral values that characterized their parents and grandparents, those great men and women who endured abject poverty, financial depression, and a terrible war. The many admirable qualities that characterized our parents and grandparents, traits such as love and honor for God, respect for His authoritative Word, revering of the Ten Commandments, and devotion to hard work and honesty—these were lost amid the moral and social upheaval in the Cultural Revolution of the '60s.

In contrast, the millennial generation will spend the greater part of their life in the 21st Century carrying the excesses of their parents and grandparents to a completely new level. The sanctity of life was lost in the last generation, when our nation witnessed in the murder of fifty-five million unborn children in the aftermath of *Roe vs. Wade 1973.* Random acts of violence, such as murder, rape, and armed robbery, skyrocketed in the sixties, seventies, eighties, and nineties. The sexually free society of those decades has eclipsed itself, to the point where fornication, adultery, sodomy, abortion, and miscegenation are the norm.

However, to the glory of God and the praise of Jesus Christ, not all Americans have chosen to go down with the *Titanic*! A growing remnant of devoted Christians has opted to hold tenaciously to the spiritual and moral values that made America the showcase nation of the earth. In an effort to transmit the moral values of former generations to today's millennial generation, Christian faith, love for God and county, and personal freedom to explore the limits of one's personal ambitions are being fiercely defended and even cultivated in this country. A few good men and women are trying very hard to drum up enthusiasm and commitment to these ageless, noble qualities. Hundreds of thousands of these children, youth, and young adults are being educated at home or in private schools and in pro-Christian colleges and universities. Somebody still cares!

This Christian remnant has made the conscious choice not to run with a multitude to do evil. They abhor abortion and are pro-life from the bedroom to the ballot box. These people, like generations before them, disdain and reject sodomy, miscegenation, same sex marriage, live-in-relationships, and all the rest of the immorality that now passes muster across the landscape of America, including much of mainstream Christianity. This growing remnant holds tenaciously to the concept of limited government, a strong work ethic, honesty, truth, self-reliance, ambition, free market enterprise, and the freedom to succeed and to fail without government bailout.

The Code of the West

A man named James P. Owen personifies this return of at least some Christian Americans to the spiritual and moral values of previous generations. After a successful Wall Street career, in

2003, Jim Owen embarked on an encore career as an inspirational author, speaker, and film producer. He also created the **Center for Cowboy Ethics and Leadership** to assist in spreading the message that *"everyone needs a code . . . a creed to live by."* James has written several books including *Cowboy Ethics*, *Cowboy Values*, and his latest book, *The Try.*

James became so dismayed at the nation's epidemic of scandals and social discord that he felt compelled to stand up and be counted and let America know about the wonderful values that once characterized the true American spirit. The *Code of the West* is a distillation of the principles to which Americans should aspire. These principles penned by James P. Owen summarize in brief what he believes America needs to recapture if we are to reclaim our country and culture and place in God's created world. In his book *Cowboy Ethics*, Owens summarized the **Code of the West** as follows:

1. Live each day with courage.
2. Take pride in your work.
3. Always finish what you start.
4. Do what has to be done.
5. Be tough but fair.
6. When you make a promise, keep it.
7. Ride for the brand.
8. Talk less and say more.
9. Remember that some things aren't for sale.
10. Know where to draw the line.

The **Code of the West** is being taught in schools throughout the West. Most recently, these ten principles written by a former Wall Street businessman were enshrined as Wyoming's official state code. Let the record show that James P. Owen strongly encourages the character qualities and criteria that enabled successive generations of Anglo-Saxon Americans to explore, settle, and civilize a vast continent stretching for 3,000 miles between the Atlantic and Pacific, land originally untamed and filled with hostile Indians, wild animals, and harsh living conditions, a land where only the tough and hardened could survive.

Many reading this article would be happy to post additions to this list of cowboy ethics. Those who have followed the footsteps of the Pilgrims, the Puritans who followed them, and the successive waves of Celtic, Anglo, Saxon, and Germanic peoples into America are keenly aware of the bravery and grit of these early pioneers. As these adventuresome Anglo Saxons cut their way through the brush, blazed trails through unmarked forests, fought off Indian massacres and disease and waged a relentless battle against harsh winter storms, the American continent was conquered foot by foot.

Men, women, and children hazarded their lives and in extraordinary physical discomfort made their way across the West by way of the Oregon Trail, the Santa Fe Trail, and many times unmarked trails. While we can never truly appreciate the horrific sacrifices these people made for the generations that would follow in their footsteps, we can do our best to honor and emulate what we do know. Out of a raw, untamed wilderness filled with hostile, uncivilized savages, our Celtic, Anglo, Saxon, Germanic forbears forged the single greatest nation ever assembled on earth.

To the God-fearing, courageous, and fearless heirs of Christianity and freedom, let us resolve that we and our children will not abandon the Christian ideals that propelled the first generations of Americans forward in history. May each of us examine the **Code of the West** and purpose to rededicate ourselves to the character qualities that made this nation so great. Now let us briefly examine each of these principles advanced by James Owens.

1. Live each Day with Courage

None of us is born into a fairy tale world, but into a fallen world where pain, suffering, and death abound. We are called to show great courage, even in the face of adversity. Each of us should aspire to face each day with resolute determination to conquer every problem that comes our way in the name and for the glory of Jesus Christ. Remember: one with God is a majority. With St. Paul, let us proclaim, *"I can do all things through Christ which strengtheneth me" (Phil. 4:13).*

The words of Moses to the children of Israel provide us with a call to courage: *"Be strong and of a good courage, fear not, nor be afraid of them: for the LORD thy God, he it is that doth go with thee; he will not fail thee, nor forsake thee" (Deut. 31:6).* Finally, these words from David, a man of indomitable courage, should inspire us to stand strong: *"Be of good courage, and he shall strengthen your heart, all ye that hope in the LORD" (Psalm 31:24).* May the lads and young men of this generation stand straight and tall and with conviction heed the instruction of the Holy Spirit when He declared through the pen of St. Paul: *"Watch ye, stand fast in the faith, quit* (act) *you like men, be strong" (I Cor. 16:13).*

2. Take Pride in Your Work

The Puritan work ethic that took root in the early 1600s became an enduring tradition in America. Taking pride in whatever task, trade, or profession a person embraced has been the American way. A passion for hard work and accepting nothing but the best: these were hallmarks of Americans' work ethic. As late as the 1950s, anything stamped "Made in the USA" was assumed to be the best of that line of products available anywhere. Sadly, this tradition is not true today. Only a fraction of the tools, goods, and other items that the American public consumes are produced in the United States. Tools, electronics, clothing, shoes, and other goods produced with cheap labor in China, Mexico, and elsewhere flood the United States where favorable import taxes encourage the flow of goods into the U. S.

Remnant Christians would do well to reaffirm the work ethic of former generations and heed the call to exercise dominion of

God's earth. Adam and his posterity were commissioned as covenant men to exercise dominion over God's earth in a fallen world. Work is essential to man's well being and is commanded of God: *"Six days shalt thou labour, and do all thy work: But the seventh day is the Sabbath of the LORD thy God: in it thou shalt not do any work . . ." (Exodus 20:9-10).* Any man who will work hard for six days each week and observe the Holy Sabbath on the seventh day will be blessed indeed. May every member of the remnant take pride in their work and heed these words from wise King Solomon: *"Whatsoever thy hand findeth to do, do it with thy might; for there is no work, nor device, nor knowledge, nor wisdom, in the grave whither thou goest"* *(Eccles. 9:10).*

3. Always Finish What You Start

Any job worth doing is worth doing well and deserves to be completed. It is not good to start a project and leave it unfinished. All of our tasks need to be brought to completion. We cannot be proud of our work until the job is done and done well. Before beginning a major work effort, recall the words of Jesus Christ when He encouraged those intending to build a tower to count the cost and determine if he had the means to finish it, lest all who beheld the unfinished project would *". . . mock him, saying, This man began to build, and was not able to finish" (Luke 14:28-30).* Most people can find many incomplete projects that they began with good intentions but left undone, forgotten.

The hardest task of most projects is just getting started. Do not allow perfectionism to get you bogged down. Once you have done your best, move on and do not continue to fuss with your project. Do not lose focus on the work before you. Remove obvious distractions and time-stealers from your life, including television, videos, excessive visiting with neighbors, etc. Do not allow procrastination to keep your project languishing. Hold yourself accountable to get the job completed. The words of the Psalmist David are appropriate to call to mind when beginning a project: *"And let the beauty of the LORD our God be upon us: and establish thou the work of our hands upon us; yea, the work of our hands establish thou it"* *(Psalm 90:17).*

4. Do What Has to be Done

There is always going to be a job that nobody wants to do, and in every career, there are times when you would like to avoid doing what absolutely must be done. Life often deals us with situations that we didn't ask for, do not want, and would like to run from. Yet, something within the fabric of our being tells us we must do what we find truly difficult, whether it be a complicated household repair or dealing with unpleasant people. Whether it is as simple as mowing the lawn, painting the house, or making repairs on a dysfunctional automobile, we must do what needs doing!

Doing what has to be done may include telling those you love what they need to hear. A friendship may be jeopardized because you have to tell someone an unpleasant truth, or because it has become a major distraction to your life, your job, or even your marriage. A young person may need to mount the courage to break off a relationship that seems to violate biblical principles. Doing what has to be done might mean rolling up your sleeves and doing your part to clean the house, spruce up the yard, wash the car, or invest in someone who is not even part of your family. Doing what has to be done might mean fixing a broken marriage or extending forgiveness to someone who has hurt you to a point that it has robbed you of your spirituality.

Doing what has to be done certainly involves doing what God commanded in His Word: feeding the hungry, assisting widows, remembering the orphans, clothing the needy, visiting the sick, and remembering those in prison. Learning how to love and serve God and the people who surround us every day is doing what has to be done. Jesus expressed it this way: *"So likewise ye, when ye shall have done all those things which are commanded you, say, We are unprofitable servants: we have done that which was our duty to do"* (Luke 17:10).

5. Be Tough but Fair

Being tough but fair also involves many aspects of our life. Parents need to be tough and uncompromising with their children and youth while at the same time being reasonable and fair. Quite early in life, children need to clearly understand what is required of them regarding behavior and consequences. They need to learn the meaning of the word "no" without the word being repeated endlessly. They need to know that obedience is required at the first command—not the second, third, or even fourth.

Children must understand that rules set by parents are unbending, immovable, and that unpleasant consequences will result when boundaries are crossed. At the same time, parents must balance their tough discipline with affection and praise when it is deserved. Parental toughness balances privileges with responsibility. When children and youth fail to be responsible, they must see the tough side of Dad and Mom and lose their privileges.

Husbands must show love and affection through their actions and demonstrate a keen awareness of what makes his wife feel loved, needed, and fulfilled. At the same time, the man of the house must maintain his headship. He must prove himself the spiritual leader. He must take the lead in family devotions, public worship, and in setting the Bible as the compass which directs the family.

The need to be tough yet fair is a necessity in almost every venue of life. Consider the military. Every classroom teacher must be tough but fair. Every athlete competing in a sport will excel only when the coach establishes a tough training program and balances the requirements with fairness. Life is like preparing for a marathon: you will not win the race by compromising in the areas of training and exercise. *"Know ye not that they which run in a race run all, but one receiveth the prize? So run, that ye may obtain"* *(I Corinthians 9:24).*

6. When You Make a Promise, Keep It

Keeping your word is a fundamental essential of building good character. In the Old West, a man's word was his bond. A verbal agreement sealed with a handshake was commonplace throughout most of our early history. Written documents were often considered unnecessary among a people who kept their promises. This brings us to the next point: we should be cautious about making promises. It is better not to promise than to break your word and cause people to lose trust in you. In every area of life, the promises we make we should keep. Children should be taught at an early age to keep their word, and parents should serve as good role models for their children in being cautious about making promises and in keeping those promises we make. When you tell someone you will do something and fail to follow through, you make a major statement about who you are. If people cannot keep a promise to their fellowman, how will they keep their promises or vows made to God? Ecclesiastes 5:2 warns that we should *". . . Not be rash with thy mouth, and let not thine heart be hasty to utter any thing before God: for God is in heaven, and thou upon earth: therefore let thy words be few."* The Holy Spirit further admonishes us in verses 5 & 6: *"Better is it that thou shouldest not vow, than that thou shouldest vow and not pay. Suffer not thy mouth to cause thy flesh to sin . . ."* Remnant Christians and their sons and daughters need to hold tenaciously to the Code of the West and keep our promises!

7. Ride for the Brand

The expression "Ride for the Brand" is derived from the days when cowboys signed on to work a given ranch, and the livestock was identified with a particular brand. The cowboy was obligated to be loyal to his employer. He rode for the brand and had to remain loyal to that outfit. He would never compromise or speak ill of his employer, because every employer deserves the loyalty of those who work under him. If you sell Ford automobiles, you should not drive another brand. If you sell John Deere tractors, you should not run a Case on your farm.

Riding for the brand translates into a love of one's own country, one's own people, one's own family, and remaining loyal to them even under duress—as long as truth is not sacrificed. Above all, a Christian must demonstrate fierce love, devotion, and conviction to ride for Jesus Christ, the "brand" of his very salvation. A Christian must be loyal to His God and the faith, doctrine, discipline, and requirements of his trust and belief in God and Scripture.

At the Church of Israel, we include as essential to our "brand" our belief in Jesus Christ, the Son of God, for salvation apart from works, allegiance to the Apostles' Creed, loyalty to the King James Bible, participation in services from the Book of Common Prayer, and corporate worship on the biblical Sabbath, among other things. When we become a Christian, we take on the name of Jesus Christ and ride for His "brand," which is our salvation. Our complete loyalty to that brand is summarized in these words from Jesus Christ: *"If any man will come after me, let him deny himself, and take up his cross daily, and follow me"* *(Luke 9:23).*

8. Talk Less and Say More

This old cowboy truism is packed with wisdom! Many people do a lot of talking but actually say very little. By His own design, God designated a woman for more talking than men. A woman will speak several thousand more words in a day than a man. I do not mean to imply, however, that the woman's words are not important. Conversation for a woman is as natural as breathing. Most men find it more difficult to converse, especially if it is simply chatter that seems to have no purpose.

Talking less and saying more simply means that instead of too much chatter and lots of fluff, you instead employ wisdom when you do speak. Proverbs 17:27 provides this sage advice: *"He that hath knowledge spareth his words: and a man of understanding is of an excellent spirit."* The words of Proverbs 17:28 indicate we should learn when to remain silent and when to speak: *"Even a fool, when he holdeth his peace, is counted wise: and he that shutteth his lips is esteemed a man of understanding."* Proverbs 10:19 is a reminder that a multitude of words is not always best and silence is often the best route: *"In the multitude of words there wanteth not sin: but he that refraineth his lips is wise."*

God reminds us that *"Death and life are in the power of the tongue; and they that love it shall eat the fruit thereof"* *(Proverbs 18:21).* Moreover, Proverbs 21:23 counsels us to know that *"Whoso keepeth his mouth and his tongue keepeth his soul from troubles."* The Apostle James devotes eighteen verses in chapter 3 of his epistle to remind us of the incredible power vested in the tongue: *"The tongue can no man tame; it is an unruly evil, full of deadly poison"* *(James 3:8).* Like the cowboys of the Old West, we need to talk less and say more. This simply means we need to weave more wisdom and useful knowledge into our conservation with others and avoid gossip no matter what.

9. Remember that Some Things Aren't For Sale

This biblical principle is a strong reminder that some things are too valuable to sell, so we need not always grab the "For Sale" sign. Esau's life would have been dramatically different if he had not sold his birthright due the firstborn son of Isaac and Rebekah. Joseph's brothers would have circumvented a lot of sorrow for their father Jacob, themselves, and Joseph personally if they had not placed a "For Sale" sign on him when traveling merchants passed. King Saul's life might have come to a much better conclusion if he had chosen not to forfeit obedience and honor to God for temporary self-satisfaction and appeasing the people under him at critical junctures of his rule over ancient Israel.

Many things in life are simply not for sale: our ethnic heritage is not for sale, so interracial marriage is off limits! The unborn children of our race are not to be expended in an abortion murder mill so the mother/father and their cohorts in crime can shirk responsibility. The moral, spiritual, and medical well being of our children cannot be sacrificed in order to accommodate the sin of sodomy. Young people cannot sell their virtue and surrender their virginity for transitory experimental pleasure. The institution of marriage cannot be sold in return for a definition of marriage that dishonors God, repudiates His Word, mocks the union of one man and one woman of the same race, and cheapens the entire concept of marriage.

The story of Esau is compelling evidence to remind us all that some things are not for sale at any price. In reference to Esau, consider also Hebrews 12:16-17, which declares that there should be no *". . . fornicator, or profane person, as Esau, who for one morsel of meat sold his birthright. For ye know how that afterward, when he would have inherited the blessing, he was rejected; for he found no place of repentance, though he sought it carefully with tears."*

10. Know Where to Draw the Line

During the conquest and settlement of the United States, the pioneers and the cowboys who followed them practiced a simple, down-to-earth moral standard of right and wrong. A sense of knowing when and where to draw the lines between good and evil was engrained in the national population. Today, America languishes in spiritual and moral apathy because parents, youth, ministers, civil leaders, and unbelievers have lost their moral and spiritual compass. Moral lines have become blurred or even non-existent.

More than all other people, Christians should know that holding our spiritual and moral priorities sacred before God cannot be compromised. Keeping our moral integrity before Jesus Christ is essential. Living in an age when most of the historic, moral, and biblical landmarks of former generations have been removed has tempted many professing Christians to simply join the crowd and erase the line between right and wrong, good and evil. Consequently, many "talk the talk" but fail to walk the walk. It is imperative that remnant Christians know when and where to draw the lines between right and wrong. Thus, St. Paul recommends that all of us *"Examine yourselves, whether ye be in the faith; prove your own selves. Know ye not your own selves, how that Jesus Christ is in you, except ye be reprobates" (II Corinthians 13:5).*

We dwell in a God-centered moral universe; in the truth and spirit of our Christian forbears, we need to heed the old cowboy adage of simply knowing when to draw the line between good and evil. A number of recent polls show that the moral standards of people inside the church are not superior to unbelieving, non-churched people. This is to our shame! Witness the divorce rate among evangelical Christians: it is slightly above the national average. This is shameful and unacceptable. Marriage is the bedrock foundation of a civilized people. The dissolution of the historic covenant of marriage between one man and one woman of the same race united for life is dismantling our culture. We need to halt this practice at once! When the marriage fails, the family fails, the church is shamed, the community suffers, and the enormous spiritual, moral, and economic consequences continue for untold generations.

The Bible is replete with commands to draw lines between right and wrong, good and evil, light and darkness: *"Be ye not unequally yoked together with unbelievers: for what fellowship hath righteousness with unrighteousness? And what communion hath light with darkness . . . Wherefore come out from among them, and be ye separate, saith the Lord, and touch not the unclean thing; and I will receive you, And will be a Father unto you, and ye shall be my sons and daughters, saith the Lord Almighty"* (II Cor. 6:14, 17-18).

A Final Admonition

Let every remnant Christian resolve to live by a creed in this day when evil and wickedness gather on every side. We dare not be a creedless people, not knowing what we believe and why. We must live by what we know in our hearts and intellect is absolute truth. Can we not join that Christian remnant tucked away in the folds of this nation and purpose to live by the **Code of the West?** This code is based upon the Bible, and these spiritual, moral landmarks set by our Christian forefathers must be restored and become alive in our hearts in this 21st Century.

22

THE SINKING
OF THE TITANIC

Spring 2012

*P*ride goeth before destruction, and an haughty spirit before a fall" (Proverbs 16:18). "Boast not thyself of to morrow; for thou knowest not what a day may bring forth" (Proverbs 27:1).

The United States of America has been referred to as the Titanic of Nations, and many do believe she is on a parallel course with the renowned *Titanic* that sank into a watery grave 12,000 feet below the icy waters of the Atlantic one hundred years ago this past April 15, 1912. This watchman on the wall feels a compelling need to compare the sinking of the *Titanic* with America's falling fortunes. One hundred years ago, the largest ship afloat the ocean, measuring 882' long by 92' wide, an amazing twenty-five stories high, and weighing 46,000 tons, set sail on the North Atlantic. We all know its unfortunate fate.

Just as that ship struck an iceberg and met a precipitous end, one has to note that our beloved America is likewise running aground. Drawing a parallel between the ship and our nation's floundering, one must question the state of the souls of the Anglo-Saxon population of America in the 21st Century, just as there was concern for the salvation of the souls aboard the mighty *Titanic* in the 20th Century. The White population of America is in desperate need of a spiritual revival, because most lack a personal relationship with Jesus Christ. The Celtic, Anglo, Saxon, Germanic, and Scandinavian population of the Christian West can be divided into two classes: the **saved** and the **unsaved**. Sadly, far too many of our racial family are unsaved.

Looking back to the Twentieth Century, let us review in brief the history of the magnificent ship *Titanic*. It had left Southampton, England on her maiden voyage to New York City with three classes of passengers. The massive liner was filled with a mixture of the world's wealthiest people, ranging from the moderately rich to the extremely rich, all relaxing in the elegance of the most luxurious ocean liner ever to ply the oceans. The opulence and grandeur of this ship were something to behold. The RMS *Titanic* was declared to be the safest ship every built, one that even God Himself could not sink. Thus, the massive liner was equipped with a mere twenty lifeboats, sufficient to carry less than half her 2,200 passengers and crew. It is said these lifeboats were included in case the crew aboard the *Titanic* had to rescue passengers from another floundering ship.

Four days into her journey at 11:04 p.m. on the night of April 14, 1912, the Titanic struck an iceberg in the icy waters of the North Atlantic. She sideswiped the massive iceberg, damaging nearly 300 feet of the hull. As water rushed into six of her sixteen watertight compartments, they flooded, causing the ship to begin listing. In a mere two hours and forty minutes, the Titanic sank, taking 1,514 passengers and crew to a cold, watery grave. The next morning, the ocean liner *Carpathia* rescued 705 survivors suffering from exposure and hypothermia from waters four degrees below freezing.

Between seven and ten warnings regarding icebergs were signaled to the RMS *Titanic* on the day she sank. Captain Edward Smith, who went down with the ship, may not have received one of the most important warnings. It is believed that he and the crew had so much confidence in the well-constructed ship that any idea of an iceberg causing much trouble was simply unthinkable. Of the 885-crew members who worked on the deck crew in engineering, the galley, or to keep the passengers fed and comfortable, only 215 survived. All of the musicians from two different bands went down with the ship, playing the hymn "Nearer My God to Thee" in the last moments before the great liner sank.

It is impossible not to compare the *Titanic* with the other even more famous ship in history: the ship Noah and his sons built to survive the most earth-shattering event two and one-half millennia prior to the birth of Jesus Christ. That ship did survive and delivered its crew and cargo safely to land one year and ten days after it began to float. Noah's Ark was designed by God, built by God-fearing engineers, and saved by Jehovah from the most turbulent, catastrophic storm ever to visit planet Earth. We are descendants of the captain in charge of the Ark, and by the grace of Jehovah God, we shall find a place of refuge before the Titanic of Nations sinks into a spiritual and moral abyss. The same Jehovah that carried Noah and his family safely through the most catastrophic event of earth's history will see His covenant people through the Time of Jacob's Trouble.

How many warnings have gone out to covenant people of America in recent decades? How many watchmen have sounded the trumpet of truth and tried to warn this country that without repentance, faith, and belief in Jesus Christ, combined with a return to the faith and covenant law of our fathers, this country was moving toward irreversible judgment? Scores of God-fearing evangelists, prophets, apostles, pastors, and teachers have warned the people that repentance toward God and faith in Jesus Christ are the only remedy that can save America.

The warnings began with the Christian patriots who crusaded long before America entered World War II in 1941. These fearless, godly men continued to warn us during the war years (1941-1945) and beyond into the Cold War era of the '50s, '60s, '70s, and '80s. Ridicule was the frequent response. But Americans at large only hardened their hearts and continued to repudiate God's Word. Much like the captain and crew that guided the great *Titanic*, those who stand in responsible positions in the church and government in America have failed to heed the warnings. All efforts to awaken the shepherds and politicians of this country have failed. The church in 21st Century America is largely unsaved, lost, and disconnected from Jesus Christ, the truth of the Bible, and the moral absolutes of God's law. The state is lost, adrift on a sea of socialism and unsustainable debt, fighting no-win, undeclared wars, and rapidly moving toward a totalitarian dictatorship. Like the sinking *Titanic*, America is beginning to tilt into the watery sea of spiritual death, moral corruption, and rot, even legalizing the murder of unborn children, sodomy, and irreversible race mixing. All this ocean of sin, combined with a tidal wave of non-White, third-world immigration, is sinking our beloved America.

The Anglo-Saxon, Germanic populations of the 21st Century are largely unsaved. The preachers abandoned God's law after World War II in 1945, and successive generations have grown up without hearing God's law preached. What is the problem with this? How can one know and define godly character and its opposite, sin, without learning God's law and recognizing that guilt has no relevance if one does not know God's precepts?

Sadly, there are no guilt, shame, or remorse among the millions of the millennial generation who languish amid drugs, alcohol, promiscuity (fornication), sodomy, lesbianism, abortion, race mixing and every other vile sin one can imagine. In this sinking sand of immorality, our people are lost souls, floundering in moral relativism. Without the moral absolutes of former generations, this generation is one of souls lost on the sea of life, without a compass or North Star to guide them. Without hearing the law preached, they can never define or understand the horrible consequences of sin and why they need Christ—the only One Who can save them from hell.

Christianity's Last Great Stand

When it became apparent that the great Titanic was sinking beneath the angry waves of the cold Atlantic, the lifeboats were lowered and with the order that women and children were the first in line. Amid tears and bedlam, husbands and wives said final goodbyes. Newlywed brides were torn from their husbands. Fathers bade their sons and daughters farewell through a veil of tears amid the frantic cries of the hundreds who were desperately searching for their loved ones or those who seemed incapable of responding to the crisis.

Consider something else that is a lost quality today. Capture the chivalry the men aboard the *Titanic* demonstrated as they valued the lives of the women and children above their own, placing them first in the lifeboats, knowing full well there would never be room for themselves. In the aftermath of this tragedy, some 700 women and children were left widowed, orphaned, and alone. The selflessness the men aboard the *Titanic* demonstrated, believers and non-believers alike, is desperately needed today. "Women and children first" seems unattainable in today's selfish, "me first" society.

In fact, contrast the chivalry and bravery of the men aboard the *Titanic* with the captain and crew of the *Costa Concordia*, a cruise ship that rent its hull against the offshore shallows on an Italian island known as Giglio in Porto, Italy on January 16, 2012. The captain and crew of that ship were among the first to leave the stranded ship while passengers were left to fend for themselves. A number of passengers died or are presumed dead. But not   Francesco Schettino, captain of the ship! He saved his lady friend and himself but was later arrested, charged with manslaughter. The captain and crew of the Costa Concordia were willing to sacrifice the lives of their passengers for their own safety. How different that is from the men aboard the *Titanic*! What happened to chivalry in the culture of the Christian West? The feminist movement has not helped women in this regard: women's mad craze to achieve equality with men has robbed women of the West of the honor and sacredness with which they were once viewed. Feminists have succeeded in removing women from the home, as millions of them pursue careers in preference to marrying and staying home with children. Women now compete with men in almost every job description you can name—including the U. S. Military.

But at what price has this liberation come? It has cost women the sacred honor of being protected and the first to be spared when danger threatens. In their search for liberation from the biblical and cultural past, women have forfeited the sacred, protected turf that once guarded them from the more vile ravages of sin. In their search for equality with men—competing for jobs in the factory and filling college classrooms, offices, and corporate rooms of America, they have abandoned the home, children, and the long-standing role of women in the Western Christian tradition. They clamor to be allowed to compete on the front line in the military and share a foxhole with their male counterparts. While we praise God that not all women are like this, we all know that far too many are—enough that the culture has shifted from one of protecting women to one of expecting them to act like equals in every sphere.

Unlike the women aboard the *Titanic*, there is no one to protect women in modern America. They now stand unprotected in a cold and cruel world filled with sin, adrift in a culture that lacks the Christian virtues and character of the past. When crisis comes, and it surely will, women will find themselves without the chivalry of bygone generations and will face the brutal world without men who will stand and die for them and their children.

Saving Souls on the Titanic

Three classes of people boarded the *Titanic*. The class you chose to travel in determined your status. One of the hundreds of passengers that boarded the Titanic was a charismatic, passionate, Scottish evangelist named John Harper, who with his six-year-old daughter, boarded the ship with an invitation to speak at the Moody Church in Chicago, Illinois. While some of the wealthiest people aboard the *Titanic* were busy talking business, other passengers were playing cards, just passing time, and still others were in the ballroom dancing and enjoying the evening's festivities.

In the brief time before the *Titanic* hit the iceberg, Evangelist John Harper had been sharing the Gospel with anyone and everyone he could. On the night of the disaster, he had said his devotions and prayers, tucked his daughter into bed, and prepared to go to sleep. Awakened from his sleep by the disaster, John Harper quickly dressed, wrapped his daughter in a blanket, and carried her up to the deck. There he kissed her goodbye and handed her to a crewmember, who placed her on lifeboat #11. By this time, Harper knew that the ship was going to sink. He knew he would never see his daughter again and that she would be left an orphan, without mother or father.

Even knowing this, Harper surrendered his lifejacket to another. He began calling out, "Women and children and unsaved people into the lifeboats." John Harper understood a simple truth: some of the passengers were not prepared to face eternity. As terror and mayhem continued, Harper spent his time leading the unsaved to confess their sins and trust Jesus Christ for their salvation.

At 2:40 a.m., the *Titanic* disappeared beneath the waters of the North Atlantic amid a cloud of smoke and steam. Tragically, over 1000 people, including John Harper, were left fighting for their lives in the icy water, struggling to find a piece of floating wreckage to hold onto. Harper moved from person to person in the cold water, asking them if they were saved or unsaved. He pleaded with the unsaved to confess their sins, believe on the Lord Jesus Christ for salvation, and beg for His mercy and forgiveness. Finally, John Harper himself succumbed to the icy sea. But know this: in the precious last minutes of his life, he was in pursuit of winning lost souls to Jesus Christ. May we all be inspired by his story!

Four years after the sinking of the *Titanic*, a survivor's meeting was held in Ontario, Canada. One of those survivors testified at that gathering that while he was clinging to ship debris, Harper swam up to him twice, challenging him with the biblical invitation to ***"Believe in the Lord Jesus Christ and thou shalt be saved."*** He rejected the offer once. But upon Harper's second trip around, the unsaved man confessed Christ. Amazingly, a returning lifeboat rescued the new believer, while Evangelist John Harper went down to his watery grave. With tears in his eyes, this now saved man declared, "I am the last convert of John Harper."

When the *Titanic* had set sail, three classes of passengers were aboard. Yet shortly after the tragedy, the White Star Line in Liverpool, England placed a board outside its office with only two classes of passengers, reading thusly: **Known to be Saved** and **Known to be Lost.** Ironically, the White Star Line seemed to acknowledge what John Harper already knew. The **saved** will spend their eternity with Jesus Christ in His Kingdom, while the **unsaved** are eternally lost in the fire of Gehenna.

Those who study religious trends in America in the 21st Century report that not more than 2% of professing Christians share their faith with other people. People are not convicted to share their faith. Apparently they feel no urgency about the state of other people's souls. Americans are growing cold and uncaring in their faith. I ask you this: does anyone who is uncaring about the state of the souls of those you love really have the precious gift of salvation? Is someone who sits in the pew, uncaring and unconcerned about the state of someone else's soul, truly saved? How long has it been since you shared your faith with another? Are you concerned for the lost souls aboard America, the Titanic of Nations? America's ship is badly listing, taking on more spiritual and moral corruption. It is in mortal danger of sinking to the bottom of the graveyard of nations. Will someone please cry out to our captain and crew for spiritual and moral reformation, revival, and renewal? Do the strangers, mamzers, misfits, and spare-parts people who man this ship have the requisite DNA to even hear the call of repentance from dead works and faith in Jesus Christ as Savior and Lord?

The Ship Is Sinking, But the Party Goes On

When the first warning calls sounded late on the night of April 14, 1912, most of the passengers paid little heed. Many continued to dance, play cards, and party on, some of them inebriated too much to be in touch with reality. Most of the passengers were from very wealthy families and were simply having a great time on the maiden voyage of the Titanic. Even after several warnings had sounded, people still did not believe anything serious could be happening to the ship they assumed was unsinkable. So, they continued their card playing, dancing, drinking, and whatever else they found entertaining.

The captain and crew of the *Titanic* were not acting responsibly, knowing they were in waters potentially concealed icebergs. Even with the warnings, the ship had changed neither its speed nor its course as it headed straight into death and destruction beneath the waters of the North Atlantic. America is much like the great Titanic. For many decades, successive Presidents from both major political parties, together with elected representatives in the House and Senate from both parties, have acted irresponsibly, without regard to the future of her people.

Moreover, pastors have utterly failed to uphold the spiritual and moral truth of God's Word and lead the people to repentance.

The warning signs are piling up, yet neither the fathers, preachers, politicians, nor educators are preparing the American public for the iceberg that lies ahead. The voices of warning can barely be heard above the clamor of the liberal press and perversion displayed on television and in the cinema. Anyone who dares expose the evil and strangers who orchestrate policy in the White House and Congress, manipulate the nation's monetary system through fractional reserve banking, and arrange for waging no-win, undeclared wars is singled out for ostracism and rebuke.

Consider the following signs of serious decline and national genocide which accompanied the decline of the Roman and Greek civilizations, and prior to that the ancient nations of Israel and Judah. While each of the following could be elongated in a detailed analysis, the brief comments will punctuate the leading causes for the sinking of the American Titanic:

1) A complete disconnection from God's Word and historic Christianity has resulted in the rapid spiritual and moral decline of the American population. Unconverted clergy leading mostly unconverted parishioners, divorced from sound Bible teaching and with little passion for Jesus Christ, have reduced Christianity to entertainment more than worship, a social agenda over Bible truth. We are languishing amid a spiritual famine.

2) We have experienced a radical change from the biblical absolutes of former generations to moral relativism, where everyone does that which is right in his own eyes. America is overwhelmed by the moral degeneracy and rot that have captivated millions with drugs, alcohol, gambling, fornication, adultery, abortion, sodomy, miscegenation, pornography, and vile sins unimaginable.

3) The dissolution of the historic covenant and definition of marriage, being that between one man and one woman of the

same flesh; the disintegration of the nuclear family; dysfunctional family units becoming the rule rather than the rare exception as in former generations—these are taking us down! Plunging birth rates, absentee fathers, working mothers, illegitimate children, sustained poverty, welfare roles, drugs, alcoholism, crime, and moral degeneracy are the legacy of broken families.

4) The change from a homogenous nation of European Caucasian people sharing the same ethnic, cultural, religious, and moral values to a nation of racially diverse people of multiple religions and opposing moral beliefs—this is where we find ourselves! The ingestion of these diverse races from the non-White Third World has radically altered the demographics of America.

5) The over-extension of our military with installations in more than 100 nations of the world, waging no-win, undeclared wars with policy decisions that are not in our best interests, and a military staffed by mercenary soldiers have accelerated our decline. We have moved from a Republic to an empire, taxing the financial resources of the country beyond its limits.

6) We have transitioned from free-market Capitalism to Fabian, European-style Socialism, gradually transforming America's economy to a state where government controls, regulations, and taxation have stifled innovation, business, and the entrepreneurial spirit.

7) Free Trade agreements that allow foreign nations to inundate the American consumer with products produced by cheap labor, with very low tariffs, have created sustained trade deficits and strangulated American manufacturing, closed factories, and caused millions to be jobless.

8) The sacredness of human life has been lost amid a barbaric culture that endorses government-sponsored murder of the unborn. This has encouraged a culture that witnesses the random urge to commit mass murder, rape, armed robbery, and other criminal acts.

9) We have lost the historic American character traits of initiative, self-reliance, personal responsibility, and innovative genius, trading them for people dependent on entitlements and pursuing a life of leisure.

10) We are witnessing a decline in the number of people who cultivate a servant spirit of serving and loving God and their neighbor.

Calling All Christians to Board the Lifeboat

Within a short time after hitting the iceberg, repeated warnings were given to the passengers aboard the *Titanic* to go to the upper deck. A few responded at once, but most passengers assumed nothing serious could be wrong with the giant ocean liner. Those who were drinking, card playing, dancing, and recreating in various ways did not bother to heed the initial warnings. However, as the ship began to list, it became obvious that something terrible was going wrong. It was not long before hysteria and bedlam were rampant. People were scrambling and crying, frantic to find loved ones and get to the upper deck.

As the ship continued to take on water, the panic only increased. People began to realize that hundreds would die for want of a lifeboat. The night was dark, moonless, the water black, icy cold, waiting to devour life. The valor and bravery of the men and boys aboard the Titanic became legendary. The call for women and children to board the lifeboats was honored. Husbands and fathers, with unbearable sorrow, bade farewell to those they loved. Newlywed brides sobbed on the shoulders of their brand new husbands, men they would never see again. It was a time that no words can describe. People who had never thought about God were calling out His name.

The distress calls the crew sent out received no response. The ships that were within range to help had essentially closed down for the night. The RMS *Carpathia* finally heard the distress call and immediately rushed to the scene, but it was too late. The *Titanic* was rapidly sinking. The last lifeboat was being lowered into the sea and the band was still playing hymns on the deck, while others went ahead and jumped into the icy sea, desperately hoping to be pulled out of the cold icy water to safety. Those who had jumped from the ship in lifejackets flayed around in the icy water, screaming and praying for help. They perished in short order, victims of hypothermia.

The lifeboats were filled with women and children, a few men, and themselves in danger of capsizing. It is difficult to imagine the stark terror of that fateful night as each porthole disappeared one by one until the once great ship slipped beneath the North Atlantic around 2:20 a.m. on Monday, April 15, 1912. The great *Titanic* sank to her resting place some 12,000 feet below. The unsinkable *Titanic* took more than 1,500 souls to their watery grave, where they will remain until the day the sea surrenders her dead in the Second Resurrection (Revelation 20:13).

The 700 souls aboard the lifeboats were weary, in shock, suffering from hypothermia, when the *Carpathia* arrived about an hour and a half after the Titanic sank. B 9:15 a.m., the final passengers aboard the lifeboats were taken aboard the rescue ship. The most tragic event in the annals of sea travel was over, with more than 1,500 dead.

What are the lessons America could learn from the sinking of the "unsinkable" *Titanic*? There are many, and course there are personal lessons for all who have a heart to respond to the day and hour in which we live. Collectively, covenant people everywhere must underscore these truths:

1)   No country or nation is so large and powerful that it cannot fall. Pride always precedes a fall. Yes, America is a superpower, and yes, America has the largest military and naval force in the world. But just like ancient superpowers of the past, America can fall more quickly than anyone could imagine. The reader is invited to examine the prophetic words of Hosea and Amos, both of whom exposed the spiritual decline and moral crisis that existed

in the Northern Kingdom of Israel and predicted the terminus there. Hosea and Amos prophesied at a time when the Northern Kingdom was reaching its zenith. Yet, in just a few years, this powerful nation would fall, and along with its population, would be carried into captivity. Recall the rapid collapse of the Soviet Communist State in 1991. Never underestimate the speed with which the U.S.A. could suffer political and military demise.

2)   All the symptoms that preceded the fall of ancient nations and empires of the past are currently present in 21st Century America. For example, every single event that preceded the collapse of the Roman Empire is present here. America is the single largest debtor nation in the world, now into year eleven in the war against Afghanistan, with absolutely no victory in sight. The signs are all there. We would be fools to believe that America can evade the judgment that befalls all other nations that forget God and His moral absolutes!

3)   Imagine yourself a passenger aboard the great *Titanic*. If any of those who lost their lives in this tragedy could have had the opportunity to re-live their lives, what choices might they have made?   What choices are we making in our lives as we see America, the Titanic of Nations, floundering in the sea of spiritual and moral debauchery?

Personally, I believe remnant Christians living in the U.S. must underscore these clear message that resulted from the tragedy of the unsinkable *Titanic*:

1) When the *Titanic* was preparing to sail, three different classes of people (based upon their choice and cost of their accommodations) boarded the Titanic. When it sank 12,000 feet to the bottom of the North Atlantic, only two postings of names appeared: the names of the lost and the names of the saved.

Today, there are only two classes of Israelites: the saved and the unsaved! The state of your soul is the most important priority of your life. Are you prepared to meet death and your afterlife?

Will your soul be numbered with the redeemed of all previous ages, now in Paradise with Jesus Christ and living in anticipation of the restored Theocratic Kingdom on earth, or will your soul be eternally separated from God, confined in a resurrected body (Revelation 20:11-15) to spend eternity in Gehenna?

2) The greatest priority of your life is the state of your soul. Have you found peace with God by turning in repentance from dead works and believing in Jesus Christ alone for your salvation? Are you certain you are saved? What about your family and extended family members? Have you personally witnessed to those you love?

3) Imagine yourself a passenger aboard the *Titanic*, with just a bit more than two hours to live. Can you sense the compelling need to win those you love to Christ (Philippians 3:8), to repent and confess their sins, to believe and trust in Jesus Christ alone for salvation, and seal this conversion with the seal of Christian baptism?

In Conclusion

The sinking of the ocean liner *Titanic* was indeed a tragedy that has been relived in a number of novels and movies. The lives that were forever changed by this event could be the subjects for endless books. But by every consideration, the future of America, the Titanic of Nations, dwarfs the event of the ill-fated ship. What is our future? Is this Superpower destined to go the way of other nations? What are you doing to demonstrate your love for this country, its Christian heritage, and the European peoples who civilized this North American wilderness? America is presently being tossed on the high sea of world intrigue while the boisterous waves of spiritual apathy, moral debauchery, political paralysis, Jewish banking cartels, special interest groups, foreign invasion, and a legion of other forces beat us.

Let us move forward with all dispatch in the search and rescue of the Lost Sheep of the House of Israel as America, the Titanic of Nations, flounders from crisis to crisis amid the turmoil of the 21st Century.

23

REVIVE OUR HEARTS O GOD OF ISRAEL

Summer 2012

F or thus saith the high and lofty One that inhabiteth eternity, whose name is Holy; I dwell in the high and holy place, with him also that is of a contrite and humble spirit, to revive the spirit of the humble, and to revive the heart of the contrite ones" (Isaiah 57:15).

Dear covenant family, thank you for allowing me to share these devotional thoughts as we engage in the journey that will lead us to everlasting life in the Kingdom of God. As I was spending time in Isaiah in the wee hours this morning, I arrived at the above Scripture and was moved to weigh carefully two expressions in the above verse. The God of Israel desires to *"revive the spirit"* and *"revive the heart"* of His redeemed people.

Look across the landscape of America and confirm for yourselves the urgent need for revival. For several generations,

Christians have been retreating before the minions of progressive, secular humanism and the anti-Christ forces of evil. It has been far too long since Americans experienced the transforming of our lives and culture by the work of the Holy Spirit, the Word of God, and the conviction to live a biblical lifestyle. A prolonged spiritual drought has settled over America. The words of the Prophet Amos describe almost perfectly the spiritual state of our country: *"Behold, the days come, saith the Lord GOD, that I will send a famine in the land, not a famine of bread, nor a thirst for water, but of hearing the words of the LORD. And they shall wander from sea to sea, and from north even to the east, they shall run to and fro to see the Word of the LORD, and shall not find it. In that day the fair virgins and young men faint for thirst"* (Amos 8:11-13).

The evidence that our hearts need revival before the God of Israel is compelling, so I need spend but a few moments on that. What we really need is the conviction to turn from the path that has separated us from God and deadened our hearts to this same God Who gave us life and marvelously provided us a pathway to eternal life through Jesus Christ, His only and eternal Son. That we absolutely need revival in our hearts is evident everywhere— even in our churches, and every denomination at that! Our churches have lost their Christian savor. The world has invaded the church, causing there to be little distinction between the lifestyles of worldly unbelievers and those who are churched. The pulpits are dead. Consequently, people in the pews suffer spiritual rigor mortis.

The moral standards of professing Christians in 21st Century America are less wholesome than the lifestyles of unbelievers in 1950. Sin has invaded the lives of church-going people at a level unknown in previous generations. The litany of sins within the churches is a true reflection of our urgent need for revival. Sin has far too comfortable a home even in professing Christians.

Fornication, adultery, divorce, miscegenation, gambling, pornography, worldly music, dress, language, the spirit of the age, and even abortion and sodomy (unbelievable!) are too common in the lives of professing Christians. When sin finds a place of honor in the hearts of professing Christians, we experience a lapse of faith, a searing of the conscience, and alienation from the Holy Spirit.

This is a generation that is determined to live beyond their financial means. Thus, debt has become a way of life. People are ever seeking but never able to find contentment. We are quite willing to mortgage our lives and our future by living a lifestyle we cannot afford. We seem helpless to rein in our spending and find contentment in the blessings that are at hand. Spiritual drought, moral lapse, and financial bondage are the outward symptoms of a deep alienation from God and His Word. Sadly, no one who professes belief in Jesus Christ is immune from this condition. Kingdom believers are especially vulnerable because they are the focus of Satan's attack and are in his crosshairs of the spiritual warfare he is waging between the Kingdom of Jesus Christ and the kingdom of darkness.

What about Kingdom Believers?

Kingdom believers living in the post-Christian history of America have just as much need for revival of the heart as anyone. Folks who lived most of their lives in the 20th Century and now are carrying over into the second decade of the 21st Century have witnessed profound transformations in their country of origin. The America of 1960 and 2012 are not the same! In fact, we bear little resemblance to the nation that came out of the 1950s and beginning in 1960 underwent a makeover spiritually, morally, economically, socially, and in every other way. Remnant Christians thus find it difficult to be optimistic about the future of their children in this country.

The moral values of America have plummeted during the lifetime of those born in 1960 and thereafter. America is on the precipice of a moral crisis that has not been witnessed since the fall of ancient Rome. This moral freefall has taken a terrible toll on the spiritual lives of all Americans, and remnant Christians grow weary in the battle to preserve the moral absolutes of God and Scripture.

In the past fifty years, technology has changed our lives in ways never known before. Nothing in the world of technology remains static. Everything is in a constant state of flux. When you buy the latest gadget produced by our technological age, it will be obsolete before you can get it unwrapped. The more technology we bring into our lives, the faster our lives become. Millions are so busy that they find it increasingly difficult to maintain a spiritual balance. It is more difficult for people to reach out and connect to God, live by faith in Jesus Christ, and allow our spirits to be one with the Holy Spirit. We desperately need a revival of the heart!

The Psalmist David addressed the heart problem of the covenant people when he said, *"Turn us, O God of our salvation, and cause thine anger toward us to cease. Wilt thou be angry with us for ever? Wilt thou draw out thine anger to all generations? Wilt thou not <u>revive us again:</u> that thy people may rejoice in thee? Shew us thy mercy, O LORD, and grant us thy salvation"* *(Psalm 85:4-7).*

Spiritual famine is not new to covenant people. History affords many examples when Israel experienced spiritual drought and suffered alienation from God. Such a time existed when the Prophet Habakkuk delivered His prophetic word to the nation of Judah about 626 B.C. In the midst of an acute state of national spiritual and moral decline, Habakkuk petitioned Jehovah, the God of Israel: *"O LORD, I have heard thy speech, and was afraid: O LORD, <u>revive thy work</u> in the midst of the years, in the midst of the years make known; in wrath remember mercy"* *(Habakkuk 3:2).*

Revival in ancient Israel generally followed a period of spiritual and moral decline. Repentance always comes before—not after—apostasy sets in. Apostasy occurs when Israel reaches a time when her sin and iniquity become willful, deliberate, and premeditated. When a nation plunges into spiritual and moral apostasy, it is **judgment**—not **repentance**, that they face. There is growing evidence that covenant people in the United States may already be in or moving toward a state of apostasy. It has been more than one hundred years since any significant spiritual awakening or revival movement swept the country. The accumulative sin and iniquity of four generations has mounted an enormous sin debt.

Summary

Christians with a heart to love God and live by Scripture are overwhelmed with the evil unfolding in our generation. Millions feel helpless in the face of terrible wickedness in our culture. These same people despair at the pathetic plight of organized churches, hireling preachers, and their willingness to compromise with sin at every turn. Remnant Christians yearn for supernatural intervention. In the midst of this spiritual depression, there seems to be no easy pathway.

Since 1960, Caucasian Americans have witnessed a veritable tidal wave of non-white immigration. In May of 2012, the U.S. Census announced that for the first time in our history, non-white children (Blacks, Hispanics, Asians, etc) outnumbered the births of White children. The demographic face of America has forever changed.

Because so many spiritual, moral, racial, and economic factors are beyond the control of remnant Christians, we suffer from chronic spiritual depression, moral lapses, and are in urgent need of revival, reformation, and renewing of the heart. What can we do to revive our hearts? As a friend and pastor, I suggest the following:

1) Turn off all the noise (TV, cell-phone, I-pod, computers, traffic, etc.) and find a quiet place where you and God can be alone (if you are married, include your spouse).

2) Enter a fast, perhaps up to three days. During this fast, pray, read Scripture, and especially read the Psalmist David aloud. Repent of all transgressions.

3) Seek God's forgiveness as well as the forgiveness of others for your transgressions brought to your mind by the Holy Spirit.

4) During this time of prayer and fasting, focus on where your life is taking you. Are you focused on good priorities? Have you become lost in the shuffle of life? Get re-oriented with Jesus Christ as your first priority. Put your prayer life, worship, and study as priorities. Reconnect to your Savior.

5) Keep the weekly Sabbath a day of worship, rest, and doing good works for Jesus Christ.

6) Make a list of the people that you need to invest time and effort to win to Christ, His Word, and His Kingdom.

7) Carefully study I Kings 17:28-34, 18, and 19 and the life of Elijah. God will always preserve a Christian remnant that holds fast to the faith. In Elijah's day, it was a remnant of 7,000 that had not bowed knee to Baal.

8) Finally, let Matthew 6:33 become the primary focus of your life. Keep in mind what Jesus told His disciples in Luke 12:32. Let us all pray this simple prayer of faith: "O God of Israel, by faith in Jesus Christ, may the person of the Holy Spirit bring revival to our hearts?"

24

THE HOPE OF THE AGES AND BIBLE PROPHECY

Fall 2012

The 21st Century has ushered in an era of unprecedented peril. Never—in all the annals of history—has there been such a complete breakdown of the spiritual, moral, social, economic, and political structure of the nations and kingdoms of this world. Few people alive would have envisioned the implosion of the Western Christian European nations in such dramatic fashion as we are witnessing. Start with the unraveling of the Soviet Empire at the end of the Twentieth Century. That was surprising enough. But that does not compare with the speed at which all of Europe and the United States of America are imploding. What in heaven's name is happening to these nations? Can we make any sense out of this chaos? You owe it to your children, grandchildren, and anyone you care about to pause and examine the consummate prophecy of the Bible and the hope of all ages.

The geo-political world has been held together for centuries by the nation States of Europe, some of the oldest and most enduring in the entire world. Now, every single European country on the map is on life support. With unspeakable sorrow, we must acknowledge that the United States is moving with incredible speed to follow suit. Remember that it took centuries for the decline and fall of the Roman Empire to complete in AD 476. The collapse of Europe began with the fratricidal years of World War I (1914-1918), and the decline and fall of the United States of America began with the extended fratricidal years of World War II (1939-1945). America's fall from glory literally can be measured in decades.

Spiritual apathy, moral rot, decadence, the tsunami of non-White hordes, plunging economic standards, and complete collapse of the biblical family communities, and extended political spheres—these are in a freefall and bear the fruit of our absolute disconnect from God. The U.S. descent into a sixteen-trillion-dollar debt hole and total rejection of biblical Christianity and America's free market system of Capitalism are plunging the nation into third world status at break-neck speed. Plunging birth rates, childlessness, and tidal wave of non-White immigration are transforming the racial face of Europe, Canada, America, and the rest of the Anglo Saxon world.

Millions of the Anglo-Saxons of Europe, the British Isles, the United States of America, Canada, Australia, and New Zealand know that something is perilously wrong; yet they continue living in a fairytale world, assuming that they have seen the worst and everything will improve soon, as it usually has. **What they fail to realize is that the *demographics* of every single western nation have been radically transformed during the past fifty years. The decline and collapse of our biblical, Christian, western culture is irreversible!** Europe is gasping for life, and America is rushing to the precipice of national suicide. It is not merely the decline of Christianity, but the corresponding loss of biblical values, character, individual incentive, ambition, and passion for excellence that is dissipating at an incredible speed.

There Is Hope for the Hopeless!

Our only hope rests upon the testimony of Jesus Christ, Who declared this in Matthew 24:14: *"And this gospel of the kingdom shall be preached in all the world for a witness unto all nations; and then shall the end come."* Jesus Christ began His ministry by proclaiming the good news of the Gospel of the Kingdom: *"And Jesus went about all Galilee, teaching in their synagogues, and preaching the gospel of the kingdom, and healing all manner of sickness and all manner of disease among the people"* *(Matthew 4:23).* St. Mark further testified that Jesus Christ, the incarnate Son of God, arrived into Galilee, *". . . preaching the gospel of the kingdom of God"* *(Mark 1:14).* St. Luke bear witness to the message that Jesus Messiah preached in Luke 8:1: *"And it come to pass afterward, that he went throughout every city and village, preaching and shewing the glad tidings of the kingdom of God . . . ."*

The hope and promise of the Kingdom of God, the full restoration of God's Kingdom on earth, with Jesus Christ ruling upon the Throne of David—this is the ultimate theme of Scripture and the destiny toward which history is moving. There is hope in a world where hope seems gone. We must stand on the promises of God! Remember that the chaos of this world is destined to ultimately end in the triumphant return of Jesus Christ, with the complete restoration of His Kingdom in a world-wide time of peace, prosperity, and moral perfection.

Every major and minor Prophet of the Bible refers to this Kingdom. The Law of God was designed to accuse, indict, and condemn sinners, leading them as a school master to Jesus Christ for salvation to the end that the redeemed children of God could inherit the Kingdom promised them from the foundation of the world: *"And he shall set the sheep on his right hand, but the goats on the left. Then shall the King say unto them on his right hand, Come, ye blessed of my Father, inherit the Kingdom prepared for you from the foundation of the world"* (Matthew 25:33- 34).

The hope and promise of the Kingdom of God rests on the consummate prophecy of the Bible tucked away in II Samuel chapter 7 and begins with David, a man after God's own heart. This is perhaps a foundational chapter in the Bible because it establishes the groundwork for the reign of Jesus Christ upon the Throne of David in a worldwide Kingdom of peace, prosperity, perfection, and utopia. The setting for this consummate prophecy was established when Jehovah God instructed the Prophet Samuel to anoint a seventeen-year-old shepherd boy named David, the son of Jesse: *"And the LORD said unto Samuel, How long wilt thou mourn for Saul, seeing I have rejected him from reigning over Israel? Fill thine horn with oil, and go, I will send thee to Jesse the Bethlehemite: for I have provided me a king among his sons"* (I Samuel 16:1).

When Samuel arrived at the home of Jesse, he examined seven sons of this distinguished Israelite but found none of them acceptable. It was then that David was called in from tending the sheep. *"And he sent, and brought him in. Now he was ruddy, and withal of a beautiful countenance, and goodly to look to. And the LORD said, Arise, anoint him: for this is he. Then Samuel took the horn of oil, and anointed him in the midst of his brethren: and the Spirit of the LORD came upon David from that day forward."* (I Samuel 16:12-13).

Years after being anointed by Samuel and after King Saul had been slain in battle, David, at age thirty, became king in Hebron over the house of Judah. He reigned in Hebron for seven years and six months, after which all twelve tribes of Israel became confederated under David's rule. Shortly thereafter, David seized the stronghold of Zion known as the city of David, and Jerusalem became the capitol of the united kingdom. David built a palatial home and in time subdued many of the enemies of Israel and extended the borders of Israel. His name and kingdom were renowned.

As David consolidated his monarchy, there came a day when he approached Nathan the prophet with the desire to build a house of worship and with it a final resting place for the Ark of the Covenant. Nathan endorsed David's desire to build a sanctuary for Jehovah but returned to David with a revelation from Jehovah that would in many ways become the consummate prophecy of divine revelation. The Living God had not only a plan for David that exceeded the mere building of a magnificent temple, but also a covenant promise to David that would extend through the corridors of history to the consummation of the ages, the return of Jesus Christ, and the establishment of Christ's Theocratic Kingdom on the earth. What a God!

The Unconditional Davidic Covenant

II Samuel 7, the consummate chapter of Bible Prophecy, lays the foundation for the coronation of Jesus Christ upon the very throne that began with David. The covenant Jehovah made with David reached far beyond David through the centuries and connects to Jesus Christ, the Branch that was destined to grow out of the roots of Jesse and his son David. Reaching far beyond His role as the Messiah/Savior of His redeemed people Israel, the Lord Jesus Christ, as the Greater David, would one day ascend to the throne of David and assume the reigns of a worldwide kingdom of peace, prosperity, and perfection.

According to the terms of this unconditional covenant, David was to be the progenitor of a line of royal seed that would culminate in Jesus Christ, Who at His Second Coming would assume the Throne of David and control the reigns of world government. The essential elements of this covenant are covered in II Samuel 7, where we shall begin where the Holy Spirit, speaking through Nathan, declares this: *"He (David) **shall build an house for my name, and I will stablish the throne of his kingdom for ever."***

Commentary: Two significant points in this divine revelation from Jehovah follow. First is the promise that a house would be built for Jehovah. David was given the blueprint for this house, and it was David who gathered the building materials to construct the magnificent temple that Solomon erected.

Second is the promise that the throne of David would continue forever: *"I will be his father, and he shall be my son. If he commit iniquity, I will chasten him with the rod of men, and with the stripes of the children of men: But my mercy shall not depart away from him, as I took it from Saul, whom I put away before thee."*

Commentary: The Holy Spirit emphasizes two points in these verses. First, there was to be an intimate relationship between David and Jehovah. Apart from David's tragic lapse into sin with Bathsheba and Uriah the Hittite, he was a man after God's own heart and lived a good portion of his life in close intimacy with Jehovah. Secondly, Jehovah promised David that he would not be without divine chastisement if he fell into iniquity; nevertheless, this chastisement would be remedial, and David and his descendants would never be without the mercy of God.

"And thine house and thy kingdom shall be established for ever before thee: thy throne shall be established for ever. According to all these words, and according to all this vision, so did Nathan speak unto David."

Commentary: This covenantal statement assures the existence of the Davidic throne in unbroken continuity to the consummation of the ages, the Second Coming of Jesus Christ, and His coronation upon that throne in a world-wide Kingdom. David himself confirmed this covenant in one of the last recorded words that David spoke prior to his death: *". . . he* (Jehovah God) *hath made with me an everlasting covenant, ordered in all things, and sure: for this is all my salvation, and all my desire . . ." (II Samuel 23:5)*. The Holy Spirit confirmed in Psalm 132:11 that a future descendant of David, the Lord Jesus Christ, would one day set upon the throne given to David: *"The LORD hath sworn in truth unto David: he will not turn from it, Of the fruit of thy body will I set upon thy throne."*

The 89th Psalm is a far-reaching prophecy that looks down the corridors of time, confirming the Davidic Covenant as well as enlarging and emphasizing the breadth and depth of this unconditional, unilateral covenantal promise to David and his posterity. The following highlights from the 89th Psalm emphasize some of the important points of the Davidic Covenant:

The Sworn Oath of Jehovah to David

The 89th Psalm begins with the fact that the Davidic Covenant is resting upon the sworn oath of Jehovah, the initiator of this everlasting covenant.

"I will sing of the mercies of the LORD for ever: with my mouth will I make known thy faithfulness to all generations. For I have said, Mercy shall be built up for ever: thy faithfulness shalt thou establish in the very heavens. I have made a covenant with my chosen, I have sworn unto David my servant. Thy seed will I establish for ever, and build up thy throne to all generations. Selah" *(Psalm 89:1-4)*. What can we learn from this divine declaration?

1) We learn that the Davidic Covenant springs from the sovereignty, mercy, and love of Jehovah for His children in confirmation of the covenant promise to Abraham.

2) The faithfulness by which Jehovah will honor this covenant can be ascertained only by looking to the heavens out of which the covenant came.

3)   The posterity of David is to be enduring through all generations to come.

4)   The throne of David has a perpetual future.

God's Sovereignty Cannot Be Abrogated

Psalm 89:29-37 establishes the Davidic Covenant as resting upon the absolute sovereignty of Jehovah. The covenant cannot be abrogated because of sin and the countless failures of David's millions of descendants.

"His seed also will I make to endure for ever, and his throne as the days of heaven. If his children forsake my law, and walk not in my judgments; If they break my statutes, and keep not my commandments;

Then will I visit their transgression with the rod, and their iniquity with stripes. Nevertheless my lovingkindness will I not utterly take from him, nor suffer my faithfulness to fail. My covenant will I not break, nor alter the thing that is gone out of my lips. Once have I sworn by my holiness I will not lie unto David. His seed shall endure for ever, and his throne as the sun before me. It shall be established for ever as the moon, and as a faithful witness in heaven."

What Can We Learn from These Sacred Pronouncements?

1)   These divine revelations confirm the enduring, unconditional covenant of both the seed of David and the Davidic throne.

2)   Sin and iniquity found in David's posterity will receive chastening from Jehovah; however, the loving-kindness and faithfulness of Jehovah will insure the unbroken continuity of David's posterity and the Davidic throne.

3)   Jehovah cannot lie unto David (Psalm 89:35; Titus 1:2; Heb. 6:18)

4)   The throne of David is as enduring as the sun and moon before the Living God.

New Testament Confirmation

The Davidic Covenant is foundational in understanding the New Testament revelation from Jehovah God. Jesus Christ came not only as the Messiah/Savior of His people, but also with inherit rights to the Davidic throne. Matthew 1:1 opens with the declaration of Jesus Christ as the son of David: *"The book of the generation of Jesus Christ, the son of David, the son of Abraham."*

The visit and annunciation of the Angel Gabriel to the young virgin woman destined to bear Jesus by means of the miraculous, supernatural act of God is not the only revelation that Gabriel delivered. This supernatural act was to be accomplished by the Holy Ghost that would overshadow this young virgin. Further, all forty-six chromosomes for the body of Jesus Christ would be supplied and imparted through this supernatural act of God, thereby insuring that the physical or Adamic/Israelite body of Jesus Christ would be without sin nature.

The annunciation went well beyond the revelation of the holy conception of the Virgin Mary. The fulfillment of the consummate prophesies of II Samuel 7 were to find completion in the incredible words from the Angel Gabriel: *"And, behold, thou shalt conceive in thy womb, and bring forth a son, and shalt call his name JESUS. He shall be great, and shall be called the Son of the Highest: and the Lord God shall give unto him the throne of his father David: And he shall reign over the house of Jacob for ever; and of his kingdom there shall be no end."*

The first advent of Jesus Christ was destined to fulfill His role as the Messiah/Savior of His covenant people. The final installment of the annunciation would be actualized at Christ's Second Coming, when Jesus, the Greater David, would ascend to the throne of a visible Kingdom on this earth and usher in a thousand-year millennial rule over all the kingdoms and nations of this earth.

The long interval between His arrival as the Savior/Messiah of His people and His ascension to the Throne of David in a worldwide Kingdom was important for more than one reason. The out calling and conversion of repudiated, divorced, and dispersed Israel of the Northern Kingdom into the church of God through grace by faith in Jesus Christ would require time. Secondly, all of the souls numbered in the elect of God the Father and chosen in Christ before the foundation of the world (Ephesians 1:4-5; II Timothy 1:9), would need to be born into this material world. Then, through grace by faith in Jesus Christ, they would receive the gift of eternal life in preparation for the Kingdom age.

Repeatedly during His earthly ministry, Jesus referenced His future in a Theocratic Kingdom on earth. Speaking to His disciples, Jesus declared this: *"Verily I say unto you, That ye which have followed me, in the regeneration when the Son of man shall sit in the throne of his glory, ye also shall sit upon twelve thrones, judging the twelve tribes of Israel"* *(Matthew 19:28).* Speaking to the apostles as recorded in Luke 22:29-30, Jesus said this: *"And I appoint unto you a kingdom, as my Father hath appointed unto me; That ye may eat and drink at my table in my kingdom, and sit on thrones judging the twelve tribes of Israel."*

Jesus made it clear that entrance into His Kingdom would not be easy: *"Verily, verily, I say unto thee, Except a man be born again,* (Again is *anothen,* a Greek root word meaning *from above* or *from the first*) *he cannot see the kingdom of God...Except a man be born of water and of the Spirit, he cannot enter into the kingdom of God"* *(John 3:3, 5).* No Israelite may **see** or **enter** into the Kingdom of God without being born from above by the regenerating power of the Holy Spirit in the providential election and calling of God.

The Apostles Confirm the Davidic Covenant

On the Day of Pentecost in AD 33, the Holy Spirit used the Apostle Peter to deliver the first major sermon in the New Testament era of church history. In his profound message, Peter examined every objection that imaginable against Jesus Christ as being the long-awaited Messiah to come and redeem Israel. Included among other great truths in this sermon was Peter's assertion that Jesus Christ rose from the dead and would ultimately sit upon the very Throne of David: *"Men and brethren, let me freely speak unto you of the patriarch David, that he is both dead and buried, and his sepulcher is with us unto this day. Therefore being a prophet, and knowing that God had sworn with an oath to him, that of the fruit of his loins, according to the flesh, he would raise up Christ to sit on his throne; He seeing this before spake of the resurrection of Christ, that his soul was not left in hell, neither his flesh did see corruption"* (Acts 2:29-31).

Confirmation of II Samuel 7 from the Prophets

Isaiah: Every major prophet in the Bible and even most of the minor prophets hold the theme of the Kingdom of God as their primary objective of salvation history. The Davidic Covenant established in II Samuel 7 is clearly the foundational cornerstone of Old Testament prophecy. Consider Isaiah 9:6- 7: *"For unto us a child is born, unto us a son is given: and the government shall be upon his shoulder: and his name shall be called Wonderful, Counsellor, The mighty God, The everlasting Father, The Prince of Peace. Of the increase of his government and peace there shall be no end, upon the throne of David, and upon his kingdom, to order it, and to establish it with judgment and with justice from henceforth even for ever. The zeal of the LORD of hosts will perform this."*

Jeremiah: In successive chorus, the Prophets predicted the ultimate appearance of the one heir of David that was destined to rule in a world-wide, Theocratic Kingdom on earth. Consider this word from the inspired lips of Jeremiah: *"Behold, the days come, saith the LORD, that I will raise unto David a righteous Branch, and a King shall reign and prosper, and* *shall execute judgment and justice in the earth. In his days Judah shall be saved, and Israel shall dwell safely: and this is his name whereby he shall be called, THE LORD OUR RIGHEOUSNESS (Jehovah-tsidkenu)" (Jer. 23:5-6).*

Ezekiel: The voice of the Prophets is one sustaining, clarion call for the son of David, the Lord Jesus Christ, to assume the reigns of world government. These words spoken by Ezekiel, the prophet of the Babylonian captivity, address the future reign of Jesus Christ, the Greater David: *"Thus saith the Lord GOD; Behold, I will take the children of Israel from among the heathen, whither they be gone, and will gather them on every side, and bring them into their own land: And I will make them one nation in the land upon the mountains of Israel; and one king shall be king to them all . . . And David my servant shall be king over them; and they all shall have one shepherd...And they shall dwell in the land that I have given unto Jacob my servant, wherein your fathers have dwelt . . . and my servant David shall be prince for ever" (Ezekiel 37:21-25).* The David spoken of here is none other than Jesus Christ, the son of David. Remember that David, the son of Jesse, had been dead for over four centuries when these words were spoken.

Daniel: The great theme of the Prophet Daniel is the Theocratic Kingdom of God and the satanic opposition to that Kingdom in the succession of world empires that would compete for the souls of men and the real estate of this earth. In the succession of world empires, Daniel foresaw the rise of a one-world confederated empire that would rise up in the latter days as a counterfeit to the true and living Kingdom of God. In the very days of this counterfeit kingdom, Daniel prophesied these incredible words: *"And in the days of these kings shall the God of heaven set up a kingdom, which shall never be destroyed: and the kingdom shall not be left to other people, but it shall break in pieces and consume all these kingdoms, and it shall stand forever" (Daniel 2:44).*

In Summary

Take heart, Israelites. There is hope in a dark world. America is a leaderless nation staggering like a drunken man without destiny or vision from God. To the glory and praise of Jesus Christ, the God of Israel is sovereign in time and history! The Lord Jesus Christ, Who appeared as incarnate God in the Person of Jesus Christ from the womb of Mary to become the Messiah and Savior of His people, is destined to fulfill His ultimate destiny as the great Prince and King of His people. Jesus Christ, the son of David, the ultimate heir of David's throne, is scheduled to return precisely on Jehovah's timetable to assume the reigns of world government. There will come a day, a moment in time, when the seventh angel will sound. There will be *". . . great voices in heaven, saying, The kingdoms of this world are become the kingdoms of Our Lord, and he shall reign for ever and ever"* *(Revelation 11:15).*

In that glorious day the words of Daniel 7:18 will find their joyous fulfillment: *"But the saints of the most High shall take the kingdom, and possess the kingdom for ever, even for ever and ever . . . And the kingdom and dominion, and the greatness of the kingdom under the whole heaven, shall be given to the people of the saints of the most High, whose kingdom is an everlasting kingdom, and all dominions shall serve and obey him"* *(Daniel 7:18, 27).*

A final word to the Christian remnant who amid tears of sorrow witness the decline and imminent fall of the United States of America and the Western European Culture in every White homeland under heaven: look to your King and remember His word to the surviving remnant of His people: *"Fear not, little flock; for it is your Father's good pleasure to give you the kingdom"* *(Luke 12:32).* *"And when these things begin to come to pass, then look up, and lift up your heads; for your redemption draweth nigh"* *(Luke 21:28).*

Made in the USA
Middletown, DE
24 May 2023

31394031R00156